THE ELECTORAL COLLEGE AND THE CONSTITUTION

THE ELECTORAL COLLEGE AND THE CONSTITUTION

The Case for Preserving Federalism

Robert M. Hardaway

Westport, Connecticut
London

Library of Congress Cataloging-in-Publication Data

Hardaway, Robert M.
  The electoral college and the constitution : the case for
preserving federalism / Robert M. Hardaway.
      p.   cm.
  Includes bibliographical references and index.
  ISBN 0–275–94569–3 (alk. paper)
  1. Electoral college—United States. 2. Presidents—United
States—Election.   I. Title.
JK529.H37   1994
324.6′3′0973—dc20   94–13730

British Library Cataloguing in Publication Data is available.

Library of Congress Catalog Card Number: 94–13730
ISBN: 0–275–94569–3

First published in 1994

Praeger Publishers, 88 Post Road West, Westport, CT 06881
An imprint of Greenwood Publishing Group, Inc.

Printed in the United States of America

∞™

The paper used in this book complies with the
Permanent Paper Standard issued by the National
Information Standards Organization (Z39.48–1984).

10 9 8 7 6 5 4 3 2

Copyright Acknowledgments

The author and publisher gratefully acknowledge permission to reprint the following previously published material: Selected passages from *A More Perfect Union* by William Peters. Copyright © 1987 by William Peters. Reprinted by
permission of Crown Publishers, Inc. and Curtis Brown, Ltd. Selected passages
from Neal R. Peirce and Lawrence D. Longley, *The People's President: The Electoral
College in American History and the Direct Vote Alternative*, rev. ed. (New Haven: Yale
University Press, 1981).

Dedicated
to
Judy Swearingen

CONTENTS

PREFACE

There have been more proposals for constitutional amendments in the area of electoral reform than in any other area. And perhaps no other aspect of government is more important than the selection of a head of state.

The debate over electoral reform has been going on ever since the Constitutional Convention of 1787. Every few years a new crop of reformers in Congress launches a new effort to alter the constitutional scheme for electing a president. After every presidential election in which a third party creates uncertainty, calls for reform inevitably resound in the halls of Congress. The 1992 election, in which Ross Perot's candidacy initially caused uncertainty about how the Electoral College would choose the president, was no exception. Dozens of bills advocating electoral reform are now pending in Congress.

I recall that as a high school senior at the St. Albans School in Washington, D.C., the question of reforming the Electoral College was the hot topic in the school's Government Class, which was held every Thursday evening. Speakers from Congress were invited to make a presentation on each side of the issue, and the rest of the evening was devoted to debate. The class was divided into two parties, and I recall my classmate, Al Gore, arguing vigorously on the side of the reformers (although I confess to having no idea what the vice president's views on electoral reform are today).

This book attempts to add something to this perennial debate by addressing the topic with a heavy historical perspective and analysis of the principles of federalism, as well as an examination of the most modern theories of political science and government. One fact that became very apparent in the course of my research was that many Americans are not well acquainted with how the Electoral College works. In one recent poll, a citizen asked to give an opinion on the Electoral College responded by saying that he thought it had an excellent football team!

Considering the importance of the topic, I was surprised by the relatively few number of books that have been written on the subject. Around the time of every presidential election, newspapers and journals begin to bulge with opinion pieces about the Electoral College, but most provide little in-depth coverage about how the Electoral College really works. In the 1992 election, the candidacy of Ross Perot provoked an exceptionally large crop of such articles in the media.

It is indeed unfortunate that so little real information has been disseminated on this much-misunderstood American institution, and it is hoped that this book will help to remedy that state of affairs. If electoral reform ever reaches the ratification process, it will be important for every American to be well informed about the issues involved.

The most in-depth coverage to date of the history and structure of the Electoral College remains Neal Peirce and Lawrence Longley's 1981 study, *The People's President*. Its appendix alone (which comprises about one-fourth of the entire book), provides a rich source of documents and statistics about past presidential elections. Although much of the raw data cited in my book comes from this rich source, I have interpreted and construed this data in a manner that leads to very different conclusions than those set forth by Peirce and Longley. However, I have endeavored to explain the conclusions of all advocates of electoral reform, so that readers may make their own judgments.

To those readers interested in further pursuit of the historical perspective emphasized in this book, William Peters' *A More Perfect Union* and Burton Hendrick's 1937 treatise *Bulwark of the Republic: A Biography of the Constitution*, are recommended as excellent supplements to the more traditional constitutional source materials, such as Max Ferrand's epic 1913 (reprinted in 1987) treatise, *The Framing of the Constitution, The Federalist Papers*, records of the Constitutional Convention, and records of the constitutional ratification debates in the state legislatures.

This book is organized in a way that reflects my view that the Electoral College should be studied at several different levels. A separate chapter is devoted to the historical and constitutional origins of the Electoral College, while another is devoted simply to explaining how the Electoral College works today. Other chapters explain how the Electoral College evolved, and how it has affected the outcome of presidential elections. Although this method of organization has necessitated some overlap, this has been minimized by reviewing only the basic features of material previously covered. It is hoped that this organization will help reveal the extent to which the electoral system is a product not only of the framers' original vision, but also of a long process of adaptation, trial and error, and compromise—a process that was itself envisioned by the framers.

The introductory chapter gives an overview of the issues raised in the remaining chapters. The reader short on time may therefore get an overview of the entire book in this chapter. However, the issues referred to in the Introduction require the exposition and in-depth clarification that the later chapters provide. Chapter Four ("Refining the Electoral Process") is somewhat technical and heavily laden with legal and judicial annotations. For this reason, the more casual reader may wish to skip this chapter.

It is strongly urged, however, that every reader read Chapter Three, which fully explains the federalist foundation of the Electoral College. The reader who is unfamiliar with the basic structure of the Electoral College may prefer to read Chapter Two first, as this chapter explains, step by step, all the phases of the presidential election process. Those already familiar with this process, but who are more interested in the arguments both in favor and against reform, may prefer to skip this chapter as well.

Although it is hoped that this book contributes to the ongoing debate about electoral reform, it is also hoped that the Electoral College will be revealed as a living, breathing American institution, with a history that is as provocative as it is fascinating.

ACKNOWLEDGMENTS

This book would not have been possible without the contributions of many people. First, I thank my dedicated cadre of research assistants at the University of Denver College of Law: Ansley Westbrook, Chris Svarczkopf, and especially Eric Sauer, who helped extensively in the editing process, and Lisa Wentzel, who prepared the Index. Each of them not only used the conventional research methods to find all available sources, but used their own imaginative methods of investigation to find sources that were difficult and, I had thought, impossible to find.

I also thank the tireless Dean of the University of Denver College of Law, Dennis Lynch, whose dedicated support of research and writing generally, and my work in particular, has made possible this book. It is only through the generous financial support of the University of Denver that studies of this kind can be seriously undertaken.

I thank my hard-working secretary Tonia Murphy for her prodigious efforts in typing the manuscript under considerable time pressure. I wish to thank my Law School colleagues William Beaney, and Jan Laitos, all of whom are experts in their chosen field of constitutional law. Each of them generously consulted with me at various stages of this project. However, all mistakes in this book are mine alone, and the views expressed herein do not necessarily reflect those of my colleagues.

At Praeger Publishers I thank Katie Chase for her careful attention to the manuscript and many helpful suggestions, and Jim Dunton for his constant support and encouragement throughout this project.

Finally, I thank Judy Swearingen, who inspired this project, supported and helped me throughout, and without whom this book would never have been written.

THE ELECTORAL COLLEGE
AND THE CONSTITUTION

Chapter One

INTRODUCTION: THE SOLAR SYSTEM OF GOVERNMENT POWER

> It is not only the unit vote for the Presidency we are talking about, but a whole solar system of governmental power. If it is proposed to change the balance of power of one of the elements of the solar system, it is necessary to consider the others.
>
> John F. Kennedy[1]

It is a rare American presidential election that does not trigger demands for reform in the manner of electing the president of the United States. The 1992 presidential election was no exception.

In May 1992 the reporting of public opinion polls by the national media sent editors and political pundits scurrying to the constitutional law books, and in particular to the all-but-forgotten Twelfth Amendment of the U.S. Constitution. The polls that so excited the pundits' curiosity about constitutional law revealed that if the election had been held on May 18, 1992, Ross Perot would have received 33% of the vote, Bush 28%, and Clinton 24%.[2] Of potentially even greater consequence was that Perot, while not receiving a majority of electoral votes himself, would receive more than enough electoral votes to deprive either Bush or Clinton of a majority. If such numbers were to hold up until election day, who would be the next president?

What the Twelfth Amendment revealed aroused not only consternation but incredulity. According to that amendment, which was ratified in 1804, if no candidate received a majority of electoral votes, the names of the top *three* electoral vote-getters would be sent to the House of Representatives, which would thereupon "immediately" elect the new president by majority vote of state delegations. Thus each state, regardless of size or population, would get one vote. Since a majority of state delegations to the House contained more Democrats than Republicans, it was widely presumed that the Democrats, who had been locked out of the White House for all but 4 of the past 20 years, would elect the Democrat Clinton, despite his third-place finish in the popular vote.

THE TWELFTH AMENDMENT SURPRISE

The Twelfth Amendment contained yet another even more startling surprise in the form of the selection of the vice president. In the case that no vice presidential candidate received a majority of electoral votes, the amendment directed that the election for vice president be referred to the Senate. However, according to the amendment's fine print, only the top *two* vice presidential electoral vote-getters would be eligible for election by the Senate, thus eliminating Al Gore as a candidate. This would leave only Dan Quayle and Ross Perot's vice presidential running mate as candidates for vice president. Although the Democrats controlled the Senate, and certainly had no love for Dan Quayle, it was difficult for most pundits to believe that the Senate Democrats, with their own candidate ineligible, would not vote with the Senate Republicans to choose Dan Quayle over the unknown quantity of Ross Perot's running mate. Thus, the likely result, if the election had been held on May 18, 1992, was that Clinton would have been elected president and Dan Quayle would have been elected as his vice president!

With regard to actual procedures, the Twelfth Amendment leaves many questions unanswered.[3] For example, it fails to indicate whether the president is to be chosen by legislators sitting in the House of Representatives at the time of the presidential election, or the incoming members of the House to be sworn in the following January. In 1992 there appeared to be an emerging consensus that the new House, rather than the old, would elect the president if no candidate obtained a majority of electoral votes. However, the Twelfth Amendment directs that in the case that no candidate receives a majority of electoral votes, the House shall "immediately" elect the president. A strict reading of this provision does not suggest that the election of the president should be delayed until the new House is sworn in,[4] and in fact in 1801 a House election was conducted by the lame-duck Federalist Congress.[5] In any case, such a delay would mean that the president-elect would have little time to form a government prior to In-auguration Day. It might even mean that no new president would be elected by January 20 of the following year, in which case (again, according to the Twelfth Amendment), the vice president would assume the office of president until a new president was elected. Nor does the amendment indicate whether a House vote shall be by secret ballot or whether the votes within state delegations are to be by majority or plurality vote.

Both of these questions were a matter of some contention in the House election of John Quincy Adams in 1824.[6] But this election was riddled with unusual events, not the least of which was the casting of a last-minute deciding vote. According to Van Buren's autobiography, the deciding vote was cast by a General Van Rensselaer, who

> wobbled back and forth right up to the time when in the House of Representatives he had to pick up a ballot and vote. At the last moment he dropped his head on his desk and made a brief appeal to his maker, as was his custom in great crises. Opening his eyes he saw a ticket on the floor beneath him bearing the name of John Quincy Adams. Taking this for divine guidance he picked up the paper and [cast the deciding vote]. "In this way" Van Buren remembered ruefully, "it was that Mr. Adams was made President."[7]

Since that election there have been no successful efforts to amend the Twelfth Amendment. It remains exactly as written 170 years ago.[8]

An election thrown into the House of Representatives in 1992 would indeed have posed considerable challenges and created deep strains within the American electoral system. There would have been powerful political incentives to support or oppose a particular House procedure, not on a principled basis but on which candidate it would favor. For example, if more Democrats were elected to the new House than were sitting in the old, there might have been partisan pressure to delay the House election until the new House members were sworn in. If the Republican candidate had gathered more popular votes than the Democratic candidate, Republicans might have favored an open ballot on the theory that Democrats might be more easily pressured to vote for the candidate who received the most votes in their particular district, even if that candidate was not a Democrat. For the same reasons, Democrats might have demanded a secret ballot. The only precedent for such procedures would have been the procedures followed in the House election of 1824.

Whatever the other merits of Perot's independent candidacy, his temporary withdrawal from the 1992 presidential campaign on, among other grounds, that his candidacy would throw the election into the House where he could not expect to win, surely spared the country what could have been a sad spectacle of electoral politics. Not surprisingly, this close call precipitated yet another round of congressional hearings on electoral reform.[9] Although the 1992 election, at least in the beginning, showed every sign of putting the electoral system to a severe test, in the end the system worked as it was designed. Indeed, it is a rare American presidential election that does not contain some unusual element that threatens to challenge the system. Third-party candidacies have abounded in presidential elections since the time of George Washington—from the third-party candidacies of Charles Pinckney and Aaron Burr in 1796 and 1800 to the more modern candidacies of Theodore Roosevelt in 1912, Strom Thurmond and Henry Wallace in 1948, George Wallace in 1968, Eugene McCarthy in 1976, John Anderson in 1980, and Ross Perot in 1992.[10] In every election since 1824, however, the Electoral college has produced a winner, and the prediction of many observers of the earliest days that most presidential elections would be decided in the House of Representatives has not come to pass.

CONTROVERSIAL ELECTIONS

Critics of the Electoral College system can point to only one fairly tallied election in American history in which the winner of the popular vote has been defeated by an opponent who garnered a majority of electoral votes— the election of Benjamin Harrison over Grover Cleveland in 1888. In that election Benjamin Harrison lost the popular vote by less than 1%, but nevertheless won a majority of electoral votes and was elected president.

Critics also point to the election of 1876 as an example of an electoral disaster. In fact, however, the debacle of 1876 was due not to any defect in the electoral system, but to a dispute resulting from fraud in the counting of the popular vote. Indeed, it has been suggested that in 1876 the electoral system saved the country from what might have flared into a second Civil War, or at least widespread violence.

In the election of 1876 it was clear that Samuel Tilden had won the national popular vote. However, on the morning after the election, the Republicans examined the returns and determined that if the popular vote counts in three southern Reconstruction states could be successfully challenged, Rutherford B. Hayes could win the election by one electoral vote. Directions were then given to Republican leaders in those states to challenge the popular vote tabulations. It was alleged that the Democrats had used threats and intimidation to prevent African Americans from voting. Democrats countered that federal army troops had been stationed near polling places to screen voters. In Louisiana there were two governors, two boards of election, and two sets of popular return tabulations.[11]

Although the House of Representatives was controlled by Democrats, a law providing that any house of Congress could disqualify the returns of any state had lapsed in 1876. Had it still been in effect, the House would surely have been able to procure Tilden's election. As it was, however, the Constitution provided that the president of the Senate (controlled by Republicans) would count the votes. There was fear, expressed by one senator, that

the Senate would declare Hayes President, the House Tilden. In that case each of the gentlemen would have taken the oath of office, and attempted to exercise its duties; each would have called upon the army and the people to sustain him against the usurpations of the other. . . . The solemn ceremonies and the grand pageant of inauguration would be only the first act in the awful tragedy and anarchy of civil war.[12]

Democrats took up the cry "Tilden or Blood" and threatened to march on the capitol.

In the end, Congress established an Electoral Commission to determine the popular vote returns in the disputed states. Although it was originally intended that the membership of the commission would consist of an equal number of Democrats and Republicans, with one independent member, the subsequent disqualification of the independent member resulted in the selection of a Republican.[13] This tilted the balance, and Hayes was declared president on an 8–7 vote of the commission. As one newspaper of the day charged, "the vote of one man nullifies the voice of [eight million voters]."[14] Although inauguration day was not scheduled until March 4, Hayes sneaked into the White House on March 3 and took the oath of office.

Although violence was averted by Tilden's graceful acceptance of the commission's decision, for years thereafter Democrats denounced the election as "fraud" on a massive scale. Even today, books and articles abound describing this contest as the "Stolen Election,"[15] a "Political Crime," and the "Master Fraud of the Century."[16] Sidney Pommerantz has described the event as an "all time low in the functioning of popular government."[17]

Paul Haworth, in his comprehensive study of the 1876 election, has observed that

had there been a fair and free election in [Florida and Louisiana], there can be little if any doubt that the result in both would have been favorable to Hayes. If there had been a fair and free election throughout the South, there can be little question that Mississippi, with its great preponderance of Blacks, and perhaps Alabama and North Carolina, would have ranged themselves in the Republican column, and that the much vaunted Democratic majority of the popular vote—which, after all stood for absolutely nothing—would have been overcome.[18]

Judith Best has observed that "in our centennial year the electoral process was so debased and dishonored by fraud and intimidation that only an eccentric majoritarian would single out the technical runner-up Presidency of Hayes as a matter of criticism and concern."[19]

Despite the evidence that fraud and political manipulation were the causes of the electoral crisis of 1876, critics of the Electoral College continue to blame its system for the debacle. Indeed there is hardly a single proposal for electoral reform that does not place the blame for the election of Hayes at the feet of the "misguided," unduly compromising, or "undemocratically inclined" constitutional framers.

In fact, the Electoral College has functioned far more successfully than was ever envisioned by the constitutional framers, and has, over the past 100 years, consistently produced clear-cut winners, all of whom received more popular votes than their opponents. In fact, the American system of electing a president has proved to be the envy of the world, thus vindicating not only the constitutional framers but the American form of government.

THE REFORM MOVEMENT

But what has been the response of legislators to this American constitutional success story? In the past 200 hundred years, over 700 bills have been introduced to either "reform" the Electoral College or do away with it entirely. In the period 1947–68 alone, there were over 265 proposed amendments introduced in Congress. In 1993 there were numerous proposed amendments pending in Congress.[20] In fact, there have been more proposed amendments to reform the Electoral College than any other proposed constitutional amendment.[21]

Congressional reformers have described the electoral system as a "loaded pistol" pointed at the American people,[22] and a "ticking time bomb."[23] An American Bar Association (ABA) Commission on Electoral College Reform has called the Electoral College "archaic, undemocratic, complex, ambiguous, indirect, and dangerous."[24] Journalists have called it an "archaic ritual and an "anachronism."[25] The framers of the Constitution who devised the Electoral College have been derided as "elitist, undemocratic thinkers."[26] Political cartoons on editorial pages have ridiculed the electoral college, as in Herblock's cartoon depicting "an old fuddy-duddy in colonial knee britches and powdered wig with an ear to a trumpet, saying 'don't expect me to get this right, bub.' "[27]

Aside from the dozens of reform proposals introduced each year in Congress, prodigious energy has been expended by numerous commissions, private studies, think tanks, and institutes issuing reports critical of the College.[28] Typical of such studies was that of the 1978 Twentieth Century Fund Task Force on Reform of the Presidential Election Process, which after years of study arrived at a compromise reform consisting of, among other recommendations, that a complex "national bonus" system be adopted.[29]

Scholars have also spent considerable time and energy on the issue of electoral reform, much of it devoted to proving by complex mathematical equations and formulae that voters in different states do not have precisely the same voting power in electing a president. John Banzhaf's oft-quoted "One Man, 3.312 Votes: A Mathematical Analysis of the Electoral College"[30] spawned a series of mathematical refutations by equally renowned scholars, such as Robert Sickels who wrote "The Power Index and the Electoral College: A Challenge to Banzhaf's Analysis."[31] Such studies incited forays into still other areas of science and mathematics, as in Carleton Sterling's "Electoral College Misrepresentation: A Geometric Analysis."[32] The latter article purported to demonstrate by a complex series of "geometric" schemes and representations that "the coincidence of electoral and popular vote outcomes is dependent on underlying cleavages among the voters" and that the ABA Report calling the electoral college "archaic . . . and dangerous" was therefore fully justified.

Such studies, however, which appear to equal in their mathematical precision the studies of the dimensions of the Great Pyramid of Giza (which claim to find significance in such facts as that half the perimeter of the pyramid is inversely proportional to some fraction of the speed of light) prove only what the constitutional framers would freely have conceded—namely, that every American citizen does not have precisely the same voting power in electing a president. Of course, the framers would have made exactly the same concession with regard to their constitutional formula for legislative representation in the U.S. Senate, in which sparsely populated small states have representation and voting power equal to large states.

Doubtless mathematical studies could prove that the framers' formula for Senate representation deprives American citizens of equal voting power in enacting legislation in Congress. Perhaps the reason that there are fewer mathematical studies of disproportionate Senate representation is that most interested observers somehow sense that voting power is unequal even without the application of calculus or mathematical formulae.

It is not only mathematicians and political scientists who have been drawn to the mathematical studies, however. Lawyers as well as constitutional scholars have claimed to find in them data and statistics to support their contention that the electoral scheme of the Constitution is unconstitutional.[33] The Supreme Court cases of *Baker v. Carr*[34] and *Westbury v. Sanders*,[35] often cited for the principle of "one man, one vote"[36] under the Equal Protection Clause of the Fourteenth Amendment, combined with the mathematical data, have been used as the basis for just such an argument. It has been suggested, for example, that if a "voter has a constitutional right to cast an effective vote for President, an elector who casts his ballot contrary to the voter's mandate may be said to be acting under color of state law to deprive the voters of that constitutional right."[37]

The claim that the unit-rule practice[38] of awarding votes in the Electoral College is unconstitutional has been made in a number of cases.[39] While the Supreme Court has struck down unit rule systems for elections to state office,[40] it has so far declined to strike down the unit rule for election of presidential electors.[41] As Justice William O. Douglas stated in *Gray v. Sanders*,[42] "the only weighing of votes sanctioned by the Constitution concerns matters of representation, such as the allocation of Senators irrespective of population and the use of the electoral college in the choice of a President."[43]

In fact, there is a third area in which unequal voting power is woven into the constitutional fabric, and that is in the area of constitutional amendments. Article V of the Constitution provides that in order for the Constitution to be amended, there must be approval by two-thirds of each house of Congress, as well as ratification by the legislatures of three-fourths of the states. There are two points in this process that create unequal voting power. First, there must be approval by two-thirds of the Senate, in which each state has equal voting power regardless of the population of the state. Second, ratification is by state, with each state having an equal voice in ratification. Again, voters in small states are given greater voting power through their elected state representatives than voters in states with large populations. (Chapter Four discusses in more detail this "one man, one vote" principle,[44] and the improbable notion that the Constitution is unconstitutional.)

THE CONSTITUTIONAL COMPACT

One may ask why it is that of the three instances of constitutional sanction of unequal voting power (presidential elections, senate elections, and amendment ratification), only the unequal voting power inherent in the presidential election process has been attacked by "reformers." In the case of unequal voting power in the Senate, there is an easy answer. The constitutional provision for equal state representation (and unequal voting power of individual U.S. citizens) in the Senate is the only provision in the entire Constitution that is immune from the amendment process. Article V clearly states that "no State, without its consent, shall be deprived of equal Suffrage in the Senate." Thus, even if there were unanimous support in both Houses of Congress for a constitutional amendment requiring the application of the "one man, one vote" principle (and thus depriving a state of its equal representation in the Senate), and even if such a proposal were ratified by the legislatures of 49 states, any one state could defeat a proposal to change its equal suffrage in the Senate. The reason for this provision is that the representatives of the small states at the Constitutional Convention in 1787 simply did not trust the big states to keep to the constitutional bargain, which induced the small states to consent to joining the union. The small states were concerned that, after they were induced to join the union by promises of equal representation in the Senate (in exchange for concessions made to the representatives of the large states), they might in the future lose the benefit of their bargain through the amendment process, stringent and difficult though that process was. In light of the attempts over the years (some of which have come very close to success), to use the amendment process to deprive the smaller states of their constitutionally conferred suffrage in the Electoral College, the small states' demand that their suffrage in the Senate be immune from the amendment process appears to have been well justified. Their progeny may very well feel today that their forebears should have been equally diligent in protecting from the amendment process their rights of suffrage in the Electoral College, which every year is subjected to renewed attacks by "reformers."

As will be seen in Chapter Three, the entire Constitution was a grand design, a sacred compact between large and small states; prior to its ratification none of the states, under the Articles of Confederation, had yielded those elements of sovereignty necessary to achieve a national state. The very integrity of the United States, its legitimacy and authority, rests on the foundations of the Constitution's sacred compact. That compact, as recognized by John Kennedy, does indeed comprise a "whole solar system of government power," no one part of which can be compromised without considering, or reconsidering, the whole.

FEDERALIST CONSIDERATIONS

The issue in electoral reform is not, however, only whether federalism should be preserved, though that issue must surely be considered. There exists the deeper issue of constitutional legitimacy and authority. Unfortunately, very little of the public debate on the Electoral College has focused on these issues. Rather the problem has been approached simplistically as in "wouldn't it be more democratic to just let the people decide?" or "why do we need electors anyway?" Myths and folklore, such as that the framers intended that an elite group of privileged electors would make a choice independent of the will of the people,[45] continue to be perpetuated as part of the ceaseless perennial campaign to create support for tampering with the constitutional plan for presidential elections.

Even scholars have not been beneath using fear to create support for abolishing the constitutional plan, as in a recent law review article that breathlessly predicted that "unrest, public clamor for reform and an atmosphere of crisis would probably ensue" if a popular vote winner were ever to lose a presidential election.[46] Perhaps the best test of such predictions is simply to look at the history of past American elections. In 1888, the last time (and only time in a fairly conducted election) in which the electoral winner was the popular vote loser, "there was hardly a ripple of constitutional discontent, not a trace of dangerous delegitimation, and nothing resembling the crisis predicted by present-day critics of the Electoral College."[47]

It is interesting to note that in parliamentary democracies such as Great Britain, it is not uncommon for the country's leader to be chosen by party members receiving a minority of popular votes in the national election. In 1974, for example, the Labour party lost the national popular vote by 1 percentage point, but nevertheless won three more seats in Parliament, with the result that it was able to form the government.[48] As far as can be ascertained from the news reports of this election, there was no mass rioting in the streets or any atmosphere of crisis. Nor were any claims made that the British government was undemocratic because of this result.

One wonders why similar forecasts of doom are not made with regard to the passage of legislation by the U.S. Senate in which voters in small states have far greater voting power than voters in the large states. Could not the prediction be made with equal overtones of doom that if the Senate ever passed legislation that directly affected all the citizens of the United States (such as an income tax law) by a margin that depended upon the votes of the senators from small states, and if the majority of Americans (as determined by polls) opposed such legislation, there would be an armed uprising at this gross perversion of democracy and this blatant disregard for the principle of "one man, one vote?" If such a suggestion seems ridiculous, it is only because this very event occurs hundreds of times each year without any noticeable protest from reformers. And yet the weighted voting taking place in the U.S. Senate every day that body is in session almost certainly has a more direct effect on the lives of individual Americans than the once-every-200-years phenomenon of the election of a president with an electoral majority who lacks a popular one. And yet the reformers still demand that the Electoral College formula, which is but one aspect of a delicately conceived balance between the states of the union, be changed to alter the balance of power worked out so meticulously by the constitutional framers.

In 1969, at the very height of electoral reform fever (a constitutional amendment to abolish the Electoral College came within a handful a votes of passing Congress that year), James Michener, the popular author whose works of historical fiction include *Hawaii* and *Iberia*, wrote a book entitled *The Presidential Lottery*, in which he claimed that he knew of "no serious student who proposes that we retain the electoral college in its present form."[49]

PUBLIC OPINION

What, then, has been the result of these popular annual deluges of anti-Electoral College rhetoric? Not surprisingly, they have had considerable effect. Peirce and Longley's 1981 study of the Electoral College revealed that "public opinion" of the Electoral College substantially paralleled the level of electoral rhetoric. It traced public support for abolishing the Electoral College back to 1945. By 1967, 58% of Americans were in favor of abolishing the Electoral College. This percentage increased to 81% in 1968, falling back to 75% by 1981.[50] Even more revealing was the breakdown of opinion by demographic groups. In 1981, 79% of Republicans favored abolition, while only 71% of Democrats favored it. While whites favored abolition by 79%, only 48% of nonwhites favored abolition. People over age 50 favored abolition by greater percentages than those under age 30.[51] Even lawyers have not been immune. A 1987 ABA law poll revealed that 69% of all lawyers believed that the Electoral College should be eliminated.[52] Political scientists, however, continue to support the Electoral College.

To some extent, these polls may reflect prevailing views in both the popular media and scholarly journals. The relatively low level of support for abolition by nonwhites, for example, may reflect the views expressed by many constitutional scholars and observers that the Electoral College gives minorities too much influence in the electoral process.[53]

Additional explanations can be found by comparing demographically adjusted opinion polls with other prevailing views,[54] such as the traditional view that the Electoral College favors small states,[55] or Banzhaf's mathematically based counterintuitive thesis that the Electoral College actually favors voters in the large states.[56] Indeed, there seems to be a theory to fit every view of whom the Electoral College favors, despite the fact that the electoral and popular vote winners have been the same in every presidential election conducted in the past 100 years. That this is so may speak more of the wisdom of the founding fathers than the reformers are willing to concede.

ELECTORAL COMPLEXITY

Not every critic has taken public opinion polls of the Electoral College seriously, however. In responding to the charge made by the American Bar Association that the Electoral College system is too "complex," Martin Diamond has retorted that

perhaps the fear is that voters are baffled by the complexity of the Electoral College and that their bafflement violates a democratic norm. It must be admitted that an opinion survey could easily be devised that shows the average voter to be shockingly ignorant of what the Electoral College is and how it operates. It all depends on what kind of knowledge the voter is expected to have. [But] however ignorant they may be of the details of the Electoral College, their ignorance does not seem to affect at all the intention and meaning of their vote, or their acceptance of the electoral outcome.[57]

To the specific charge that the Electoral College is too complex, Diamond has noted that

the Electoral College is only one example of the complexity that characterizes our entire political system. Bicameralism is complex; federalism is complex; judicial review is complex; the suspensory executive veto is a complex arrangement; the Bill of Rights introduces a thousand complexities. If a kind of prissy intelligibility is to be made the standard for deciding what should remain and what should be simplified in American government, how much would be left in place?[58]

Diamond might also have added that one of the least "complex" proposals made at the time of the Constitutional Convention was that the United States become a monarchy. Max Farrand, professor of history at Yale University, reported in his 1913 (1987 reprint) treatise *The Framing of the Constitution of the United States* that "the records show frank expressions by certain members that they considered a limited monarchy the best form of government."[59] Needless to say, this proposal, despite its "simplicity," was given short shrift at the Constitutional Convention.

CLOSE CALLS

But even taking into account the questionable accuracy of polls on such matters as the Electoral College, it remains clear that a large number of Americans favor doing away with the Electoral College. How then has the Electoral College managed to remain intact? There are several answers to this question.

First, it must be recalled that there have been several close calls. In September 1969 a proposed constitutional amendment passed the House by a vote of 338–70. Senator Birch Bayh explained what followed: "(D)uring Senate debate the following year we came within a handful of votes of breaking a filibuster [conducted by representatives of small states] that prevented a veto. I believe that only the extreme time pressures at the end of the session kept us from bringing direct popular election to a vote."[60]

Second, opponents of retaining the Electoral College in its present form have not all agreed on how it should be reformed. Thus, opposition has been split among those who favor direct popular election, a proportional plan, a district plan, an automatic plan, and those who favor only tidying up the loose ends of the Twelfth Amendment. In this regard it may be noted that the reformers have failed to achieve the one thing that the Constitutional framers did achieve: a consensus.

Nevertheless, the battle over electoral reform continues, its flames fanned almost every presidential election year by fears of how some third-party candidate might affect the election process. In 1992 it was the candidacy of Ross Perot, but in future elections there will doubtless be some new and unexpected factors that will continue to fan the flames.

In each battle, however, considerations of federalism are given little attention. Rather, the issue of electoral reform is treated as if in an historical vacuum—indeed as if the question were being considered in isolation, apart from all the other provisions of the Constitution that were conceived as part of a sacred compact. In response to attacks, defenders of the Electoral College therefore have no choice but to address the specific pro's or con's of electoral reform as if it were being considered for the first time at a new constitutional convention. What is remarkable is that the Electoral College, even today, can stand on its own merits as superior to any of the new systems proposed, including direct election.

MAJORITARIANISM AND THE "WRONG PRESIDENT" SYNDROME

A recent book entitled *The Wrong Winner* catches the reader's eye with this opening paragraph:

It finally happened. Scientists had been issuing warnings about it for years but the politicians and business leaders and media people had not taken the warnings very seriously. There had been occasional references to the danger in newspaper columns and on the Sunday morning interview shows, but nobody seemed very worried about it. And, of course, it happened in California. The Great San Andreas earthquake? No, scientists had been predicting that for years, too. . . . In 1996 the electoral college had selected the wrong president![61]

And just what is the "wrong president"? Well, claim the authors, a wrong president is one who has received an electoral majority without a majority of popular votes. Such claims, however dramatically made, nevertheless raise the perfectly legitimate question of what is a "majority." More precisely, one may ask, a majority of what?

The drafters of the Constitution assumed that it would be very unlikely that any presidential candidate (after Washington) would ever actually achieve a "majority" of votes, even in the Electoral College. There were delegates at the Constitutional Convention who initially favored a Western parliamentary style of democratic government, in which the chief executive was elected by the legislature. Indeed, many thought Congress should appoint the executive, since the chief reason for having an executive was to carry out the will of Congress.[62]

Other delegates opposed this idea, believing it would make the executive "a creature of the legislature" who would be "beholden" to it, and thus jeopardize the delicate balance and separation of powers envisioned as the heart of the constitutional fabric. James Madison, for example, stated that "an election by the legislature is liable to insuperable objections. It not only tends to faction, intrigue, and corruption, but leaves the executive under the influence of an improper obligation to that department."[63]

A number of proposals regarding the chief executive were proposed and considered at the Convention, among them the proposal made by Thomas Paine (outlined in *Common Sense*) that the president be chosen from delegates of a colony that should be selected by lot.[64] Other proposals, seriously considered, included that the executive should consist of three members from different parts of the country, that the executive should serve on "good behavior" (a euphemism for serving for life), and that the executive should be selected by direct vote of the people. Although all these proposals were eventually voted down, the proposal for direct election was the most severely defeated, receiving only one affirmative vote (from Pennsylvania).[65] Indeed, it received even less support than the similarly minded proposal to eliminate the states entirely and proceed with forming a national, rather than federalist, republic. Had the direct election proposal been approved, the participation in the union by the smaller states would at best have been problematic, at least without considerable concessions in other areas.

Although Madison initially favored direct election, he was later converted to an active supporter of the electoral system, having apparently been convinced that the interests of the small states demanded an election system other than direct election.[66] In the end, the Electoral College system was overwhelmingly approved, not so much as a compromise but as the result of a realization on the part of the delegates that it offered the best of both legislative and direct election proposals. On the one hand it insulated the executive from undue influence by the legislature, while on the other hand it promised to reflect the will of the people while still providing protection to the smaller states sufficient to induce their participation in the union. Though hailed as part of the "Grand Compromise," which included the equal representation of the states in the Senate, it in fact reflected far more—namely, the vision and genius of the constitutional framers. The Electoral College was to become a bulwark and foundation stone of a new federal system that was to become the envy of the world.[67]

Although the Electoral College system was the end product of extensive discussions and debate among the framers at the Convention, once it was agreed upon it was perceived by the framers and their supporters with considerable pride as one of the most important accomplishments of their constitutional mission. Alexander Hamilton spoke glowingly of their accomplishment, writing in *The Federalist* that "the mode of appointment of the chief magistrate of the United States is almost the only part of the system, of any consequence which has escaped without severe censure or which has received the slightest mark of approbation from its opponents."[68] Iridell, at the North Carolina Convention debating the ratification of the new Constitution, stated that "in all human probability no better mode of election could have been devised,"[69] and Davie declared it "impossible for human ingenuity to devise any mode of election better calculated to exclude undue influence and combination."[70]

Of course no provision of the proposed Constitution ever enjoyed absolute unanimity of support, and the Electoral College was no exception. As Jeane Kirkpatrick has noted, however, the charges against the Electoral College have been "precisely those made against the Constitution itself by its detractors," and indeed continue to be made today by its detractors: that it is "undemocratic, complex, ambiguous, and dangerous."[71] It may be recalled that the most ferocious American patriots opposed the whole idea of a strong national government, and viewed the whole Constitution as an invitation to tyranny. Patrick Henry, of "Give me liberty or give me death" fame, refused even to attend the Constitutional Convention. When asked why, "Henry's reply was succinct but hardly enlightening. 'I smelt a rat' he replied."[72] Were he alive today, he would, like today's "reformers," very likely continue to smell a rat in the Electoral College.

This, then, is the plan that has been attacked as undemocratic and dangerous because it may result in the selection of the "wrong" winner who has not received a majority of popular votes. But would a direct election really provide a true majority?

THE CONCEPT OF THE MAJORITY

In fact the notion of a "majority" is an elusive concept. It is rare that any one person in a largely populated society rises to the level of being favored for high office over all other candidates combined. Of course, it does sometimes happen even in democratic societies, as in the case of George Washington, who was the only obvious candidate to be the first president of the United States. More often, however, the existence of only one candidate is indicative of an authoritarian society in which choice is influenced more by fear or self-preservation than by free will—witness the charade of past "elections" in some Communist countries in which the head of state was purportedly elected by 99.7% of the popular vote.

The critical stage of any selection process that calls itself "democratic" is primarily in the intermediate stage. The primary stage is usually self-selective—that is, candidates select themselves as candidates by putting themselves forward, seeking support, and asserting their positions. In the intermediate stage, however, the vast number of self-elected candidates are culled to a manageable handful—that is, reduced to a number that can practically be listed on a paper ballot comprehensible to the average voter. Over the centuries, those few countries that have professed a dedication to democratic ideals have experimented with a variety of culling methods. Many of the parliamentary democracies elect, by district or county, representatives to a national parliament. These representatives then select a leader who proceeds to put together a government.

Such parliamentary systems of selection share one essential feature with the American Electoral College: both systems rely on a majority vote within a district or political subdivision to determine the identity of the legislator or elector who will in turn select the national leader. In theory, therefore, although certainly less often in practice, both systems can produce a minority national leader in cases where thin majorities in a barely sufficient number of districts serve to elect electors who thereupon vote for a leader who is opposed by vast majorities of voters in a minority of districts.

Indeed, these parliamentary systems are much more likely to produce minority leaders than the Electoral College system. This is because the average political subdivision in most modern parliamentary democracies generally contains far less than one-fiftieth of the total number of citizens in the country. Each subdivision is less likely to represent a representative sample or cross section of the country as a whole. Thus, a candidate enjoying only a small percentage of support from the country at large is more likely, if he or she nevertheless commands allegiance in one small locality, to be able to command a majority or plurality in one particular district than a candidate in the United States will be able to command in any particular state.

The results of these differences can best be demonstrated by comparing the makeup of legislative bodies (which select the executive) in such parliamentary democracies as Italy or Israel with the makeup of the Electoral College in the United States. Since it is far easier for candidates with only local or regional appeal to be elected to the legislatures of the parliamentary democracies, small and minority parties abound, thus depriving the major parties of the majority needed to govern or elect a leader with broad national support.

Under the Electoral College system in the United States, however, electors pledged to candidates with only regional or local appeal have far less chance of election by the people, since they must command the allegiance of a plurality of voters in a relatively large region of the country (i.e., an entire state). Thus, while minority or extremist parties might have a chance of being elected in a small subdivision (such as a town or county), they rarely, in the United States, can command the allegiance of a majority or plurality of an entire state. The result, doubtless envisioned by the constitutional framers, is that candidates commanding a majority, or at least a substantial plurality of popular votes countrywide are ultimately elected, and smaller parties representing narrow interests must either compromise or merge with a major party.

This electoral culling process also has the healthy side effect of constantly rejuvenating and infusing the major parties with new ideas, interests, and programs, without which the major parties might wither and die. In parliamentary societies, where little incentive exists to compromise or merge, small parties are often relegated to the fringes of society where in isolation they harden their positions, but nevertheless bide their time to exert influence far beyond their numbers in time of extreme crisis when their support is desperately needed to help shore up a minority government.

Some parliamentary governments have actually made the situation worse by experimenting with proportional representation, in which a certain small percentage of the overall popular vote is automatically translated into a certain number of seats in the legislature. This even further fosters the proliferation of parties and virtually guarantees that no one party will receive a governing plurality, much less a majority.

Many parliamentary democracies have learned to cope and live with the consequences of unstable minority governments. Italy, for example, has learned to live with the trauma of constant transition and the rise and fall of as many as three or four different ruling coalitions in the space of a few months. Citizens have learned not to count on the policies of their elected government, since a new one might come to power at virtually any time. In Israel, citizens have learned to live with the possibility that even a very tiny political party representing the most narrow interests might, in the aftermath of an election, demand the most extreme concessions as the price for providing crucial votes for a ruling coalition. Great Britain, with its relatively homogenous population, and thousand-year history of stable monarchial rule and evolved democracy, has perhaps coped best with the vagaries of parliamentary rule. And yet, no nation in the world is the subject of as much awe and admiration as the United States when, like clockwork, at noon on January 20 of each fourth year, the greatest executive power in the world is peacefully transferred to the winner of the most votes in the Electoral College.

It is suggested, however, that this awe and admiration is not due to the Electoral College or the efforts of the constitutional framers, but rather exists in spite of it; that while our constitutional election system may be more democratic and superior to that of the parliamentary democracies, it is inferior and certainly less democratic than direct popular election. It is to this suggestion that we now turn.

THE "DIRECT VOTE" PLANS

Most of the "direct vote" plans propose that the winner of the most popular votes be elected president, unless no candidate receives at least 40% of the vote, in which case there would be a runoff election of the two highest vote-getters. At first blush this plan would appear to guarantee a president who received a majority of the popular vote. A closer look at such plans, however, reveals the illusion of any notion of a majority.

A Twentieth Century Fund Task Force has recognized that

direct election does not guarantee that the candidate with the most support wins if there are more than two candidates . . . since direct election measures only first choice preferences, it cannot directly reflect intensities of preference or distaste and therefore cannot assure that the candidate with the most votes is the most preferred. The run-off between the top two candidates is designed to deal with the possibility that a candidate with a mere plurality will not be able to win unless he prevails over opponents who have an opportunity to unite against him. However [under conditions of multiple candidacies], there is no way to guarantee his election.[73]

The following hypothetical example illustrates this point, and demonstrates the inherent democratic weaknesses of a "direct" election and its illusion of plurality or majority:

Suppose that there is no Electoral College mechanism to foster the two-party system or deter the proliferation of minor parties. Even the smallest and most extreme parties know that each and every vote they receive will show up on the final tally sheet and serve to reduce the plurality of the most popular candidates. As a result, dozens or even a hundred different parties serve up candidates. Assume there are up to a hundred candidates, no one of which commands an allegiance of over 2% of the voters. However, two small but fanatical and highly organized parties, headed by a Joe Hitler and an Edward Mussolini each manage to garner 2% of the vote, while all the other parties (none of which individually gets as much as 2% but which together constitute the mainstream), divide up the remaining 96%. Under the direct election plan proposed by such democratic reformers as Senator Birch Bayh, the election would proceed to a runoff between Joe Hitler and Edward Mussolini. Although three-fourths or more of the electorate might sit out the runoff election in protest, those who actually voted in the runoff would indeed give either Hitler or Mussolini a majority vote.

Presumably this outcome would satisfy our electoral reformers, who would beam that the system had reflected the principle of "one man, one vote," and had therefore produced a majority candidate.

This brings us back to the question of what is meant by "majority." In most instances the use of this term only begs the question of how a field of candidates is narrowed down to a small number such that one candidate has the opportunity to gain a majority or substantial plurality of votes. The Electoral College system meets this question head on; the direct election system does not.

A typical response of some electoral reformers to a hypothetical situation such as that posed above is "well, it couldn't happen, the hypothetical isn't realistic." In fact, such situations have occurred frequently in the twentieth century.

Consider the manner in which the Nazis rose to power in the 1930s by taking advantage of a direct popular election. Although the Nazis never came close to receiving a majority of votes, they were highly organized and commanded a fanatical and loyal following. The mainstream parties divided the majority of voters opposing the Nazis, allowing the Nazis to establish a minority power base from which they ultimately seized total power.

A more modern example can be found in the Russian election conducted on December 14, 1993. In that election, dozens of parties participated, and 13 parties received significant numbers of votes. Of these, the "liberal Democratic" party led by Vladimir Zhirinovsky received 23% of the vote. (Despite its label, this party's platform was fascist in nature, blaming Jews for starting past wars, and advocating the military take-over of Finland, Poland, and even Alaska. In January 1994, Zhirinovsky was kicked out of Bulgaria for advocating that a former Waffen SS officer become dictator of Bulgaria.)

The Communist party received 11% of the vote, while other more moderate parties split the remaining vote. Fortunately, the reformist People's Choice party edged out the Communists by 2%. A swing of but 2% of the vote would have meant that the two top vote-getters would have been Fascists and Communists. In such a situation, had this been a presidential, rather than legislative election, and if Russia had adopted the ABA's proposal for a direct election (with a runoff between the two top vote-getters), the Russian people would have had a choice between a Fascist and a

Communist, despite the fact that a vast majority of Russians opposed both Fascism and Communism.[74]

In claiming that these scenarios could not occur in the United States, many advocates of direct elections cling to a number of unrealistic assumptions. The first of these is that the abolition of the Electoral College would not bring fundamental changes in the two-party system. It is possible, of course, that the two-party system, which is the result of over 200 years of evolution and development under the rubric of the Electoral College, might continue on for an election or two by the sheer weight of its own momentum. Very soon, however, the lure of getting a piece of the national popular tally would be too great for a multitude of minor and extreme parties to resist. The incentive to compromise, to give and take, to come to terms with major parties, would soon vanish. The evidence for the Electoral College's dampening effect on the growth of factionalism is manifest from the annals of past presidential elections.

In July 1977 Senator Birch Bayh conducted hearings of the Electoral College. A former member of the National Executive Committee of the Socialist party testified before Senator Bayh's committee. In referring to his former colleague and Socialist leader Norman Thomas, he testified:

One thing we all had in common was an absolute detestation of the electoral college. It was one of the chief barriers to the success of minor parties. . . . We knew that we didn't have a snowball's chance in the nether regions to . . . win any states. Whereas, under the system you propose [direct popular election], we would have made hay while the sun shined during the late autumn. We always started with 5 or 6 or 7 percent who said they were for Norman Thomas. And I'm quoting Thomas: About the third week in October, it would be down to 2 percent; on the first day in November it would be down to 1 percent; and on the first Tuesday after the first Monday in November, it would be down to about 150,000 votes. Period. The reason was that there was no chance for victory in any state. Your 40 percent provision, with the contingency runoff election was precisely what we prayed for. Unfortunately, the manna from heaven came too late for my use in the socialist days.[75]

When Senator Bayh replied that "It's interesting for me to see how you make a parallel of going from 5 to 1 percent and going from 5 to 20 percent or more which you have to do if everything else was mathematically equal in order to cause a run-off," the witness responded without hesitation.

I can handle that one, sir, I believe. You see the Socialists could go to 5 percent, but there's no reason under your proposed system, as I understand it, why 20 percent has to be garnered by one party. I believe that the 20 percent would be garnered by 15 or 20 parties. I can name 4 or 5 of them: Wallacites, Henry and George; McCarthyites, Eugene and Joseph; Socialists, Trotskyites, Communists, black militants, yellow militants, green militants, purple militants . . .

After interruption, the witness went on to explain:

It's not hard to create the French Chamber of Deputies in a multiparty system. We've seen it happen everywhere. It can be done by fiddling with the constitutional structure that undergirds and constrains and channels the two-party system. . . . Every minority party would have no reason for the chastening constraint of the need to win in the first election. There would be a kind of victory for everybody. And then they'd stay in business, to get the federal financing again in the next election. We would simply create a multiparty system.[76]

It may reasonably be asked to whom the 4% or 5% of voters who evaporated from the Socialists' polls ultimately gave their support. In the 1932 election Franklin Roosevelt received 57.4% of the vote and Herbert Hoover received 39.6% (for a combined total of 97%). It is probable that these 4% or 5% of Socialist voters found an accommodation with one of the major parties, most likely the Democratic party.

Evidence that the Electoral College inhibits fractionalism can be found in a number of other presidential elections. It has already been noted that in 1992 Ross Perot initially dropped out of the presidential race because, among other reasons, he could not hope to gather a majority of electoral votes, and also he could not hope to win in the House if he deprived the major party candidates of a majority. When he later changed his mind and re-entered the race, he encountered the electoral phenomenon that had confronted Norman Thomas—a gradual erosion of his popular support as election day drew near and voters declined to throw away their vote on a candidate who now had no hope of winning any electoral votes. Once again the Electoral College had done its job of insuring the election of a candidate with either a majority of popular votes or a substantial plurality of popular votes.

From time to time, however, some presidential candidates have tried valiantly to buck the Electoral College system and pursue a fractionalist course. In 1860 Stephen Douglas and John Breckinridge split the Democratic vote and handed the election to Lincoln, who thereby gained the distinction of winning an electoral majority with the lowest popular vote in American history (39.8%).[77]

In 1912 Theodore Roosevelt, who had won the 1904 election with a stunning 56% of the popular vote and a 336 electoral-vote majority, refused an accommodation with his Republican party, which nominated the incumbent President William Taft. Roosevelt and Taft ended up splitting over 50% of the popular vote and handed the election to the Democrat Wilson, who had received but 42% of the popular vote.

The Electoral College lesson has been clear throughout American history: accommodate, compromise, merge, persuade, build, and achieve a consensus. It is surely a far different one from that taught by a system of direct election: stick to your guns, harden your position, remain in isolation, refuse to accommodate or compromise in the hope that you may ultimately gain leverage out of all proportion to the level of your popular support.

The Electoral College has proved to be a flexible system, evolving, growing, and adapting to meet the needs of the election process (see Chapter Four). That its lessons have been learned is demonstrated by the fact that, since evolving into its present form, it has never once failed to produce a clear-cut majority winner of electoral votes.[78] Only on occasion, as in 1992, have its lessons had to be repeated.

Again, we must return to the concept of the majority. Advocates of direct election claim that "resort to a runoff election would be a relatively rare occurrence."[79] This assumption is apparently based on the fact that, since 1860, no winning presidential candidate has ever received less than 40% of the popular vote. What the advocates of direct election fail to take into account, however, is that *these consistently large pluralities and majorities are the result of the very Electoral College system they are seeking to destroy.*

One has only to look at sister democracies that lack such a system (the parliamentary democracies or the French Chamber of Deputies) to see that the two-party system is a rare phenomenon. Indeed, one may look at early American elections, before the Electoral College evolved into what it is today, to see that the two-party system was not the norm. In 1824, for example, President Adams received only 31.9% of the vote (Jackson, Crawford, and Clay split the rest).

As will be seen in Chapter Four, the Electoral College today is the result not only of the Constitutional Convention, but the result of over 200 years of evolution, trial and error, and adaptation. The Twelfth Amendment provision for joint tickets, the state-evolved unit rule, and the popular election of electors have all evolved as essential ingredients in the American plan for electing a president. Like the Constitution itself, which has proved itself marvelously flexible and adaptable to changing times, each of these developments evolved in response to particular needs, and represents more than mere fine-tuning.

That the Electoral College must continue to adapt is not in dispute. Some reforms are necessary to address such problems as the "faithless elector," the lack of uniformity in state unit-rule provisions, and the failure to provide for such contingencies as the death of a candidate after election but before inauguration. In addition, the Twelfth Amendment procedures for reference of an election to the House where no candidate receives a majority of electoral votes need to be reexamined, particularly those provisions that permit the election of a president and vice-president of different parties. (i.e., the Twelfth Amendment surprise that so shocked students of the "Perot factor" in the 1992 election).

If these problems have not in recent times been seriously addressed, however, it is in large measure due to the advocates of direct election who feel that any such modest reforms would freeze the essential ingredients of the Electoral College into the Constitution, and thus defeat their ultimate goal of abolishing the Electoral College altogether and instituting direct election. Many such advocates appear to be adherents of the philosophy of Viscount John Mosley (who asserted that "the small reform may become the enemy of the great one")[80] and thus refuse to countenance any reform less than direct election of the president by popular vote. This attitude on the part of many direct election advocates has effectively created a stalemate in which responsible reform is consistently blocked.

CLAIMS OF ELECTORAL BIAS

Another tactic of the advocates of direct election has been to claim that the Electoral College system unfairly favors one group or prejudices another.[81] It has already been noted that some scholars claim that the Electoral College favors small states, while others claim that it favors voters in large states.[82] Depending upon which of these groups the advocates are trying to persuade, it has variously been claimed that the Electoral College creates a bias against rapidly growing states,[83] states with high voter turnout,[84] Northern African Americans,[85] Southern African Americans,[86] Mexican Americans,[87] Mormons,[88] and homosexuals.[89] It has been claimed that the Electoral College favors Italians,[90] suburbanites,[91] Jews,[92] and "Narrowly Defined economic interests."[93]

All of these studies are apparently based on the theory that certain narrowly defined groups either hold the critical balance of electoral power in particular states or are victimized by others that hold the balance of electoral power. In most cases, however, these claims appear to be based on highly subjective analyses of demographic patterns and how certain groups are inclined to vote. Inasmuch as these voting patterns as well as the underlying demographics may change and have changed considerably over periods of time, none of these claims is particularly persuasive of any underlying unfairness in the Electoral College.

Although vast amounts of time and energy have been expended by scholars bent on demonstrating statistical anomalies in voting patterns under the Electoral College, the fact remains that in only one fairly conducted election in the past 200 years has the winner of an electoral vote majority not also received the majority of popular votes. Therefore, it is difficult to see how a case of actual bias could be made in any election other than the 1888 election in which Benjamin Harrison defeated Grover Cleveland with less than a 1% minority of popular votes. Since there is little data now available on how homosexuals or Mormons voted at that time, there appears to be little upon which to base a case of bias even in that election.

Just as many Egyptologists have spent lifetimes trying to prove a statistical relationship between the dimensions of the Great Pyramid and such physical constants as the speed of light, scholars conducting additional studies of Electoral College voting patterns doubtless might, if sufficient energy and time were expended, reveal biases against tall people, people with red hair, and people with large feet.

In any case, however, it does not appear that any of the claims have made much impression on the groups involved. Although such groups as homosexuals have asserted a number of grievances, it does not appear, judging from national media coverage, that the Electoral College is one of them. It is suggested that the energies spent on such studies might be more usefully directed toward the study of how parliamentary democracies and countries with direct elections cope with unstable minority governing coalitions.

More important, however, such studies focus on the wrong issue. The point is not whether one group or state might, at one period in time, have a theoretical voting advantage. Nor should arguments for or against the Electoral College rest on the validity of such claims. Groups, voting patterns, and demographics all change over time. The ultimate issue is which system is best for the entire country, for all the people. More recent debates have indicated a recognition of this. It is true that in 1979 (the last time Congress gave considerable attention to the Electoral College), two-thirds of the Senators from the ten smallest states voted against a proposed constitutional amendment for direct election.[94] However, many states, even some of the smaller ones, split their votes, indicating that the issue was perceived not as one of local or regional advantage, but of what was best for the country.

It is true of course that some groups feel that they have a vested interest in the current system, which they would lose if a direct election were imposed. Vernon Jordan (president of the National Urban League, one of the leading civil rights organizations) testified at the 1979 congressional hearings: "Take away the Electoral College and the importance of being black melts away. Blacks, instead of being crucial to victory in major states, simply become 10% of the total electorate, with reduced impact."[95] (This view is, incidentally, contrary to that of some scholars who maintain that African Americans are disadvantaged by the Electoral College.)[96] It has also been reported that "White Senators like Moynihan of New York and Sarbanes of Maryland normally in the forefront of legislation to democratize American politics were responsive to pleas from Black and Jewish leaders concerned about losing the advantage they thought the Electoral College gave them."[97]

The fact that even members within groups or representatives of states cannot agree on whether they are advantaged or disadvantaged perhaps speaks more of the vision of the constitutional framers than any one other feature of the Electoral College. In truth, the case for preserving the Electoral College is the case for preserving the integral ingredients of the solar system of government power envisioned by the framers. The fact that the Electoral College also happens to be the best method within the American system for manifesting the will of the majority only serves to reinforce the primary reason for its preservation.

ABA CRITICISM OF THE ELECTORAL COLLEGE

It remains to discuss two additional criticisms of the Electoral College made by the American Bar Association—namely, that it is "archaic" and "ambiguous." "Archaic," as the term is used by the American Bar Association, appears to be equated with old. That it is. But it must be considered that the very oldness of the American tradition of electing a president has much to do with the unquestioning acceptance of its results by the American people.

Consider for a moment the example of the Russian attempt in the early 1990s to establish a rule of law and ordered liberty. Lacking a tradition of absolute adherence to constitutional provisions, the government was torn apart when warring political factions ignored their constitution and relied on the loyalty of the military. Merely having a constitution is not sufficient. It must be accepted, revered, obeyed, without even the thought of any other course of action. Such acceptance is not the historical norm of human conduct, and it does not come overnight. It takes time. Today Americans would be truly shocked were a president to proclaim, as Andrew Jackson allegedly did 150 years ago, that the Supreme Court has made their ruling; now let them enforce it.

As Americans we now take for granted that if a party in power is defeated in an election, it will gracefully, peacefully, and without question give up all its power to the electoral winner. The most critical days for the American Republic were its very first; for in those days there was no tradition, no history of adherence to constitutional principles. That the constitutional framers were able to create a document under which sovereign states would give up many of their powers to a federal entity was only the beginning of their task. It remained to persuade those with power to give it up, and to begin a tradition of adherence to constitutional law.

James Madison knew that a procedure for amending the Constitution was necessary to insure that it would be flexible enough to adapt to the needs of the Republic. But he also knew, as he stated in *Federalist* No. 49, that tinkering with the essential elements of Republican government deprives that government of "that veneration which time bestows on everything, and without which perhaps the wisest and freest government would not possess the requisite stability."[98]

Martin Diamond has further observed that "a long standing Constitutional arrangement secures, by its very age, that habitual popular acceptance which is an indispensable ingredient in Constitutional legitimacy, that is, in the power of a Constitution to be accepted and lived under by free men and women."[99]

With regard to the charge that the Electoral College is "ambiguous," it is submitted that the exact opposite is true. Indeed, one of the most critical features of the Electoral College is that it almost always provides a prompt and unambiguous result. This feature has been most pronounced in elections in which the popular vote has been very close.

In the 1960 election, for example, history has recorded the final vote tally as giving Kennedy a popular vote margin of 112,000 out of 69 million votes cast. In fact, however, this popular vote count was only one of three separate tallies of popular votes. Peirce and Longley's study of American elections has observed that "it was impossible to determine exactly what Kennedy's popular vote plurality—if it existed at all—really was."[100] The problem arose in Hawaii and Alabama, where "unprecedented difficulties arose in determining the popular vote."[101] One vote tally, using a method developed by the Congressional Quarterly to count the Alabama votes, showed that "Nixon was the popular vote winner by a margin of 58,181 votes"[102] (see Chapter Five).

Fortunately for the country, however, a constitutional crisis was averted because of the clear and unambiguous results provided by the Electoral College, which gave Kennedy an overwhelming electoral majority regardless of how the Alabama popular votes were counted. One reason this potentially explosive glitch in the electoral process has faded into a footnote in history is that the popular vote in Alabama would have made absolutely no difference in the outcome of Kennedy's overwhelming victory in the Electoral College.

Another reason the incident has been forgotten is because, as Peirce and Longley have explained,

Nixon never sought to use these figures to argue that he had been the people's choice for President in 1960. Since Kennedy was clearly the electoral college winner, Nixon may have felt that claiming a popular-vote victory would simply have made him out as a poor loser. Moreover, the complex issues raised by the Alabama count were not the kind that many people would fully understand. Thus, little public debate took place on the question of how Alabama's votes should be counted, and it seemed likely that the issue would not be raised again.[103]

Although the glitch in counting popular votes in the 1960 election was, of course, related to the electoral process,[104] one lesson that may nevertheless be learned from that election is that in very close elections, exact popular vote tallies may take days, weeks, or even months to ascertain if there are any voting irregularities. While such irregularities would certainly deserve the most complete and comprehensive investigations, the country cannot afford the luxury of such delays in determining who has been elected president. Any substantial delay in determining the new president would put the nation into a state of intolerable limbo, which would be particularly unnerving and destabalizing in a day of nuclear weapons. Unlike the pseudo constitutional crises conjured up by advocates of direct election, a substantial delay in modern times in determining who has been elected president would create a true constitutional crisis.

Most American elections, even when the popular vote is extremely close, result in very lop-sided and decisive victories in the Electoral College. It has already been noted that the 1960 election, one of the closest in history in terms of popular votes, was nevertheless won by Kennedy by a 303–216 margin in the Electoral College, giving him an immediate and decisive win and the mandate he needed to govern. In 1844 Polk won by a scarce 1% of the popular vote, but nevertheless won by a decisive 170–105 tally in the Electoral College. In 1968 Nixon won by less than 1% of the vote, but nevertheless carried a 301–191 electoral mandate into the White House.

Consider how the Electoral College system and a direct election system would work in a hypothetical close election. Assume an election in which the popular vote is as close or closer than the election of 1960—that is, on the morning after the election the candidates are within a few thousand votes of each other. A few late tallies are still dribbling in from rural counties, there are absentee ballots from overseas, and there is a claim of a fraudulent vote count in three states with a total of 23 electoral votes.

Under the Electoral College system there would still be a decisive electoral vote winner, as there has been in almost all close presidential elections (303–219, in the 1960 election). Regardless of the final popular vote tally, the loser knows he or she would still be beaten even if he or she were to successfully challenge the popular vote tallies here and there, pick up some extra thousands of popular votes, or even, after a prolonged period, win a reversal of the popular vote counts in the three states where fraud was alleged. With no conceivable way to challenge the overwhelming electoral count of one's opponent, the loser gracefully concedes and congratulates the winner. The winner proceeds to start picking a cabinet and forming a government, and the country goes back to doing whatever it was doing before the election.

Now consider the likely consequences if, the year before the election, the reformers have been successful in abolishing the Electoral College and instituting a system of direct election. First of all, since the popular vote is so close, the loser (or who would have been the loser were there still an Electoral College) refuses to concede the election. Why should he or she? Votes from a few far-flung rural counties are still dribbling in, and vote recounts, if conducted around the country in every hamlet and county, might result in locating the few thousand votes needed to win the election. Of course the loser demands, as is one's right, a recount in the three states where there are serious questions of voting irregularities. While there would be no incentive to do so under an Electoral College system (since 23 extra electoral votes would make no difference in the outcome), it could make a crucial difference in a direct election, since finding only a handful of votes in those states could make the difference in the popular vote tally. If this avenue is pursued diligently (which could, of course, take weeks or months), the "loser" might find what is needed to win. And, unlike Nixon, one needn't fear looking like a sore loser, since he or she might, after all, come up a winner!

Although the damage to the country of the delays brought about by recounts over the entire country might be evident, the stakes would simply be too high for most politicians to relinquish. (It will be recalled that Nixon declined to demand a recount in Illinois, despite the obvious voting irregularities there, because he knew he would lose in the Electoral College even if he gained the Illinois votes). At this point the reader is spared a vivid description of the political horrors that would ensue while the nation, in limbo, waited for Congress to pick up the pieces, and the holder of the nuclear keys wandered around looking for the next person to give the codes to. Such a scenario would result in a true constitutional crisis.

The fact is that as Americans we have been spoiled by 200 years of peaceful elections in which an immediate and clear-cut winner has almost always been produced by our Electoral College. It is doubtful if even the framers could have predicted the success of this system conceived in the heated atmosphere of the Constitutional Convention. What the framers would surely not have predicted, however, was that many of the very citizens who benefited most from the peaceful transfer of power over the course of two centuries would seek to destroy it.

It may be countered that the constitutional crisis described above would occur only in close elections, and that most presidential elections are not as close as that described in the hypothetical scenario. While this is true, it is also true that close elections of the type described have occurred—in fact two of the last nine elections have been decided by less than 1% of the popular vote (1960 and 1968), and another by less than 2% (1976). The 1960 election was decided by less than .2% (depending upon which popular vote tallies are used).

It is also true that additional hypotheticals may be considered in which popular vote totals are very close in a large number of states. In that case popular vote reversals in each of those states might be sufficient to change the outcome of the election, and the determination of a winner might be delayed even under the Electoral College system. Indeed, a variation of this actually occurred in the election of 1876, in which voting fraud was alleged in four states, the combined electoral vote of which was just sufficient to change the electoral outcome by one vote. It is, of course, possible that such a situation could occur again.

However, it should be recalled that the 1876 election occurred just as many Southern states were beginning to assert themselves against the powers of Reconstruction, and the efforts to prevent voting by African Americans in those states were by all accounts blatant and fraudulent. In today's modern era of electronic voting machines and computers, the likelihood of widespread fraud in a large number of states simultaneously is greatly diminished.

The point to be made is that while simultaneous voting fraud across a whole region of states (such as the South) is a possibility, it would be an exceptional event; an election that is simply very close in terms of the popular vote would not be so exceptional, and has in fact occurred on an almost regular basis in recent years. Thus the chances of a constitutional crisis arising under the Electoral College are substantially less than the chances arising under a system of direct election.

It will again be recalled that in the 1960 election there were allegations of voting irregularities in Illinois, and that controversial popular vote counting procedures were used in Alabama. Nevertheless, Nixon declined to demand a recount or investigation in both instances because, as both Abbott and Levine as well as Peirce and Longley have noted, a change in those outcomes would not have affected the Electoral College verdict.[105]

Had a direct election system been in effect during the 1960 election, it is clear that, even without allegation of voting irregularities, no clear winner would have been known for a very long period of time, and Nixon would have had every incentive to challenge the popular votes in Illinois and demand an investigation of the voting irregularities there. Although his refusal to demand a recount there certainly gave him the appearance of a graceful loser, it must be recalled that he had lost in any case; it is difficult to imagine, however, that he would have passed up the opportunity to challenge the Illinois votes if there had been a direct election system in effect and there existed a distinct possibility of winning the presidency. Any challenge of this kind would certainly have delayed the determination of a winner for weeks, months, or longer. It should also be recalled that the 1960 election took place at the height of the cold war and nuclear tension.

THE ELECTORAL MANDATE

One might assume that the immediate and decisive effect of an Electoral College verdict would be universally conceded, even by its opponents, to be one of the primary advantages of the Electoral College system. Amazingly, however, advocates of direct election have chosen to find fault even with this undeniable feature of the Electoral College.

Abbott and Levine, for example, claim that electoral mandates in close popular vote elections are "misleading" to the American people. Noting that Roosevelt in 1936 got 98% of the electoral vote (but only 61% of the popular vote), and that Reagan in 1980 received 489 electoral votes (but only 50.1%) of the popular votes, they assert that such "magnified majorities"[106] create the "illusion of landslides."[107] As a result, even marginal popular vote winners are perceived as having a mandate to govern.

And why is this bad (according to Abbott and Levine)? "It may enable the [President] to push through political agendas which are opposed by the majority."[108] It may also "endo[w] the President with excessive power,"[109] and "demoralize"[110] losers who will have the "illusion" that they have been totally wiped out.

First, the basic assumption implicit in this view appears to be that no one, including the president, will bother to read the newspapers and determine the popular vote—or if anyone does, he or she will not be able to understand the popular vote tallies. In fact, the average citizen may be more impressed by the closeness of the popular vote than by the overwhelming electoral vote. Even today, if one asked the average middle-aged adult what he or she remembers about the 1960 election, they would probably recall that it was a very close election, and would probably not recall that Kennedy won an overwhelming 303–216 electoral vote. As for the loser being demoralized,[111] it is doubtful if Nixon took the view that he had been wiped out. Rather, he was perceived as having come so close that he could win if he tried again (which, of course, he did in 1968).

Second, even if it were true that an electoral count gave an "illusion" of a mandate, would the alternative be preferable—that is, that the president be perceived as lacking a mandate to govern? Would it have been preferable had Kennedy been perceived as lacking a mandate to govern the country and deal with the Soviets?

Third, although it is not conceded that overwhelming electoral votes are necessarily viewed as mandates, it is submitted that they should be. An overwhelming electoral vote, even in cases of a close popular vote, indicates that a candidate's support is broad as well as deep. An election in which a candidate receives substantial popular pluralities in many states across the country should be perceived as a greater electoral achievement than, say, obtaining an overwhelming popular vote in only one region of the country (as in the South), even though such an overwhelming popular vote in one region might give one an impressive overall popular margin of victory. Thus, if it is not, a substantial electoral majority should be perceived as a mandate to govern the entire country, and not just one part or region of it where the candidate is particularly popular.

Finally, but by no means least important, the federalist foundations of the Electoral College must be considered. In order to insure support and legitimacy for the new institution of the presidency, the constitutional framers gave to the states, through the institution of the Electoral College, an important role in the election of that president. To say that winning the support of the people in States across the nation is an illusion, and not deserving of a mandate to govern, is to deny full credit to the federalist foundations of the institution of the presidency.

THE RISKS OF TAMPERING WITH THE CONSTITUTION

It remains to balance the risks of the advantages and risks of both the Electoral College and direct election. Advocates of direct election rely heavily on the specter of the wrong president—that is, the possibility that a winner of the popular vote would lose in the Electoral College, and thus cause an alleged constitutional crisis. Although this has indeed happened once in the past 200 years in a fairly conducted election (in 1888), it caused barely a ripple at the time and no one thought much of it. Any constitutional crisis caused by that 100-year-old event appears to be only in the minds of those who today attack the Electoral College.

Some scholars have defended the Electoral College by relying on the fact that the "wrong president" has been selected only once. Such a defense, however, concedes that an electoral winner lacking a popular majority would indeed be the wrong President. It is submitted, however, that no president receiving a majority of electoral votes is any more a wrong president than a piece of legislation passed by the Senate (in which voters of small states enjoy disproportionate voting power) is the "wrong legislation," or a constitutional amendment (ratified in part by small states enjoying disproportionate voting power) is the "wrong amendment."

If the advocates of direct election truly believe a president duly elected under the Electoral College is wrong, they must, as John Kennedy suggested, open up the whole question of the federalist compact, and not just the part that meets their fancy.

In any case, as one scholar has noted,

historically the problem of democracy was not about minute margins of electoral victory but about whether, say 5 percent [the rich and the wellborn few] should rule over 95 percent [the poor many] . . . only a severe case of doctrinaire myopia makes us imagine that democracy is at stake in the minute statistical margins that might conceivably, though improbably, elect a President who did not enjoy a margin in the popular vote.[112]

The claimed "bias" in the Electoral College system would have more force if the alleged disadvantaged groups could even agree that they are so victimized. Although advocates of direct election should be sensitive to the claims of some African American leaders that the abolition of the Electoral College would unfairly reduce their electoral influence, they should also not rely on any claims of bias based on the shifting sands of constantly changing voting patterns and demographics.

Balanced against these dubious alleged risks of retaining our present constitutional system, the risks of direct election must be considered. These include the risk of a delayed presidential verdict in close elections, the rise of minority parties depriving major candidates of a majority or substantial plurality, the elimination of the role of the states in choosing a president, and the undermining of the foundation of legitimacy for our federalist democracy.

Balancing these risks and advantages weighs heavily on the side of retaining the underlying characteristics of the system of presidential elections. Although the Electoral College should be allowed to adapt, it has served this nation well. As one critic has noted, if a

realistic rather than utopian standard is applied, the Electoral College has to be rated an unqualified success. To betrays this betrays a reluctance to credit the Electoral College with any merit at all. Or perhaps it is another propensity, remarked on by Hobbes, to attribute all inconveniences to the particular form of government under which one lives, rather than to recognize that some inconveniences are intrinsic to government as such regardless of its form.[113]

One is reminded of what Winston Churchill said about democracy—that it is the worst system of government devised by man, except for every other system of government.

PROPOSALS FOR REFORM

There are several other alternatives to the Electoral College that have been proposed in a variety of different packages. For example, the proportionality plan would break down the electoral votes according to the percentage of popular vote received by a candidate in each state. Although it does have the redeeming feature of preserving the fundamental elements of federalism envisioned by the framers, it provides no more protection against factionalism and the rise of third parties than a direct election. For those concerned that the present system may select a wrong winner, it may be of interest that the proportionality plan would have elected at least three popular vote losers to the presidency (Hancock in 1880, Bryan in 1896, and Nixon in 1960).[114]

The district plan would award one electoral vote to the winner in each congressional district, and two electoral votes to the popular vote winner in the state. Besides being an invitation to gerrymandering of the worst kind now plaguing congressional elections, this plan would also cater to minor parties intent on depriving major candidates of a mandate. It would also not satisfy direct election advocates who fear a wrong winner (Nixon would have been elected under the plan).[115]

Among the hundreds of electoral reform bills and proposed constitutional amendments that have inundated Congress, there have also been a number of hybrid plans proposed. Note has already been made of the Twentieth Century Fund Task Force, which proposed a system providing for two extra electoral votes for each state, which, it is claimed, would reduce the chances for a wrong president.

All of these various reform proposals are discussed in more detail in Chapter Six. The details of the Electoral College system, its origins and evolution, as well as the effect of the Electoral College on past presidential elections are discussed in the remaining chapters of this book.

NOTES

1. Michael J. Glennon, *When No Majority Rules: The Electoral College and Presidential Succession* (Washington, D.C.: Congressional Quarterly, Inc., 1992), 76, citing Congressional Record, Senate Bill 150, 84th Cong., 2nd sess., March 20, 1956.

2. See, for example, Charley Roberts, "The Perot Factor at Work," *Los Angeles Daily Journal* (May 27, 1992): 1.

3. See, R. Hardaway, "How Would House Pick the President?" *The Plain Dealer* (Cleveland) (June 25, 1992).

4. In the presidential election of 1800, the House voted on February 11, 1801; the new Congress did not take office until March 4, 1801. See, Neal R. Peirce and Lawrence D. Longley, *The People's President: The Electoral College in American History and the Direct Vote Alternative*, rev. ed. (New Haven: Yale University Press, 1981), 39–40.

5. *Id.*

6. See, American Law Division, Congressional Research Service, "Majority or Plurality Vote Within State Delegations When House of Representatives Votes for the President," (Washington, D.C.: Library of Congress, unpublished document, June 10, 1980). See generally, *Memoirs of John Quincy Adams: Comprising Portions of His Diary from 1795 to 1848*, Charles Francis, ed. (New York: J. B. Lippincott, 1875), 501–505; Samuel Flagg Bemis, *John Quincy Adams and the Union* (New York: Alfred A Knopf, 1956); Arthur M. Schlesinger, *The Age of Jackson* (Boston: Little, Brown, 1945).

7. *Memoirs of John Quincy Adams, supra* note 6, at 501.

8. The Twelfth Amendment has, however, been augmented by the Twenty-third Amendment (1951), which limits presidential terms to two; the Twenty-fourth (1961), which provides three electors to the District of Columbia; and the Twenty-fifth (1967), which provides for succession in cases of presidential disability and in cases of a vice presidential vacancy.

9. *The Electoral College and Direct Election of the President*, Hearings Before the Subcommittee on the Constitution of the Committee on the Judiciary, U.S. Senate, 2nd Sess.; S.J. Res. 297, 302, and 312: measures proposing amendments to the Constitution relating to the direct election of the president and vice president of the United States (Washington, D.C.: U.S. Government Printing Office, July 22, 1992).

10. Peirce and Longley, *supra* note 4, at app. A.

11. See, Louis C. Kleber, "The Presidential Election of 1876," *History Today* 20 (1970): 806; Peirce and Longley, *supra* note 4, at 52–57.

12. John Hampden Dougherty, *The Electoral System of the United States; Its History, Together with a Study of the Perils That Have Attended Its Operations, an Analysis of the Several Efforts by Legislation to Avert These Perils, and a Proposed Remedy by Amendment of the Constitution* (New York: Putnam, 1906); Peirce and Longley, *supra* note 4, at 54.

13. The independent member, U.S. Supreme Court Justice David Davis, became disqualified when he was named a U.S. senator by the Illinois legislature. The Commission members, including the Democratic members, thereupon selected Justice Joseph Bradley, apparently unaware that he was in fact a Republican. Peirce and Longley, *supra* note 4, at 55.

14. *Id.*

15. See, for example, Bernard A. Weisberger, "The Stolen Election," *American Heritage* 41 (July/August 1990): 18

16. Roy Morris, Jr., "Master Fraud of the Century: The Disputed Election of 1876," *American History Illustrated* 23 (July 1988): 28. See also A. M. Gibson, *A Political Crime: The History of the Great Fraud* (New York: William S. Gottsberger, 1969).

17. Sidney I. Pommerantz, *The Coming to Power: Critical Presidential Elections in American History*, Arthur M. Schlesinger, Jr. and William P. Hansen, eds. (New York: Chelsea House Publishers in association with McGraw-Hill, 1972).

18. Judith Best, *The Case Against Direct Election of the President: A Defense of the Electoral College.* (Ithaca, N.Y.: Cornell University Press, 1975, citing Paul Haworth, *The Hayes-Tilden Disputed Presidential Election of 1876 (Cleveland: Burrows Brothers, 1906).*

19. *Id.* at 53.

20. The following bills were introduced in the 103rd Congress:

• H.J. Res. 28 Wise, amend Constitution to abolish electoral college & to provide for direct popular election for President & Vice Pres; House C/Judiciary. Source: 103–001 Page: H86 Subfile: House Proceedings History: Introduced January 5, 1993, and referred to the House Committee of the Judiciary.

• H.J. Res. 42 N. Smith, amend Constitution re nomination of individuals for election to offices of President & Vice Pres of U.S.; House C/Judiciary. Source: 103–001 Page: H86 Subfile: House Proceedings History: Introduced January 5, 1993, and referred to the House Committee of the Judiciary.

• H.J. Res. 60 Kleczka (Durbin, McNulty), amend Constitution to provide for election of President & Vice Pres by direct popular vote: House C/Judiciary. Source: 103–003 Page: H114 Subfile: House Proceedings History: Introduced January 7, 1993, and referred to the House Committee of the Judiciary.

• H.J. Res. 65 Wheat, amend Constitution to provide for direct popular election of President & Vice Pres; House C/Judiciary. Source: 103–003 Page: H114 Subfile: House Proceedings History: Introduced January 7, 1993, and referred to the House Committee of the Judiciary.

• H.J. Res. 169 Orton, amend Constitution re election of President & Vice Pres; House C/Judiciary. Source: 103–042 Page: H1739 Subfile: House Proceedings History: Introduced March 30, 1993, and referred to the House Committee of the Judiciary.

21. Congressional Research Service, *supra* note 6, at CRS-18.

22. See, Walter Berns, ed., *After the People Vote: A Guide to the Electoral College*, with essays by Norman J. Ornstein and Martin Diamond, 2nd ed. (Washington, D.C.: AEI Press, 1992), 55.

23. Final Report of the Commission on National Elections, Georgetown University, *Electing the President: A Program for Reform*, Robert E. Hunter, ed. (Washington, D.C.: The Center for Strategic and International Studies, 1986).

24. "Electing the President: Recommendations of the American Bar Association's Commission on Electoral College Reform." *American Bar Association Journal* 53 (March 1967): 219.

25. William Schneider, "Electoral College's 'Archaic Ritual,' " *National Journal* 20 (December 10, 1988): 3164.

26. Thomas M. Durbin, "The Anachronistic Electoral College," *Federal Bar News & Journal* 39 (October 1992): 510.

27. Cited in, Martin Diamond, "The Electoral College and the Idea of Federal Democracy," *The Journal of Federalism* (Winter 1978): 63.

28. *Id.*

29. Report of the Twentieth Century Fund Task Force on Reform of the Presidential Election Process, *Winner Take All*, background paper by William R. Keech (New York: Holmes and Meier, 1978). (The system set forth proposes that each state be given two extra electoral votes, thus increasing the total number of electoral votes from 538 to 640.)

30. John F. Banzhaf, "One Man, 3.312 Votes: A Mathematical Analysis of the Electoral College," with comments by the Honorable Birch Bayh, the Honorable Karl E. Mundt, the Honorable John J. Sparkman, and Neal R. Peirce. *Villanova Law Review*, 13 (Winter 1968): 304. See also, John F. Banzhaf III, "Weighted Voting Doesn't Work: A Mathematical Analysis," *Rutgers Law Review*, 19 (1965): 317; John F. Banzhaf III, "Multi-Member Electoral Districts—Do They Violate the 'One Man, One Vote' Principle?" *The Yale Law Journal* 75 (1966): 1309.

31. Robert J. Sickels, "The Power Index and the Electoral College: A Challenge to Banzhaf's Analysis," *Villanova Law Review*. 14 (Fall 1968): 92.

32. Carleton W. Sterling, "Electoral College Misrepresentation: A Geometric Analysis." *Polity* 13: 1981, 425–449.

33. *Id.* at 449.

34. 369 U.S. 186 (1962).

35. 376 U.S. 117 (1964).

36. Michael J. O'Sullivan, "Artificial Unit Voting and the Electoral College," *Southern California Law Review* 65 (July 1992): 2421, 2433 .

37. Albert Rosenthal, "The Constitution, Congress, and Presidential Elections." *Michigan Law Review* 67 (November 1968):1, 26.

38. Under the unit rule, *all* of a state's electoral votes are awarded to the winner of the popular vote.

39. See, for example, Richard Claud, *The Supreme Court and the Electoral Process* (Baltimore: Johns Hopkins University Press, 1970); cited in O'Sullivan, *supra* note 36, at 2441.

40. *Gray v. Sanders*, 372 U.S. 368 (1963).

41. See O'Sullivan, *supra* note 36, at 2441, citing *Delaware v. New York*, 385 U.S. 895 (1966).

42. 372 U.S. 368 (1963).

43. *Id.* at 380.

44. The author uses the phrase "one man, one vote" only because that phrase has taken on a life of its own in the law and legal literature. "One person, one vote" is to be much preferred.

45. *Id.*

46. John D. Feerick, "The Electoral College — Why It Ought to be Abolished," *Fordham Law Review* 37 (1968): 1.

47. Diamond, *supra* note 27, at 63.

48. *Id*. at 54, note 10.

49. *Id*.

50. James A. Michener, *Presidential Lottery: The Reckless Gamble in Our Electoral System* (New York: Random House, 1969), 137.

51. Peirce and Longley, *supra* note 4, at App. N, 296.

52. Paul Reidinger, "Still Ticking After All These Years," *ABA Journal* (September 1, 1987): 42.

53. See Chapter Six.

54. See Chapter Six.

55. See Chapter Six.

56. Banzhaf, "One Man, 3.312 Votes," *supra* note 30.

57. Diamond, *supra* note 27, at 58–59.

58. *Id*. at 59–60.

59. Max Farrand, *The Framing of the Constitution of the United States* (New Haven: Yale University Press, 1987 [originally published in 1913]. Farrand gives the details as follows:

When McHenry returned to the convention on August 6, he reports that he saw his colleague Mercer making out a list of members in attendance with "for" or "against" marked opposite almost every name. On being asked what that meant, Mercer laughingly replied that those marked with a "for" were for a king. McHenry copied the list, and on learning what it was Luther Martin copied it likewise. There were said to be over twenty names favoring a royal government. Mercer later claimed that he said these delegates were in favor of a national government, but his statement is not very convincing and leads one to think that McHenry reported the incident in substance correctly (*Id*. at 174).

Farrand further notes that: "Richard Kruel in the *American Historical Review, XVII,* 44–51 presents interesting evidence to show that Nathaniel Gorham in the latter part of 1786 actually wrote to Prince Henry of Prussia with regard to the 'Possibility of his becoming the monarch of the United States.' "

Farrand also reports that during the sessions of the convention, but it would seem especially during the latter part of August, while the subject of the presidency was causing so much disquiet, persistent rumors were current outside that the establishment of a monarchy was under consideration. The common form of the rumor was that the Bishop of Osnaburgh, the second son of George III, was to be invited to become King of the United States.

60. Birch Bayh, "Electing a President—The Case for Direct Popular Election." *Harvard Journal on Legislation,* 6 (January 1969): 127.

61. David W. Abbott and James P. Levine, *Wrong Winner: The Coming Debacle in the Electoral College* (Westport, Conn.: Praeger, 1991), 1.

62. Durbin, *supra* note 26, at 510.

63. Lolabel House, "A Study of the Twelfth Amendment," Ph.D dissertation, University of Philadelphia, 1901, 1.

64. *Id*. at 11.

65. *Id*. at 12.

66. *Id*. at 12, 15.

67. Best, *supra* note 18, at 15.

68. House, *supra* note 63, at 22.

69. *Id.*

70. *Id.*

71. Jeane J. Kirkpatrick, "Martin Diamond and the American Idea of Democracy, " *The Journal of Federalism* (Summer 1978): 7.

72. William Peters, *A More Perfect Union: The Making of the United States Constitution (New York: Crown Publishers, 1987)*, 23.

73. *Winner Take All, supra* note 29, at 59.

74. Rocky Mountain News (Denver) (December 24, 1993), 36A.

75. Hearings on S.J. Res. 1, 8, and 18 before the Subcommittee on the Constitution of the Committee of the Judiciary, U.S. Senate, 95th Cong., 1st sess. (July 22, 1977); transcription set forth in Diamond, *supra* note 27, at 75-76.

76. *Id.*

77. John Quincy Adams became president in 1824 after having received but 31.9% of the vote, but he did not obtain an electoral majority. The election was thrown into the House of Representatives, where he won by one vote.

78. The unique circumstances of the 1876 election do not detract from the fact that an electoral mandate was ultimately achieved and a crisis thereby averted.

79. Lawrence D. Longley and Alan G. Braun, *The Politics of Electoral College Reform*, foreword by U.S. Senator Birch Bayh (New Haven: Yale University Press, 1972), 67.

80. Michener, *supra* note 50, at 138.

81. See *generally*, Abbott and Levine, *supra* note 61, at 82–83, and references cited therein, including Banzhaf, "One Man, 3.312 Votes," *supra* note 30; John H. Yunker and Lawrence D. Longley, *The Electoral College: Its Biases Newly Measured for the 1960s and 1970s*, Randall B. Ripley ed. (Beverly Hills, Calif.: Sage Publications, 1976). G. Rabinowitz and Stuart Elaine McDonald, "The Power of the States in U.S. Presidential Elections," *American Political Science Review* 80 (March 1986); Harvey Zeidenstein, *Direct Election of the President* (Lexington, Mass.: D. C. Heath, 1973); Mark Levy and Michael Kramer, *The Ethnic Factor* (New York: Simon and Schuster, 1973). Similar claims have been made by others, and it is not suggested that Abbott and Levine, or any of the others cited in their work, were appealing to any particular group in advocating direct election. Rather they appear only to be making the point that the Electoral College is fundamentally unfair. Abbott and Levine's fine work is cited specifically in notes 80–90 only so that those interested in the reasoning behind each claim can find it in one handy reference source.

82. Banzhaf, "One Man, 3.312 Votes," *supra* note 30.

83. Abbott and Levine, *supra* note 61, at 82–83.

84. *Id.* at 83–84.

85. *Id.* at 90.

86. *Id.* at 93.

87. *Id.* at 91.

88. *Id.* at 94–95.

89. *Id.* at 94.

90. *Id.* at 87–88.

91. *Id.* at 88–89.

92. *Id.* at 86–87.

93. *Id.* at 89.

94. *Id.* at 144.

95. *Congressional Quarterly Guide to American Government* (Washington, D.C.: Congressional Quarterly, 1979), 78, and cited in Abbott and Levine, *supra* note 61, at 144.

96. *Id.* at 90.

97. *Id.*

98. *The Federalist* No. 49, quoted in Lucius Wilmerding, Jr., *The Electoral College* (Boston: Beacon Press, 1958), 2. See also Martin Diamond, *The Electoral College and the American Idea of Democracy.* (Washington, D.C.: The American Enterprise Institute for Public Policy Research, 1977); and Martin Diamond, "The American Idea of Equality: The View from the Founding," *The Review of Politics* (July 1976): 314.

99. Diamond, *supra* note 27.

100. Peirce and Longley, *supra* note 4 at 67.

101. *Id.* Alabama Law provided that electors would appear separately on the ballot.

All the Republican electors were pledged to vote for Nixon. . . . However a Democratic primary had resulted in six unpledged and five [Kennedy] elector candidates to compose the 11 man Democratic slate. . . . On election day the highest unpledged elector on the Democratic slate received 324,050 votes, while the highest [Kennedy] elector received 318,303 votes"(*Id.* at 66).

Those methods were used to count these votes. The nine services credited Kennedy with 318,000 votes (the highest of any Democratic elector), making it appear that he had won the popular vote by 115,000 votes. The Congressional Quarterly method, however, divided the Democratic votes proportionately between Kennedy and the unpledged electors, giving Kennedy only 147,295 popular votes. Under this method, Nixon was the popular vote winner by 58,181 votes.

102. Peirce and Longley, *supra* note 4, at 67.

103. *Id.*

104. *Id.*

105. Abbott and Levine, *supra* note 61, at 103.

106. *Id.* at 100.

107. *Id.* at 103.

108. *Id.* at 108.

109. *Id.*

110. If Nixon was ever "demoralized," it was due to a disappointing loss in the California election for governor some years later.

111. Abbott and Levine, *supra* note 61, at 103.

112. *Id.*

113. Quoting Chapter 18 of Thomas Hobbes, *Leviathan.* (Oxford, The Clarion Press, 1909), 141, and cited by Diamond, *supra* note 27, at 61.

114. Abbott and Levine, *supra* at p. 123.

115. *Id.* at 128.

Chapter Two

THE ELECTORAL COLLEGE: HOW IT REALLY WORKS

Every four years, on the first Monday after the second Wednesday in December, at or about the lunch hour, a little-known but fascinating ceremony takes place simultaneously in 51 different selected locations across the United States. Each ceremony is attended by invited guests who, although by no means household names, are upstanding citizens of the community. In many cases, their presence at the ceremony is a reward for their past dedication and service. Some are young, but most are older (93, in the case of the master of a ceremony held in Massachusetts in 1960).[1] Sometimes they are not sure why they are there. If one chosen for the honor of being present fails to appear, it is permitted to find a substitute wandering about in the area, or in the hallways. They must then be told what to do, and sometimes they resist instructions. (At a ceremony in Michigan in 1948, six invited guests failed to appear and substitutes had to be quickly found to fill in.)

The purpose of these unlikely gatherings? Nothing less than the election of the president of the United States. The titles of the invited guests? Presidential electors of the Electoral College.

ELECTING THE PRESIDENT OF THE UNITED STATES

It has been charged that the Electoral College is complex. In fact, the Electoral College system itself is simple and straightforward, though the entire process of electing a president can indeed be complicated. The Constitution simply provides that each legislature shall appoint electors, who will subsequently meet in their respective states and elect the president.

It must be recognized, however, that the procedures used today are the product not only of the simple system outlined by the framers in the Constitution and in one paragraph of the Twelfth Amendment, but of tradition and a long history of trial and error over the course of two centuries. The courts (both state and federal), state legislatures, Congress, and the major political parties have all played important roles in devising the system used today in electing a president.

Thus Article I, Section 1 of the Constitution no more sets forth the entire body of law relating to the election of the President than the 45 words of the First Amendment constitute the entire body of the law relating to freedom of speech and religion.

A basic understanding of the Electoral College and how it works is a necessary prerequisite to evaluating the many current proposals for reform. It has been revealed that many of those expressing an opinion with regard to electoral reform (such as those who advocate direct popular election) in fact have little understanding of how the Electoral College actually works today in electing a president.

The Constitution provides no method for selecting the final candidates for election to the office of president. In part this is because the formation of political parties was still in its infancy at the time of the Constitutional Convention, and the subsequent rise of the importance of political parties was not envisioned.

In many ways, the preelection selection procedure is the most important part of the process, for it is from a relatively small group of selected candidates that the people, through the presidential electors, express their final choice. As political scientist Donald Mathews has observed, "nominations are more critical than elections."[2] It is the nomination phase of the process that narrows the field from a potential pool of millions of eligible candidates down to two (sometimes, but rarely, three or four) major candidates. In practical terms, the Electoral College only provides for the procedure for selection from among these final candidates.

After the preelection process has chosen the candidates, the process for final selection of the president under the Electoral College can be divided into nine separate steps, or stages. Not all of these stages are directly mandated by the Constitution, but rather are determined by judicial interpretation of the Constitution, federal and state laws, or by tradition. Nevertheless each stage is an essential feature of the Constitutional process of electing a president under the Electoral College system. Not all nine steps are followed in every election, since following some of the steps is contingent upon the occurrence of an electoral event that may or may not take place. Indeed some of the steps have not been utilized in any election, since the contingent events provided for have never occurred.

The nine stages, discussed more fully in the sections of this chapter, are as follows:

1. Nomination of Presidential Electors
2. Election of Presidential Electors

3. Election of the President by Electors

4. State Certification of the Electoral Slate

5. Transmission of Certificates to U.S. Senate President

6. Counting of Electoral Votes by Congress

7. Referral of the Presidential Election to the House (if no candidate receives a majority of electoral votes)

8. Referral of Vice Presidential Election to the Senate

9. Election of the President Pursuant to the Automatic Succession Act (if no selection of president is made by House)

THE PREELECTION PROCESS

Since nothing is said in the Constitution about how presidential candidates are to be selected, this process is determined primarily by party politics. However, state laws also play an important role in the selection of candidates, particularly in governing many of the rules for the selection of party delegates at national conventions.[3] The result is an exceedingly complex nominating process that makes the final selection process (i.e., the Electoral College) look quite simple by comparison.

It has been observed that "the United States must have the most elaborate, complex, and prolonged formal system of nominating candidates for chief executive in the world."[4] Austin Ranney has described the nomination process as the "most elaborate, variegated, and complex set of rules in the world. They include national party rules, state and local party rules, state statutes, and a wide variety of rulings by national and state courts."[5] The system is indeed a virtual labyrinth, for each state has its own laws, customs, and political procedures. The American Bar Association, which has criticized the Electoral College for being "too complex,"[6] might do well to concentrate on proposing simplifications to the maze of present procedures for nominating, rather than electing, presidential candidates.

The first phase of the preelection process is informal; it involves the ability of a citizen seeking nomination to become visible as a candidate, and to be perceived by a broad base of the electorate as a potential and viable candidate. (In modern times, the biggest role in this process is played by the media.)

If one considers the preselection support of 1% of the population (as reflected in public opinion polls) as the threshold for viability, it is interesting to note that in the past 60 years, only 109 Americans have been given this measure of support by partisans of the two major parties.[7] Those receiving this threshold measure of support have been primarily past or present public officeholders. Of these 109 Americans, 36% have been U.S. senators, 23% governors, 17% cabinet officers, 6% House representatives, and 2% vice presidents.[8]

Although not all citizens receiving this measure of support in prelimi-
nary public opinion polls choose to actively run, those who do face a
daunting gauntlet posed by a variety of state and party rules and procedures.[9] While it is beyond the scope of this book to fully review those laws
and procedures, the broad outlines of those procedures are considered
here.[10]

NATIONAL CONVENTIONS

The next step in the nominating process is to begin the cultivation of
support from those who are likely to become delegates to a national party
convention. In the case of a candidate for nomination by an out-of-power
party, this may involve appearing at party fund-raising events, or in support of local party candidates. (Richard Nixon, for example, spent years
performing such functions prior to his 1968 Republican nomination.) During the first years of the Republic, the newly evolving parties' function of
channeling support to one competitive candidate was performed by Congressional Caucuses, which provided a convenient national forum before
the days of reliable travel by rail.[11] It was recognized, however, that Congressional Caucuses violated the spirit if not the letter of the framers' intent
to insulate the institution of the presidency from the Congress. By 1824 this
system had given way to a hybrid system reflecting the choice of local party
conventions, state legislatures, and other party meetings.[12] The first national convention was held by the anti-Mason party in 1831.[13] By 1856
national conventions had become the norm for both the Democratic and
Republican parties.

Delegates to national conventions, chosen under a variety of different
sets of state and political rules, consist largely of public officials, governors,
congresspersons, and other party leaders. Although participation by such
officials has continued over the years, both the states and the major parties
have adopted a number of rules to insure fair prepresentation among
delegates of women, minorities, and young people.[14]

Prior to 1950 the manner in which delegates were to be selected was
primarily at the state level, both by statute and party rules. By 1964 there
was a definite trend toward the imposition of national party rules regarding
the selection of delegates.[15] National party rules have also been imposed
determining whether delegate votes shall be proportional or by unit, and
the amount of delegate support necessary to place a candidate's name in
nomination. Although federal regulatory participation in the nomination
process is minimal, tension and conflict between national party rules and
state and local party rules continue, and resort has often been made to the
courts to resolve these conflicts.[16]

A much more important question than how delegates are to be selected,
is how they are to vote once they arrive at the convention. It has been noted

that delegates are chosen pursuant to a variety of local state and party rules. A delegate's preference for a particular presidential candidate has traditionally been but one factor in his selection. While delegates were technically free to vote for any candidate, in practice their primary loyalties were to party leaders. This led to the much maligned practice of a handful of party leaders choosing a candidate in a "smoke-filled room."

THE PRIMARIES

By 1912, however, about 17 states were holding popular vote primaries and binding delegates, regardless of their personal preference, to vote for the winners of the state primary at least for a certain number of ballots at the convention.[17] Between 1920 and 1968, however, more states abandoned primaries than instituted them, so that by 1968 only 15 states conducted primary elections for President.[18] By 1976, 8 more states instituted primaries, and the percentage of delegates bound to vote for the primary winner on the first ballot approached 70%. The modern trend is for even more states to adopt primaries. As a result, the selection of a nominee in recent years has been a virtual foregone conclusion by the time the convention actually takes place.

In order to assert a greater regional influence in the selection of a presidential candidate, some states (such as a number of Southern states) in recent years have chosen to conduct their primaries on the same day ("Super Tuesday"). Others have chosen to assert disproportionate influence by conducting a primary before any other state. (New Hampshire, for example, has insisted on conducting its primary first.)

In recent presidential contests, the early primaries have proved to be critical to presidential aspirants. Sources of funding tend to wait until a front-runner emerges, and the winner in New Hampshire often becomes the first front-runner. Media attention and the release of funding resources can then build a momentum in later primaries that can carry a candidate through to victory at the convention.

This system has been criticized on grounds that it gives undue weight and influence to the presidential choice of one small or particular state such as New Hampshire, which may not be representative of the country as a whole. Thus a candidate whose appeal might be much greater across the rest of the country might be delivered an unfairly fatal blow by the voters of New Hampshire, to whom his appeal might be very limited.

A national primary, in which every state conducts its primary on the same day, has been suggested as an alternative.[19] Like the direct election proposed by electoral reformers, however, a national primary might bring unintended results. A national primary would contain many of the weaknesses of direct election. Since there would not be a significant reduction of the field prior to the primary, voters across the country would be asked to vote for one candidate among many on one particular day. The top vote-getters in the primary could win with a relatively small plurality, even though they might be the third, fourth, or fifth choices of a large majority of voters.

Under the present system, it is true that losers in the first primaries may be at a disadvantage in pursuing the party nomination. While some early candidates might indeed be eliminated by a poor showing, others who did not participate in the early primaries might be encouraged to enter the race, replacing candidates who had not shown the ability to win the confidence of voters. Also, losses in the first primaries usually constitute a knock-out blow only to the very worst losers, and candidates known to have broad appeal elsewhere can usually survive to test their appeal on more fertile territory.

The present system also gives a chance to candidates who can not afford to fund a national primary campaign at the outset. Rather it allows candidates to test their appeal in a relatively small and inexpensive campaign, obtain media coverage and funding if they are successful, and gradually build momentum to challenge candidates with greater sources of funding. It may therefore present more practical opportunities for a direct appeal to the people, rather than making a candidate dependent on internal party resources, and the support of party bureaucrats. John Kennedy's 1960 campaign revealed the opportunities a staggered primary system affords to a youthful and energetic candidate (though there were fewer primaries at that time).

Finally, a national primary would afford few second chances to the losers. Staggered primaries, on the other hand, permit impressive losers in one primary to redeem themselves later in a second primary and to show their mettle over a period of time. Though certainly a grueling process, the system of staggered primaries performs the critical function of narrowing the field, while at the same time providing a proving ground for many of the qualities thought desirable in a president: stamina, fortitude, poise and grace under pressure, and sheer physical and mental energy. Indeed, more than one presidential candidate has been eliminated after failing to show one or more of these qualities over the course of a long primary campaign— probably to the benefit of the Republic.

In most states, however, primary results bind the votes of national convention delegates only for one or a limited number of ballots. If, after a certain number of ballots, no candidate receives a majority of votes, delegates may be free to search for a majority consensus. Although this has rarely been necessary in recent years, it has frequently occurred in earlier conventions.[20] Ironically, the claimed function of the earliest presidential electors (that is, exercising independent judgment) has, over the course of American history, devolved in not infrequent practice upon delegates to national conventions.

In fact, the American primary and convention system as it has evolved over two centuries has served us well in providing presidential candidates for consideration by the Electoral College. We turn now to the nine stages of that final electoral process.

NOMINATION OF PRESIDENTIAL ELECTORS

Article II, Section 1(2) of the U.S. Constitution provides that "each state shall appoint, in such manner as the Legislature thereof shall direct, a number of electors, equal to the whole number of Senators and Representatives to which the state may be entitled in the Congress." While the Constitution provides that the ultimate appointment of electors is left to the state, it does not, however, specifically direct how electors shall be nominated for consideration for appointment by the state.

As a result, the nomination of electors is performed pursuant to state laws. In about 37 states, each party is required to nominate electors at a state convention. In 10 states, the nominations are made by a party committee. In Florida, the nomination of electors is done by the governor upon recommendation of each state party committee; Arizona conducts a separate primary; Mississippi uses a combined convention-primary system; and Pennsylvania allows the party's presidential nominee to appoint the electors.

ELECTION OF PRESIDENTIAL ELECTORS

It has been noted that although the Constitution does not direct how electors shall be nominated, it does direct that their ultimate appointment shall be by each state as its legislature directs. It also provides how many electors each state may ultimately appoint.

The Twenty-third Amendment gives the District of Columbia electors equal in number to those given to the least populous state (3). Since there are 465 House representatives, 100 senators, and 3 electors for the District of Columbia, there are a total of 538 electors, a majority of whom (270) will elect a president. However, the Constitution does not specify how the state legislatures are to appoint the electors allocated to their state. In fact, the plain words of the Constitution appear to give each state legislature plenary power to determine the method of appointment.

In the first few elections after the ratification of the Constitution, most state legislatures chose to select the electors themselves, either by vote of both houses of the state legislature, or by majority vote of the two state houses voting in joint session. As early as 1788, however, some state legislatures began to provide for appointment by direct election of the people (notably New Hampshire).[21] A variety of other intermediate methods, involving both the electorate and the legislature in the selection process, were also employed during these early elections.[22] More and more states began to adopt the popular vote method of electing electors, however, and by 1820 all but nine states provided for popular election of presidential electors. By 1832, only one state, North Carolina, had refused to adopt the direct election of electors (North Carolina did not provide for direct election of electors until after the Civil War).

Although every state after 1865 provided for the direct election by the people of presidential electors, it was never doubted that each state legislature had the power to change its method of selecting presidential electors, and to use virtually any method of selection it chose.

In 1874 the U.S. Senate Committee on Privileges and Elections confirmed that

The appointment of these electors is thus placed absolutely and wholly with the legislatures of the several states. They may be chosen by the legislature, or the legislature may provide that they shall be elected by the people at large; [it] is no doubt competent for the legislature to authorize the governor, or the Supreme Court of the State, or any other agent of its will, to appoint these electors.[23]

The report also asserted that even if a legislature adopted a method of direct popular election of electors, "there is no doubt of the right of the legislature to resume the power at any time, for it can neither be taken away nor abdicated."[24] Indeed, on several occasions prior to 1832, state legislatures did exactly that.[25]

Any doubt of the legislature's power to determine the manner of selection was resolved by the Supreme Court in the 1892 case of *McPherson v. Blacker*. In that case the Court reaffirmed that Article II, Section 2 confers "plenary power to the state legislatures in the matter of the appointment of electors."[26]

Since no state has since attempted to take away from the people the right to elect presidential electors, the issue of legislative prerogatives to determine the method of selecting electors was not again pressed until 1968, when the Ohio American Independent party and the Socialist Labor party attempted to get on the Ohio Presidential ballot.

In that case, *Williams v. Rhodes*, the State of Ohio had, in the opinion of the Supreme Court, made it "virtually impossible for a new political party, even though it had hundreds of thousands of members, or an old party, which has a very small number of members, to be placed on the state ballot to choose electors pledged to particular candidates for the Presidency and Vice Presidency of the United States."[27] Although the two major parties were automatically put on the primary ballot, Ohio election laws not only required that a new party obtain signatures of qualified electors totaling 15% of the ballots cast in the last gubernatorial election, but also required that a long series of other requirements be satisfied, such as appointment of 1,200 committee members who had not previously voted in primary elections for another party. The parties excluded by such requirements claimed that their rights under the Equal Protection Clause of the Four-teenth Amendment were violated by such discriminatory requirements.

Nevertheless, the Court was faced with its prior decision in *McPherson v. Blacker*, in which it had said that the states had virtually unlimited discretion in determining the method of appointment of electors. Since that time, however, the Twenty-third Amendment of the Constitution had been ratified, which provided that the right to vote for "electors for President or Vice President shall not be denied ... by reason to pay any poll tax or other tax." Thus, this amendment confirmed that there were at least some limits to the state power to appoint electors.

However, the Court pointed out, "the Constitution is filled with provi-sions that grant Congress or the States specific power to legislate in certain areas; these granted powers are always subject to the limitation that they may not be exercised in a way that violates other specific provisions of the Constitution."[28] For example, the Constitution gives the Congress plenary power to "lay and collect taxes," but the taxing power cannot be invoked in such a way that only minorities are taxed, or that citizens are denied their rights against self-incrimination. Thus the Court held that the Ohio voting restrictions violated the voting, associational, and Fourteenth Amendment equal protection rights of the plaintiffs.[29]

Taken together, the *McPherson* and *Williams* cases confirm the principle that the states are still free to choose any method they wish to appoint presidential electors (such as appointment by the legislature, the governor, or the State Supreme Court). But if a state chooses to appoint the electors by means of popular election, it is not permitted to employ election laws that violate the Equal Protection Clause of the Constitution.

Before proceeding further, it may be helpful to briefly pause and review the electoral process up to this point. The Constitution simply provides that each state will appoint electors who will subsequently meet and choose the president. Through a natural political process, parties have formed that nominate candidates to be considered for election by the electors. By tradition, that process of nomination is by a national convention of each party. At that convention, delegates chosen by the party vote for a nominee. According to state laws and party rules, delegates may be chosen by a variety of means, including caucuses conducted by party members. A recent trend is to conduct a popular primary vote that binds respective delegates to vote for the primary vote winner for a certain number of ballots at the national convention.

Parallel to the nomination process is the actual election process. Each party may nominate candidates to be electors. (Care must be taken not to confuse the process of nominating presidential candidates and the process of nominating electors.) However, under the Constitution, the actual ap-pointment of electors is left up to the states, which now all provide that the "appointment" shall be by popular election of the people. Once a state decides to use the election method of appointment, it must not employ election laws that violate the Equal Protection Rights of all eligible voters.

It remains to examine what might appear to be a mundane aspect of electing the electors—namely, the mechanics and logistics of their selection. In fact, this aspect has become the very heart of the Electoral College as it functions today.

Consider the variety of ways in which a large number of electors can be chosen by popular vote. One way would be to put on a ballot the names of each individual elector nominated by each party. In a state like California, that would mean that there would be 54 names on the ballot for each party, or 108 names of electors representing both major parties. In addition each minor party qualifying to be on the ballot would also have 54 names. For obvious reasons few states (and none of the largest ones) have chosen this method.

The method overwhelmingly preferred by the states is the "general ticket ballot" method, whereby all the electors nominated by a party in a state are lumped together as a unit, or elector slate. Thus voters are not given the option of voting for, say, one elector they may like from the Democratic slate, one from the Republican slate, and so on. Rather, they are given only the option of voting for a party's entire slate. In fact, in states employing the "short ballot," the individual names of the electors are not even listed. Instead the entire slate is simply given a label (usually the name of the presidential nominee of the party that chose the elector slate). What voters see when they look at the ballot is, in tiny letters, "electors for," and then in big type the name of the party's nominee. Some states have even eliminated the reference to "electors for" and list only the name of the presidential nominee. This has led some voters to believe they are actually voting directly for a presidential candidate rather than for the electors.

If the electors are chosen on a statewide basis, the general ticket ballot has a most important consequence—namely, that the presidential choice of the winning slate gets all the electoral votes allocated to that state, and the losing slate gets none. It is this particular feature of the Electoral College that has caused the most controversy, since it means that a candidate's slate can receive millions of popular votes, but not receive a single electoral vote to show for it. Although advocates of direct popular election have focused on this particular feature to support their argument for a constitutional amendment, this feature is not in fact a part of the Constitution at all. Rather, it is a feature chosen by each individual state.

A few states have chosen actually to list on the ballot each individual elector, and permit voters to pick and choose between electors on each slate.[30] One state even permits the listing of individual electors without requiring a designation of which presidential candidate each elector favors.[31] In such a state a premium is obviously put on voters having done their homework, and determined ahead of time whom each elector favors.

Two states avoid the "winner take all" consequences of the general ticket ballot by conducting the election of electors on a district basis rather than on a statewide basis. The Constitution distributes electoral votes to a state based on the number of senators and members of Congress to which it is entitled. Thus, if a state is entitled to two senators, and two members of Congress, a state is entitled to four electoral votes. The state of Maine has chosen to elect two of its electors (representing its senators) on a statewide basis, since the senators themselves are chosen on a statewide basis. The remaining two electors (representing the members of Congress from each district within Maine) are elected within each district. That is, each district votes separately for each elector. The result is two possible electoral vote tallies in Maine: either 4–0, or 3–1.

Nebraska also has chosen this district system of electing presidential electors. In 1992 Florida considered adopting such a system but finally decided against it. Thus, in all but two states it is the combination of the general ticket ballot and election of electors on a statewide basis that results in the "winner take all" feature of the Electoral College.

During the first elections of the Republic, many states adopted the district system now used by Maine and Nebraska. Gradually, however, the states switched over to the general ticket system of statewide voting, apparently on the theory that by casting its state's electoral vote as one large bloc, the state's influence on the election would be enhanced. Once one state went to that system, the others felt compelled to follow so as not to be at a disadvantage. Nevertheless, it is entirely within a state's prerogative to switch back to a district system at any time, as Maine and Nebraska have done.

By 1892 the general ticket ballot had become so widely adopted by the states that it was argued it had become an integral part of the Electoral College system. It was this very argument, however, that was rejected by the Supreme Court in *McPherson v. Blacker*, in which Michigan attempted to revert back to a district system. It was entirely permissible for Michigan to choose such a system, said the Court, since the Constitution permits the states to appoint its electors in any manner it chooses.[32] (Michigan has since gone back to the general ticket ballot.)

Finally, it remains to determine the credentials of electors, and what they must do to qualify for election. The Constitution only sets forth the requirement that they not be a senator or member of Congress, or a person holding an office of trust under the United States. Political parties, however, have imposed an important additional requirement on their own chosen electors: prior to their election, they pledge to cast their vote for their party's presidential nominee.

In 1952 the practice of a party requiring an elector to pledge, in advance of nomination and election, to support the party's presidential nominee was challenged in the Supreme Court case of *Ray v. Blair*.[33] In that case an elector, otherwise qualified for nomination and election, was denied certification by his party as an elector nominee on grounds that he refused to pledge to vote for his party's nominee in the Electoral College. The plaintiff's argument was that the Constitution places no limitation on how an elector must cast a vote in the Electoral College, and that it is therefore an infringement on an elector's constitutional right for a party to demand, as a condition of an elector's election, a pledge that he or she will vote for a particular candidate.

The Court flatly rejected this argument, noting that neither the Constitution nor the Twelfth Amendment "prohibits an elector's announcing his choice beforehand, pledging himself" nor does it "forbid a party to require from candidates in its primary a pledge of political conformity with the aims of the party."[34] In other words, the court made a distinction between the constitutional right of an elector, once chosen, to vote for whomever he or she pleases, and the right of a party, before nominating that elector, to demand in advance a pledge to vote for a particular candidate.

While many states have been content to rely on party loyalty to insure that an elector votes for the presidential candidate of the party that nominated him, a growing number of states have required that electors give pledges in advance to their party to vote for the party nominee.[35] Some have gone even further, and provided that violation of the pledge is a crime (punishable in some states as a misdemeanor, and in at least one state as a felony).[36]

Not answered specifically by *Ray v. Blair* is whether such laws punishing "faithless electors" are constitutional. It does appear clear, however, that even if such laws were enforceable, they could not change a faithless elector's vote. The only recourse would be to punish the elector after the fact. The electors meet at a specific time and place to cast their ballots for president. The whole ceremony is over in a matter of minutes. There is simply no time to rush to court and obtain a court order to vote for a particular candidate. Once the vote is cast, it is not retractable.

Even if an elector were to announce prior to the meeting of electors that he or she intended to violate the pledge, it is unlikely that any court would order them to vote in accordance with the pledge. To do so would clearly violate the Constitution, which places no restrictions on for whom one can vote. It is only the violation of the pledge that can be made a crime, and not the actual vote.

The problem of the faithless elector has not been a major one in past presidential elections. Of the 17,397 votes cast by electors during the years 1820–1980, only 7 have been cast by electors for other than their party's candidate.[37] Nevertheless, this is an area in which responsible reform would be appropriate (see Chapter Seven).

ELECTION OF THE PRESIDENT BY ELECTORS

Article II, Section 2 states simply that "the electors shall meet in their respective states, and vote by ballot for two persons. . . . The person having the greatest number of votes shall be the President, if such number be a majority of the whole number of electors appointed." The Twelfth Amendment modifies this procedure to require balloting for president and vice president separately. It was thought by the framers that by requiring the electors to meet in their respective states, rather than in one large gathering, intrigue, combination, and corruption would be effectively avoided, and a "free and pure election of the President of the United States made perpetual."[38] In the days before the railroad, it also was far more convenient than having all the electors meet at the seat of government.

The U.S. Code directs that the electors shall meet on the first Monday after the second Wednesday in December to cast their votes "at such place in each state as the legislature of such state shall direct."[39] In most states the electors meet in the state capitol, the office of the secretary of state, or in the governor's chambers. In some states a ceremonial ritual of electing chairpersons, giving speeches, and benedictions is prescribed.

The decorum of the electoral meetings is not always appropriate to the solemnity of the occasion. At the 1976 Wisconsin meeting of the Electoral College, the invited speaker told the electors that they were "little more than a state by state collection of political hacks and fat cats."[40] In fact it is true that electors are often loyal political functionaries whose appointments as electors are rewards for past dedicated service to the party. It has been said that they are "usually selected for their devotion to party, their popular manners, and a supposed talent for electioneering."[41] However, electors have also been defended as "among the state's ablest men" who go "among the people to instruct, excite, and arouse them on the issues of the campaign."[42] Elector (and author) James Michener claimed that his credentials as an elector were that "every year I contributed what money I could to the party."[43]

The U.S. Code provides that when the electors meet, they shall make and sign six certificates that shall contain two distinct lists, one of the votes for president, and the other for vice president.[44] The electors then seal up the certificates [45] and send one by registered mail to the president of the Senate (i.e. the sitting vice president) in Washington, two to the secretary of state of the state, two to the archivist in Washington, and one to the judge of the district in which the electors have assembled.[46]

Although the reference in the Constitution to the electors casting a "ballot" might suggest that their vote be secret, by custom the electors' votes have not been secret since 1800 (when a New York elector who insisted on a secret ballot was faced down and obliged by fellow electors to reveal his choice).[47]

The U.S. Code permits states to provide for filling any vacancies that might occur in the Electoral College.[48] Since the electoral vote must occur on the date set by statute,[49] any vacancies occurring on the day of the vote must be quickly filled. When six electors failed to appear in Michigan in 1948 on the date of the election, substitutes had to be found immediately from those wandering about in the area. One of those recruited did not understand that as a substitute for an elector pledged to vote for the Republican nominee he was bound to vote for the Republican who had carried the state, and tried to vote for Truman (who had in fact lost the state of Michigan). Later the substitute elector explained that "I thought we had to vote for the winning candidate."[50]

STATE CERTIFICATION OF THE ELECTORAL SLATE

Section 6 of Title 3 of the U.S. Code states that it is the duty of the governor of each state not only to certify the electoral votes of his or her state, but also to certify that, if a dispute has arisen as to which electoral slate has been elected, a final determination has been made according to established state procedures for resolving the dispute.[51] Section 15 further binds the U.S. Congress to accept the state governor's certification of the state's electoral slate, so long as the electoral votes had been "regularly given" by the electors.[52]

These Code provisions were first promulgated after the 1876 election debacle between Tilden and Hayes. It will be recalled that in that election several states submitted two sets of electoral returns, reflecting the dispute over the popular vote count in their states. Congress then had to appoint a commission to determine which of the two sets of electoral slates would be authenticated.

In the aftermath of the debacle that followed, Congress enacted a law that it hoped would avoid the need for congressional involvement in the certification of state electoral returns. The idea was that this distasteful task would be performed by each state rather than Congress. Thus the states were to establish their own internal procedures for resolving any disputes, and any resolution of a dispute over which an electoral slate had been elected would be certified by the state governor and transmitted to the president of the U.S. Senate, who would then accept the governor's certification as binding. Congress would then be spared the potentially explosive task of having to certify the returns itself.

The problem with this scheme, however, was that Congress was not quite willing to give up all its power to accept or reject the states' certified returns. The statute it enacted hedged by saying that only electoral votes "regularly given" would be accepted. The exact words of the statute read as follows: "(N)o electoral votes or votes from any state which shall have been regularly given by electors whose appointment has been lawfully certified to according to Section 6 of this title from which but one return has been received shall be rejected."[53]

There are several interpretations that may be given to this language. One is that Congress will consider itself bound by the selection of an appointed slate certified by a governor, but will not consider itself bound if a particular elector on that slate has voted in a manner inconsistent with constitutional requirements.

Although there have arisen few occasions since 1876 in which there has been a need to interpret the language of Section 15, a problem did arise in 1969 when a North Carolina elector (Dr. Lloyd Bailey) on a slate appointed to vote for Nixon (the popular vote winner), decided to vote for George Wallace instead. Representative O'Hara from Michigan and Senator Muskie from Maine objected and proposed that Dr. Bailey's vote not be given on grounds that it was not "regularly given." The dispute triggered a heated debate among those in Congress who felt the objection well founded, and those who did not.

Opponents to the objection argued that the Constitution clearly imposes no restrictions on an elector's vote, and that Congress therefore had no right to reject Dr. Bailey's vote. Proponents of the objection conceded that this was true, but argued that Dr. Bailey had restricted his own freedom to vote for anyone other than the popular vote winner by representing to the people of his state that he would vote for the candidate of the party on whose slate he was appointed, and therefore his vote should be rejected on general equitable principles of estoppel and detrimental reliance.[54]

In the end the objection was rejected and the vote for Wallace counted in the final tally of electoral votes. However, the line between state and federal certification of electoral votes remains gray and should be addressed as part of responsible reform.

TRANSMISSION OF CERTIFICATES TO U.S. SENATE PRESIDENT

The Twelfth Amendment directs that after the electoral counts are certified, they are to be transmitted to the seat of government and directed to the president of the Senate.

The President of the Senate shall, in the presence of the Senate and the House of Representatives, open all the certificates and the votes shall then be counted; the person having the greatest number of votes for President shall be the President, if such number be a majority of the whole number of electors appointed. . . . The person having the greatest number of votes as Vice-President shall be the Vice-President, if such number be a majority of the whole number of electors appointed.

Title 3 of the U.S. Code gives more specific instructions, directing that on the sixth day of January following every meeting of electors, the Senate and the House of Representatives are to meet in the House of Representatives at precisely 1:00 P.M., and that the president of the Senate will be the presiding officer.[55] Two "tellers" from the House and two from the Senate are to be appointed to receive the electoral certificates, which shall then be "opened, presented, and acted upon in alphabetical order of the states, beginning with the letter A. The tellers shall then make a list of the votes as they appear on the certificates, and the tally then delivered to the president of the Senate who shall thereupon announce the results and declare the elected President and Vice President."[56]

It may be recalled that in the election of 1876 a serious question arose about the authority and responsibility of the president of the Senate in counting the votes. One view was that by being given the responsibility to count the votes, the president of the Senate by implication was also given authority to authenticate them as well and determine their validity. Others took the view that the Senate president's duty to count the votes was purely ministerial and that it was the responsibility of Congress to determine the ultimate validity of the returns. This latter view was, at least in part, codified in a law passed the year after the 1876 election (now Title 3 of the U.S. Code).

COUNTING OF ELECTORAL VOTES BY CONGRESS

It will be recalled that Congress attempted to relieve itself of the political responsibility of certifying state electoral slates by providing by law that no electoral votes that have been "regularly given" shall be rejected by the Congress. However, after the president of the Senate has announced the electoral results, Title 3 now provides that he (or she) shall "call for objections, if any."[57] Written objections, signed by at least one member of the Senate and House, will then be entertained. The Senate and House shall then withdraw to consider the objections. The two houses concurrently may reject the contested electoral votes if they agree that they have not been "regularly given."

Title 3 further takes into account the need for a prompt and expeditious resolution of any electoral dispute. When the two houses withdraw to consider an objection, each senator and representative may speak to the question, but for no longer than five minutes, and no more than once.[58] If the matter has not been resolved within five days after the first meeting in the two houses, no recesses are permitted, and the houses must stay in constant session until the matter is resolved.[59]

REFERRAL OF THE PRESIDENTIAL ELECTION
TO THE HOUSE

The Twelfth Amendment provides that if, after the electoral votes are counted, "no person [has] a majority, then from the persons having the highest numbers not exceeding three on the list of those voted for as President, the House of Representatives shall choose immediately, by ballot, the President. But in choosing the President, the votes shall be taken by states, the representation from each state having one vote." The amendment further requires a quorum of a "member or members from two-thirds of the states, and a majority of all the states."

It has been over a century and a half since this procedure has been utilized. The last time a presidential election was referred to the House was in 1825, when John Quincy Adams was elected by one vote. In every election since then, no presidential candidate has ever failed to get a majority of electoral votes. It will be recalled that the problem in the election of 1876 was not that there was no obtainable majority of electoral votes. (No candidate other than Tilden and Hayes received any electoral votes.) Rather the problem was that the popular vote returns in several states were disputed, thus casting doubt as to whom the electoral votes of those states should be awarded.

It is perhaps not coincidental that after 1825 the general ticket system was widely adopted, becoming almost the exclusive method of tabulating electoral votes. Perhaps no other feature of the Electoral College has performed so well in insuring the prompt and orderly election of a president.

Because there has been no occasion in the past 169 years to apply the House election provisions of the Twelfth Amendment, there has been little federal law enacted on the subject. This is indeed unfortunate, since it would be far better to enact rules and procedure for such a contingent election at a time when there was no immediate possibility of such an election, rather than waiting until it becomes a distinct possibility, in which case political factors would no doubt become paramount. Thus if Congress waits until it becomes clear that such an election must take place, rules and procedures will be put forth and opposed not on their merits, but rather on the basis of which party and presidential candidate they will favor.

The only precedent, other than the Twelfth Amendment, relating to how a House election would be conducted are the rules adopted by the House of Representatives in 1801[60] and 1825.[61] In both those years none of the presidential candidates received a majority of electoral votes, and the election was referred to the House of Representatives.

Neither set of rules adds much to the Twelfth Amendment. In the 1801 House election the vote of each state was determined by a majority of votes within each state delegation. The rules, however, do not require a majority decision. The 1825 rules direct that doors of the House shall be closed during balloting, and they provide a procedure whereby each state first conducts a vote within its delegation and then later casts its ballot as a state. If the balloting within a delegation produces a majority winner, that winner becomes the selection of that state. If no candidate receives a majority within the state's delegation, the ballot for that state will read simply "divided," and its vote will not count in the final balloting of states.

The 1825 rules, having never been changed, would presumably be binding on a House election conducted today if new rules were not promulgated. It is unlikely, however, that new rules would not be adopted if there arose the likelihood of a deadlock in the Electoral College. In 1992 the House began deliberations on the adoption of new rules when it became apparent that the candidacy of Ross Perot might produce just such a deadlock. However, these deliberations were terminated when Perot dropped out of the race in July 1992. When Perot later reentered the race there was no longer the threat of an electoral deadlock, and the deliberations of new House rules were not resumed.

Even if the 1825 rules were to remain in effect, however, there are a number of procedural issues that are not clearly resolved by either the Constitution or the Twelfth Amendment. Those issues, discussed separately in this section, are as follows: Would the votes within each delegation be by plurality or by majority? Would the votes be by open or secret ballot? Would a quorum be required of delegates within a delegation? Would the House election be by the House sitting at the time of the presidential election, or the new House not yet sworn in at the time of the meeting of the Electoral College in December?

Majority Versus Plurality

The Constitution does not indicate whether a majority or plurality of votes within a state delegation is sufficient to cast a vote for that state in the House election. The 1801 House election rules state only that "in case the vote of the state be for one person, then the name of that person shall be [the vote of the state]; and in case the ballots of the state be equally divided, then the word 'divided' shall be written on the state's ballot." Despite the ambiguity in this language on the question of whether a majority or plurality would be required, the Congressional Research Service now records that in fact "a majority decision determined each state's result."[62]

The 1825 rules are more explicit, clearly stating that "in case one of the persons from whom the choice is made shall receive a majority of the votes given . . . the name of that person shall be [the choice of that state]."[63] Although this rule would be subject to the Twelfth Amendment, the amendment states only that the House "shall choose immediately, by ballot, the President," and that the "vote shall be taken by states, the representation from each state having one vote." There therefore appears to be no constitutional barrier to requiring either a majority or a plurality in the voting of a delegation.

In 1980 the Congressional Research Service responded to a congressional inquiry about the constitutional requirements of either a majority or plurality. Its report, which exhaustively researched the records of the Constitutional Convention and the legislative history of the Twelfth Amendment, concluded that "legally there is no reason why a plurality vote in a delegation cannot be adopted. Politically and psychologically problems might arise because of the absence of the aura produced by a majority but they are policy matters primarily and have to be considered in such light absent a legal examination."[64] In the unlikely circumstance that a House election would be held without revising the 1825 rules, a majority within each delegation would be required. If new rules were adopted, it is most likely that the requirement of a majority would be retained.

The problem posed by the issue of whether a majority or plurality would be required is directly related to the provision in the Twelfth Amendment that permits the top three electoral vote-getters to be candidates in the House. This provision can be explained in part by the fact that in every election conducted after 1792 and before the Twelfth Amendment was ratified in 1804, there were three or more major candidates for the presidency. Since 1804, however, the Electoral College evolved and developed to the point where it was very successful in narrowing the field to two major candidates in most elections. An appropriate matter for responsible reform of the Twelfth Amendment would therefore be an amendment providing only that the top two, rather than top three, electoral vote-getters be eligible for election in the House. Obviously if only two candidates are eligible for consideration by the House, the issue of majority or plurality becomes moot.

The Secret Ballot

There are two questions relating to the issue of a secret ballot. The first is whether each representative within a state delegation may cast his or her ballot in secret; the second is whether the ballot of the state taken as a whole shall be secret.

It has been argued that the use of the term "ballot" in the Twelfth Amendment implies that any votes by House members are to be secret, since "ballots" are traditionally cast in secret. There are two problems with this view. First, the Twelfth Amendment states only that the House "shall choose . . . by ballot." It does not indicate whether it is referring to the ballots cast within a state delegation to determine the state's vote, or to the vote of the state itself. Second, while ballots cast by voters have traditionally been secret votes, this does not mean a ballot must per se be secret. Otherwise the adjective "secret" to describe a ballot would be superfluous.

It is therefore reasonable to conclude that the Constitution itself neither requires nor forbids a secret ballot, thus leaving that issue open to congressional rule-making. However, the 1801 and 1825 rules cast little additional light on the question of secrecy except to clarify that the vote within a delegation shall be by ballot. The 1825 rules state that the House shall "proceed, by ballot, to choose a President," and that the "Representatives of each state shall, in the first instance, ballot among themselves." Nevertheless, it was the view of many members of the House during the 1801 and 1825 House elections that there was a right to a secret ballot, and indeed in both elections neither the individual votes of representatives nor even the votes of individual voters were recorded.[65] The official House journal records only the final number of state votes for each candidate. Nevertheless, somehow the votes of both delegates and states leaked out, and several newspapers of the day reported how both delegates and states voted.[66]

If a House election were held today without modifying the 1825 rules, it could reasonably be argued that since the House of Representatives in 1825 interpreted their own rules as giving representatives the right to a secret ballot, this interpretation should continue to apply. It may also be relevant that some House members at the time felt that the Constitution itself provided the right to a secret ballot, presumably on the theory that a ballot was per se a secret one.[67] The fact that 169 years ago some House representatives thought that the word "ballot" meant "secret ballot," however, should not be considered binding on representatives today, who presumably would be free to take a contrary position and adopt rules requiring an open ballot. Just as in 1801 and 1825, however, the practical chances of keeping all the ballots secret might be very small in any case.

Aside from the legal question of whether House ballots may be secret is the broader political question. On an issue as important as the election of the president it is doubtful that public opinion would support a secret ballot, and most voters would insist on knowing for whom their elected representatives voted. Of course, it is possible that some representatives might support a rule permitting a secret ballot, hoping to avoid the political consequences of an open choice. Doubtless representatives would be torn by countervailing political considerations in casting their votes. Should they vote for their own personal choice, the choice of the voters in their districts, the nominee of their own political party, the national popular vote winner, or the candidate who received the most electoral votes? One can understand why members of Congress might want to keep their votes to themselves under such circumstances, but it is doubtful if their constituents would stand for it. In any case, a responsible constitutional amendment should specifically address and resolve the issue of the secret ballot.

The Quorum Within Delegations

The Twelfth Amendment states that in a House election "a quorum shall consist of a member or members from two-thirds of the states, and a majority of all states shall be necessary to a choice." The 1825 rules further provide that when a vote is taken within a delegation, the choice of the delegation is the candidate who receives a "majority of the votes given."[68] The Twelfth Amendment provision clearly states that a quorum shall consist of "a member" from two-thirds of the states. This implies that even one member of a delegation will constitute a quorum for the delegation. It is also very clear that there must be two-thirds of the states present and voting.

Nevertheless, some scholars have suggested that the Twelfth Amendment language addresses only the question of the quorum in the House and not the question of a quorum within a delegation. Under this interpretation a House rule could require a two-thirds quorum within each delegation.[69] Aside from the apparent conflict with the Twelfth Amendment, such a requirement would also almost certainly be bad policy. Michael Glennon has pointed out that if there were a two-thirds quorum requirement in a delegation, a minority of representatives within a delegation (who constituted more than a third but less than half of the delegation) could subvert the will of the majority of representatives in the delegation by simply not appearing, and thereby nullify the vote of their state for the candidate they oppose.[70]

Which House Shall Elect the President?

In order to resolve the question of whether the old House or the newly elected House chooses the president, it is first necessary to review the following six relevant dates relating to the presidential election:

The Popular Vote Election Day. Title 3 of the U.S. Code sets the date for the appointment of the presidential electors as the "Tuesday next after the first Monday in November, in every fourth year."[71] Since every state in the union has delegated the appointment of the electors to the people, this date is more popularly known as the presidential "election day." It is also, of course, the day on which all representatives, and one-third of the U.S. senators are chosen.

The Electoral College Election Day. The electors, by law, cast their votes for president on the "first Monday after the second Wednesday in December next following their appointment."[72]

The Date Electoral Votes Are "Opened, Presented, and Acted Upon" in Congress. Pursuant to Section 15 of Title 3 this occurs on January 6th following the election.

The Date the New Congress Is Sworn In. The Twentieth Amendment provides that the new Congress shall be sworn in at noon on January 3rd following the election.

The Date the New President Takes Office. The Twentieth Amendment provides that the new president shall take office on the 20th day of January following his election.

The Date on Which the House Shall Select a President Where No Candidate Receives a Majority of Electoral Votes. The Twelfth Amendment sets forth no exact date, but states that

the person having the greatest number of votes for President, shall be the President, if such number be a majority of the whole number of electors appointed; and if no such person have such majority, then from those persons having the highest numbers not exceeding three on the list of those voted for as president, the House of Representatives shall choose immediately, by ballot the President.

Most scholars and observers have analyzed these dates and concluded that the newly elected House, rather than the lame-duck Congress, would elect the president if no candidate receives a majority of electoral votes in the Electoral College. Peirce and Longley, for example, have stated firmly that

If a presidential election should ever be thrown into Congress again, at least the decision would not be made by lame-duck legislators as it was in 1801 and 1825. Under the 20th Amendment, ratified in 1933, a new Congress—elected the same day as the presidential electors—takes office on January 3, three days before the official count of the electoral votes.[73]

Glennon has opined that "Federal law currently provides that electoral votes will be counted on January 6, three days after the new Congress is sworn in. To permit the Congress to choose the president, this statute would therefore have to be changed, placing the electoral count on a date before January 3."[74]

Both of these views appear to rest on the assumption that January 6, the date on which the electoral votes shall, by law, be "opened, presented, and acted upon" by Congress, is the date on which it is determined that "there not be a majority of the whole number of electors appointed." In fact, however, this date is almost entirely ceremonial, and the duties of the president of the Senate are purely ministerial. It is true that it is the first date upon which members of Congress have the opportunity to formally raise objections to electoral votes on grounds that they were not "regularly" cast. But the fact that no candidate has received a majority of electoral votes is determined on election day—the first Tuesday after the first Monday in November. To assume that January 6 is the critical day, a day that receives little attention, would appear to elevate form over substance.

It is true that in the House elections of 1801 and 1825 it was the old House rather than the new House that elected the president. Unfortunately, however, those elections do not provide any guidance today, because prior to the ratification of the Twentieth Amendment, inauguration day was March 4, and under no interpretation of relevant dates could there have been an election by the new House.

It is submitted therefore that the popular election day is the date on which it is determined that no candidate has received a majority of electoral votes, and that the old House rather than the new House would select the new president if no candidate received a majority in the Electoral College.

REFERRAL OF THE VICE PRESIDENTIAL ELECTION TO THE SENATE

The Twelfth Amendment states that the "person having the greatest number of votes for Vice-President shall be Vice-President, if such number be a majority of the whole number of Electors appointed, and if no person have a majority, then from the two highest numbers of the list, the Senate shall choose the Vice-President."

The Senate election of the vice president involves fewer of the problems associated with the House election of the president. Election is by the whole number of senators, so there is no question about majority or plurality within state delegations, or a quorum within delegations. The Senate has had occasion to select a vice president only once in American history (it chose Robert Richardson in 1837 when Richardson failed to get a majority of electoral votes).[75]

Although few records have been left describing the circumstances of this little-known Senate election, it does not appear that any serious disputes arose over issues of a secret ballot. Since the wide adoption of the general ticket ballot, there has been little likelihood that a vice presidential election would be referred to the Senate without the presidential election also being referred to the House.

Nevertheless, were a Senate election of a vice president to occur today, issues of a secret ballot would also have to be resolved. However, since the Twelfth Amendment does not use the term "ballot" in describing the Senate election, there could be no argument that the Constitution requires a secret vote.

The issue of whether the new Senate or the old Senate would not be as critical as the issue of whether the old House or the new House would elect the President, since there is only a turnover of one-third of the Senate every two years. Nevertheless, there would still be a different composition of senators, and the issue of whether the old or new Senate would elect the vice president would still have to be addressed.

The most troubling feature of the Senate election is that it may preclude the election of the running mate of the candidate elected to president. This is because the choice in the Senate is limited to the top two electoral vote-getters, whereas the House election is open to the top three electoral vote-getters.

It will be recalled that in the months prior to the 1992 election, polls showed that Perot would have received 33% of the vote, Bush 28%, and Clinton 24%. They also revealed that no candidate would have received a majority of electoral votes. Had these numbers held up until election day the presidential election would have been thrown into the House of Representatives (where Clinton would have been the most likely winner), and the vice presidential election into the Senate (where Gore would have been ineligible, and Quayle would have been the most likely winner). The likely winners (Clinton and Quayle) would have been from opposing parties and would certainly have made an unlikely pair.

Responsible reform would reduce the possibility of the president and vice president being of different parties. The best way of accomplishing this would be to limit the number of presidential candidates in the House to the top two electoral vote-getters.

Many reformers argue that direct election would eliminate the need for a referral of any election to the House or Senate, and they propose a runoff where no candidate receives at least 40% of the popular vote. It has already been pointed out, however, that a popular election, even with a runoff, would not necessarily result in the election of the first choice of the American people (see Chapter One). There are also important reasons why the presidential election should continue to be referred to the House where no candidate receives a majority in the general election. Indeed, this feature of the Constitution should be retained even if reformers are successful in amending the Constitution to provide for direct popular election.

The House referral provision of the Constitution plays an important role in preserving the two-party system, and reinforces the incentives for compromise and accommodation provided by the Electoral College itself. It will be recalled that one of the reasons given by Perot when he first dropped out of the presidential race was that he could not hope to win a majority of electoral votes, and that he had even less hope of being elected if the election were referred to the House of Representatives, where he had no party support. Without the prospect of a House election, Perot might have stayed in the race, and the American people would have been saddled with a minority president who might have received as little as 24% of the popular vote. (It will be recalled that when Perot returned to the presidential race he was no longer perceived as a threat to deprive a major party candidate of a majority of electoral votes.)

Although reformers generally view the prospect of a House election with horror, in most democracies in the world today the head of government is elected by the legislature. To view this procedure as inherently undemocratic is to take an extremely chauvinistic view of democracy. So even if an American presidential election were ever referred to the House, it would certainly not be the death knell of democracy as claimed by some advocates of direct election. In any case, it has not occurred in over one and a half centuries, and is not likely to occur as long as the two-party system is not crippled by the passage of an amendment abolishing the Electoral College and substituting direct election. And as long as the general ticket ballot is retained, it is extremely unlikely that a House election will ever again be necessary.

Some more moderate reformers have suggested that the contingent House election be retained, but that the system giving each state one vote should be eliminated on grounds that it gives voters in small states a disproportionate influence in the election of the president. Martin Diamond, for example, though favoring retention of the Electoral College and a contingent election by the House, has advocated that the state unit rule be abolished and that a contingent election in the House be by individual vote of the Senate and House in joint session.[76]

The problem with Diamond's suggestion is again the problem of federalism. The state unit rule was part of the Great Compromise, which induced the small states to join the union, and a change in the unit rule should therefore be considered in the context of all of the other aspects of the Great Compromise, including the small states' representation in the U.S. Senate. Moreover, the state unit rule is an appropriate counterpart to the Electoral College itself. That is, the president was to be the president of all the states, and not just the choice of citizens, though their number be great, concentrated in a few large states. That very simply was not the "deal" as agreed to by the participants at the Constitutional Convention. The state unit rule in a House election is no more undemocratic than giving small states disproportionate representation in the U.S. Senate, or giving each state an equal role in ratifying constitutional amendments. Again, John Kennedy's perspicacious observation about the nature of the solar system of government power must be carefully considered.

Nevertheless, the ambiguities in House procedures for a contingency election should be addressed, preferably by constitutional amendment, but, where possible, at least by new House rules. Candidates in the House election should be limited to the top two electoral vote-getters, quorum requirements should be relaxed, the secret ballot should be prohibited, and a definite choice should be made between the old House and the new House in electing the president. Reducing the number of eligible candidates in the House and modifying the quorum requirements would require a constitutional admendment.

The quorum requirements deserve attention because, as currently provided, they leave open the possibility of considerable political mischief. A party fearing a loss in the House election might deliberately fail to appear for a vote in order to deny the House a quorum. This might be done with the purpose of delaying the House election until after January 20, with the hope that a member of that party might assume the duties of president under the Automatic Succession Act (see next section of this chapter). If the election is to be conducted by the old House, the lack of a quorum might delay the election until the new House is elected (which would presumably be more favorable to the party denying the quorum).

Rather than giving a party the incentive to commit political mischief by delaying the House election, the incentive should be to hold the election as soon as possible. This would be done by significantly reducing the quorum requirement. It is difficult to imagine, even if the quorum requirement were reduced, that many House members would choose not to participate in what would probably be the most important legislative responsibility of their term.

Secret ballots should be expressly prohibited. Provision could possibly be made to permit secret ballots until a final ballot—in order to induce compromise and prevent deadlock. If the candidates were limited to the top two vote-getters, however, even this concession would be unnecessary. In no case, however, should a representative's final vote for president be hidden from scrutiny, as this would allow a representative to escape ac-countability to the people for his or her vote.

With regard to the issue of whether the new House or the old House should elect the president, a strong argument can be made that the new House should elect the president, since the new House would be more reflective of the current will of the people. However, there are problems with this procedure. It is recalled that the new House is not even sworn in until January 3 following the presidential election. Many of these new members will be serving in the House for the first time, and will not be familiar with House procedures. Many will be busy just trying to settle into their new offices. Committee assignments may not be complete. And yet this new House will be under pressure to immediately convene to elect a president. Even if the new members act with great immediacy and dispatch, there will be little time to convene, adopt special procedures, debate, and vote prior to January 20 when the new president is to be inaugurated.

In the meantime, the entire country, and the candidates, would remain in limbo, waiting for the new House to convene. Even when a candidate becomes the clear winner of the presidential election in early November, the president-elect is hard-pressed to form a government during the period between the date of the election in November and inauguration day (as-suming, of course, that he is not the incumbent president). Even if a new House were able to elect a president within, say, two weeks, this would allow the president-elect only three days to form a government. It might even be the case that the House would be unable to elect a president prior to January 20, and the vice president would have to assume the duties of acting president. None of this seems worth the theoretical advantages of election by a new House.

Rather, it would be far better to have the House convene the day after the November election, and, as the Constitution requires, "immediately" meet to elect the new president. This procedure would promptly end the uncertainty and give the president-elect ample time to form a new government.

ELECTION OF THE PRESIDENT PURSUANT TO THE AUTOMATIC SUCCESSION ACT

If no president or vice president is elected by January 20 of the year following the general election, the Twentieth Amendment states that "Congress may by law provide . . . declaring who shall then act as President." Congress has so provided in Section 19 of Title 3 of the U.S. Code, which states that if by reason of "failure to qualify, there is neither a President or Vice-President to discharge the powers and duties of the office of President, then the Speaker of the House shall . . . act as President."[77] Presumably this section refers to the Speaker of the House on January 20, and not the Speaker at the time of the general election. If the Speaker of the House fails to qualify or rejects the office, the president pro tempore of the Senate shall act as president.[78] After the president pro tempore, cabinet members are designated in chain of succession.[79]

These provisions make reform of the "three candidate" and quorum provisions of the Twelfth Amendment all the more urgent. By denying a quorum, a party is given the means to delay an election in the House and assure that a member of their own party will assume the duties of the presidency under the Automatic Succession Act.

In this chapter, the broad outlines of the Electoral College procedures for election of the president have been reviewed. However, a deeper understanding of these provisions, and the purposes behind their enactment, requires a knowledge of the men and women who created them, as well as a review of their motives, hopes, and vision. This is the subject of the next chapter.

NOTES

1. William T. Gossett, "Electing the President: New Hope for an Old Ideal." *American Bar Association Journal*, 53 (December, 1967): 1103.

2. Donald Mathews, "Presidential Nominations: Process and Outcomes," in *Choosing the President*, James Barber ed. (Englewood Cliffs, N.J.: Prentice-Hall, 1974), 36.

3. *Id* at 56.

4. *Id*.

5. Austin Ranney, "Changing the Rules of the Nominating Game," in Barber, *supra* note 2, at 72.

6. Gossett, *supra* note 1.

7. Mathews, *supra* note 2, at 39–40.

8. *Id.* at 45, Table 1.

9. Ranney, *supra* note 5, at 72.

10. For an excellent and comprehensive study of the factors involved in the nomination of presidential candidates, see 1936 research conducted at the Brookings Institution and summarized in Mathews, *supra* note 2.

11. Neal R. Peirce and Lawrence D. Longley, *The People's President: The Electoral College in American History and the Direct Vote Alternative*, rev. ed. (New Haven: Yale University Press, 1981), 88.

12. *Id.*

13. *Id.*

14. See, for example, 1972 Democratic Party Convention.

15. *Id.*

16. *Id.*

17. Ranney, *supra* note 5, at 87.

18. James Davis, *Springboard to the White House* (New York: Thomas Crowell, 1967), 24–37, cited in Ranney, *supra* note 5, at 87.

19. Ranney, *supra* note 5, at 87.

20. *Id.*

21. Laws, New Hampshire, November 12, 1788 (Codified 1789, p. 169).

22. See a summary and history of selection methods in *McPherson v. Blacker*, 13. U.S. 3 (1892) at 7–9.

23. Senate Rep. 1st sess. 431 Cong. No. 395 (May 28, 1974).

24. *Id.*

25. Peirce and Longley, *supra* note 11, at 45.

26. Williams v. Rhodes, 393 U.S. 23, at 28.

27. *Id.* at 32.

28. *Id.* at 29.

29. For technical reasons the court did not require the name of the Socialist Labor Party to be placed on the ballot. *Id.* at 35.

30. In 1981 Mississippi, Louisiana, and South Carolina used this method. Peirce and Longley, *supra* note 11, at App.J., 295.

31. Mississippi does permit the designation of a preferred candidate if the elector is so pledged. *Id.*

32. But see *Williams v. Rhodes, supra* note 26.

33. *Ray v. Blair*, 343 U.S. 214 (1952); see also *Ray v. Garner*, 57 So. 2nd 824 (Al. 1952).

34. 343 U.S. 214, at 224, 226.

35. 24 states plus the District of Columbia require such pledges. Michael J. Glennon, *When No Majority Rules: The Electoral College and Presidential Succession* (Washington, D.C.: Congressional Quarterly, Inc., 1992), 34.

36. *Id.*

37. Peirce and Longley, *supra* note 11, at 99.

38. 3 USC § 7.

39. Rufus King, Annals of Congress, 18th Cong. 1st sess. 1., p. 355, cited in Peirce and Longley, *supra* note 11, at 102.

40. Peirce and Longley, supra at 103.

41. Senate Report No. 22, 19th Cong. 1st sess. (January 19, 1826), cited in *Id*. at 92.

42. *Id*.

43. James A. Michener, *Presidential Lottery: The Reckless Gamble in Our Electoral System* (New York: Random House, 1969), 9.

44. 3 USC § 9.

45. 3 USC § 10.

46. 3 USC § 11.

47. James Cheetham to Thomas Jefferson, Proceedings of the Massachusetts Historical Society, 3rd Series, 1, p. 47, cited in Peirce and Longley, *supra* note 11, at 104, note 52.

48. 3 USC § 4.

49. If for any reason the vote fails to take place on the date by law, it is permitted to vote on a subsequent day. 3 USC § 2. Any delay would obviously be awkward, however.

50. *Ann Arbor News* (December 14, 1948), cited in Cong. Rec. (April 13, 1949) at p. 4449, and cited in Peirce and Longley, *supra* note 11, at 103.

51. 3 USC § 6.

52. 3 USC § 15.

53. *Id*.

54. *See* Glennon, *supra* note 35, at 37–40.

55. 3 USC § 15.

56. *Id*.

57. *Id*.

58. 3 USC § 17; 62 Stat. 626, ch. 644 § 1 (June 25, 1948).

59. 3 USC § 16.

60. American Law Division, Congressional Research Service, "Majority or Plurality Vote Within State Delegations When House of Representatives Votes for the President" (Washington, D.C.: Library of Congress, unpublished document, June 10, 1980), 292–293, reproduced in App. I in Peirce and Longley, *supra* note 11, at 273–274.

61. *Id*. at 1.

62. *Id*.

63. *Id*.

64. *Id*. at 14.

65. Glennon, *supra* note 35, at 51–52.

66. *Id*.

67. *Id*.

68. American Law Division, *supra* note 60.

69. *Id*. at 53.

70. *Id*.

71. 3 USC § 1.

72. 3 USC § 7.

73. Peirce and Longley, *supra* note 11, at 108.

74. Glennon, *supra* note 35, at 47.

75. Edward Stanwood, *A History of the Presidency from 1788 to 1897* (Boston, 1898), 187–188, cited in Peirce and Longley, *supra* note 11, at 108.

76. Martin Diamond, "The Electoral College and the Idea of Federal Democracy," *The Journal of Federalism* (Winter 1978): *70*.

77. SC § 19 (A) (1).

78. 3 USC § 19 (B).

79. 3 USC § 19 (d) (1).

Chapter Three

ORIGINS: THE CONSTITUTIONAL CONVENTION AND THE TWELFTH AMENDMENT

I do not, gentlemen, trust you.

Delegate Dunning Bedford of
Delaware to delegates from the large states
at the Constitutional Convention of 1787.

It was all of very doubtful legality. The three bedraggled men who met for drinks at George Mann's Tavern in Annapolis, Maryland, in August 1786 had no legally recognized agenda. They had come to discuss trade problems and perhaps enter into some kind of agreement they could take back to their home states. Any agreement they came to, however, would be clearly illegal, since the Articles of Confederation strictly forbade any such agreements without the consent of the Confederation Congress.

The last of the three to arrive at the Tavern was James Madison, who had somehow convinced his Virginia Assembly to call for a meeting to talk about problems of interstate trade. Invitations had been sent to all the states. Madison and the other two "delegates" waited a week for others to come, at which time they planned to convene at the Annapolis State House. But only nine more delegates, representing five states, showed up. None of the Eastern states made an appearance. It appeared that this "Annapolis Convention" would be recorded as just another feeble and aborted attempt to do something about the intolerable state of commerce and trade between the former colonies.

It was a tremendous disappointment to Madison, who had used all his wiles and powers of persuasion to arrange the meeting. Madison knew such a meeting might be the last chance to prevent the 13 former colonies from breaking up into separate amalgamations and confederations. Maryland had already invited Virginia, Pennsylvania, and Delaware to form a commercial alliance. Originally, the union was to consist only of Virginia and Maryland, who would agree to eliminate tariffs between the two states, and form a common monetary system. But Virginia's main navigation arteries connected with those of Pennsylvania, and so it was deemed necessary to invite Pennsylvania to join the alliance. Delaware was invited when it became apparent that a scheme to build a canal linking the Susquehanna River with the Delaware River would have to include Delaware.

A federation of states south of Virginia was being proposed as a counterweight to that of Maryland's four-state nation, and it was assumed that states north of Pennsylvania would then form their own nation—minus Rhode Island, of course, which was known to favor union with no one.

It was not, however, a case of the union breaking up, for there had never been a union. The "Articles of Confederation" had created a "league of friendship" under which each state would retain its "sovereignty, freedom, and independence."[1] But the Confederation had no power to raise money, regulate commerce, or even enforce its own laws. Its "president" had no executive powers, and was simply one chosen to preside over the Congress. When the Congress needed money, it had to assess each state. Often the states simply declined to pay, and on many occasions the states neglected even to send delegates to the Congress, thus depriving it of a quorum and the ability to conduct any business at all. Each state had one vote in the Confederation Congress, and unanimity was required to pass such measures as an import duty.[2] Meanwhile, states imposed protective tariffs on each other and issued their own paper money.

Soon after gaining independence, the former colonies were at the mercy of Great Britain's policy of economic strangulation aimed at coercing the colonies back into the royal fold. After the colonies gained their independence, there had been a proposal in Parliament to conduct normal trade relations with the former colonies. King George adamantly refused, calling the Americans "knaves" and their departure from the empire "good riddance . . . the American cannot expect nor will ever receive any favor from me."[3]

There followed a British policy of prohibiting the import of all American goods into Great Britain. "America was to be treated as an 'alien' country, totally shut off from that commerce which had been the cause of all its prosperity and on which its very existence seemed to depend."[4] Payment of debts to the British could not be paid with goods, but had to be paid in specie—of which the American continent was soon stripped bare. The only way to obtain reciprocal trade rights was to retaliate by imposing trade barriers on the import of British goods. But when the Confederation Congress sent John Adams to Great Britain to negotiate an agreement, he was, literally, laughed out of London. "What did [Adams] represent? One, or thirteen nations? What was the use of making an agreement with Congress, when each state could repudiate it? Congress had power to contract loans, but no power to pay them."[5]

With Congress having no power to act, Britain knew it had its former colonies over a barrel. Indeed, many in Britain fully expected that a slow policy of strangulation would make the Americans realize how good they had it before the Revolution, and that they would now seek readmittance to the empire. A royal advisor wrote in 1784 that

if the views of his Majesty's ministers extend towards the recovery of the sovereignty of the [colonies], or towards a dissolution of their confederation, these ends will best be promoted by an adherence to the system of excluding American shipping from the advantages of being sold in this Kingdom. Such exclusion will render the situation of many states much worse than when they were subject to the British crown. If such exclusions be continued, the [Americans] will, in less than twelve months, openly concert measures for entering into something like their former connections with Great Britain.[6]

By 1786 the British economic strategy for regaining its colonies was working. Benjamin Franklin stated that he knew of a plan to make one of the "numerous progeny King of the old-time transatlantic possession."[7] Although several of the American states attempted to form an alliance and agreement among the states to retaliate against the British, renegade states could not resist the temptation to decline such alliances and gain economic advantage over their sister states. Retaliatory tariffs were erected, but against sister states, not Great Britain. Some states even began to charge higher duties on the goods of their sister states than on those of Britain.

As economic chaos deepened, and Great Britain gloated, states began to fight among themselves over boundaries and navigation rights. Hard-pressed state assemblies raised revenues by imposing steep property taxes, provoking in Massachusetts Daniel Shays' armed rebellion, which soon spread throughout the country.

These events alarmed George Washington, who wrote:

What astonishing changes a few years are capable of producing! I am told that even respectable characters speak of a monarchial form of government without horror. From thinking, proceeds speaking, and thence to acting is often but a single step. But how irrevocable and tremendous! What a triumph for our enemies to verify their predictions! What a triumph for the advocates of despotism to find that we are incapable of governing ourselves, and that systems founded on the basis of equal liberty are merely ideal and fallacious! . . . Thirteen sovereignties pulling against each other.[8]

It was amid such events that Madison, on the last day of the Virginia Assembly's 1786 session, slipped in a resolution accepting Maryland's invitation for a four-state "river and harbor" convention in Annapolis. But he added a short sentence inviting all the other states as well; more important, he envisioned that the meeting might turn into something far more important: the binding of the states into a union.

Historian Burton Hendrick has observed that "Madison's ruse succeeded; on the last day of the session the resolution was called from the table and rushed through the house."[9] Apparently Madison's foes had either not noticed or not appreciated the significance of Madison's rapidly scrawled addendum to the resolution.

THE ANNAPOLIS CONVENTION

And yet, on that hot August day in Annapolis in 1786, all Madison's hopes appeared dashed. Obviously no important work on trade, let alone union, could be accomplished with only twelve delegates representing but five states. And even among the twelve there appeared to be little enthusiasm for cooperation in trade or any other matter. Doubtless annoyed by the time they had wasted in making the journey to Annapolis, eleven of the twelve delegates at George's Tavern consumed their final mugs of ale and prepared to go home.

At this critical moment in American history there leaped onto the stage a man still in his twenties—the delegate from New York who, it was soon to be revealed, had a vision of his own. Alexander Hamilton had attended a number of gatherings, both official and unofficial, and at each he had pressed his vision of a union of the American states. He was not about to pass up the opportunity to press it at this one. As one historian has noted, the Annapolis "convention demonstrated that it could not agree on anything, and would soon have broken up in sullenness had not the New Yorker suddenly assumed command."[10]

Hamilton prevailed upon his fellow delegates to remain. He had found, he claimed, a phrase in the written instructions to the New Jersey delegate authorizing the negotiation not only of commercial matters, but of "other important matters." Historians have since noted: "Never has a parenthesis in a state paper served a grander historic end."[11]

Waving the New Jersey addendum, and relentlessly pressing the advantage, Hamilton aroused the other delegates and argued vigorously that the problems confronting them extended beyond simply matters of trade. (Madison, of course, needed no such arousing, but completely relinquished the floor to Hamilton.) In the end, the Annapolis Convention unanimously issued a recommendation that a

convention of all the states be held at Philadelphia on the second Monday of May next, to take in consideration the situation in the United States, to devise such further provisions as shall appear to them necessary to render the Constitution of the Federal government adequate to the exigencies of the Union, and to report such an act for that purpose to the United States in Congress assembled as, when agreed to by them and afterwards confirmed by the legislature of every state, will effectually provide for the same.[12]

In the end, Madison's ruse, with the aid of a young and energetic Alexander Hamilton, had achieved its purpose. A convention to which all states had been invited (although most had never shown up) had called for another convention to "take into consideration the situation in the United States" and "render the Constitution . . . adequate."

With disorders spreading, and the British economic policies continuing to take their economic toll, the call was taken up by others, including George Washington, who urged that all states send delegates to Philadelphia. When seven states jumped the gun and began selecting delegates for the Philadelphia Convention, the Confederation Congress, belatedly, felt obliged to approve the call for a convention. However, perhaps alarmed by the open-ended nature of the Convention's avowed purpose, and the manner in which its own authority was being bypassed, the Confederation Congress issued a directive specifically restricting the purpose of the convention to "the sole and express purpose of revising the Articles of Confederation." In other words, no funny business. (One can perhaps imagine the discomfiture of the Confederation Congress by considering how Congress might feel today if delegates outside of Congress began meeting to consider a new form of government.)[13]

Today, it is apparent that neither Madison nor Hamilton had any intention of abiding by the letter, much less the spirit, of the congressional directive restricting the convention agenda to "revising" the Articles of Confederation. If Madison at first played along, it was only so as not to spook those who considered the congressional directive to be the primary source of the Convention's legitimacy. As in the case of his Annapolis ruse, Madison knew that the first order of business was to convene the Convention. After that, events would take their own course.

THE CONSTITUTIONAL CONVENTION

One wonders how Madison must have felt when he first arrived in Philadelphia on May 3, 1787. He was, of course, the first out-of-towner to arrive. He went immediately to the boardinghouse of Mrs. Mary House, where four years earlier he had stayed when he was a delegate to the Continental Congress. It had been there that he had fallen in love with 16-year-old Catherine Floyd, who was half his age. Although they had planned to get married, Catherine fell under the influence of a clergyman who wooed her by "hanging around her at the harpsichord."[14] Soon after, she later wrote a letter to Madison "informing him that he had been dismissed."[15] Madison had taken the rejection very badly, but was consoled by his friend Jefferson, who wrote him that "firmness of mind and unremitting occupation will not long leave you in pain."[16]

Like Voltaire, who had observed that the Holy Roman Empire had been neither Holy, Roman, or an Empire, Madison knew that the Confederation's "firm league of friendship" was neither firm, a league, or very friendly. He knew that what was needed was an entirely new form of government, with a Constitution at its heart.

Although the Convention had been scheduled to begin on May 14, few delegates had arrived by the evening of May 13. Washington did appear on the 13th, although he had initially declined the invitation. Washington had already declined to attend another convention being held in Philadelphia at the same time—the Society of the Cincinnati, which was to convene on May 15. This society was comprised of officers who had fought in the Revolutionary War and provided for hereditary membership. Although Washington had joined the Society out of loyalty to his former comrades, he felt uncomfortable about attending its meetings because of its hereditary membership policy. He therefore made an excuse not to attend its May 15 meeting. The problem, however, was that it would now be very awkward for him to attend the Constitutional Convention. He therefore declined to attend either convention, and it was only after Madison's persistent requests that he finally relented and agreed to attend the Constitutional Convention.[17] (How his comrades in the Society of the Cincinnati took this snub has not been recorded by history, but presumably they got over it.)

On the morning of May 14, the day the Convention was to begin, Madison must have feared that there would be a repeat of the fizzled Annapolis Convention. Some states had not even bothered to appropriate travel funds for their delegates. Two bedraggled delegates from New Hampshire had been obliged to hitchhike at their own expense, and arrived two months late.

Although Madison patiently waited for new arrivals, by May 16 most of the 13 states were still absent. Delegates soon began to get bored loitering about at the Philadelphia tavern. Benjamin Franklin had them over to his house for dinner to relieve the monotony, "tapping a cask of English porter."[18]

On May 18 Alexander Hamilton, and his codelegate from New York, Robert Yates, arrived in Philadelphia. Yates was known to oppose any significant changes in the Articles of Confederation, and was prepared to oppose any measures that might inhibit New York from imposing its lucrative import fees on sister states transporting goods through New York.

By May 21 six states had voting quorums. But Rhode Island refused to send any delegates, and the Delaware delegate ominously presented credentials that "forbade the delegation's participation in any attempt to change the one state, one vote provision of the Articles of Confederation."[19]

On May 25 storm clouds were gathering and a torrential rainstorm drenched the delegates as they made their way from the tavern to the State House. There were now 7 states present, a majority of the 13. However, there was only one delegate representing all of New England, and it appeared that the Philadelphia Convention would be a repeat of the Annapolis debacle.

At Madison's urging, the 29 drenched delegates who had now arrived decided to go ahead and start the meeting. By the time the Convention dissolved some four months later, some 55 delegates had made an appearance on at least one day the Convention was in session. Nineteen of the appointed delegates failed to appear at all, and the average daily attendance never exceeded the 29 who convened on May 25. It was a better turnout than the 12 who appeared at Annapolis, but not by much.

About half of the delegates had attended college, and many of them were young. Jonathan Dayton of New Jersey, for example, was 26, Alexander Hamilton had just turned 30, and Madison was 34. However, older delegates, like Benjamin Franklin who was 81, served to round out the average age.

Once Washington had been prevailed upon to appear, there was no question but that he would preside. One historian has recorded that "the extent to which Washington swayed the deliberations is not known. Washington was no debater, but he had his way, by nods of approval or deprecating shrugs, of expressing his opinion—signs that would have infinitely greater weight upon the body than a thousand fiery orations."[20]

Benjamin Franklin was, by all accounts, ineffective (except for one very important compromise he submitted at the very end of the convention, relating to how the Constitution should be subscribed). Historians have described him as "so feeble that his speeches were read by a close colleague; his ideas made no impression, although he was heard with the respect due his years of fame. His interventions were mainly of a conciliatory nature, intended to calm an excited atmosphere, but his proposals for the most part were futile and even, at times, absurd."[21]

John Dickinson was said to have "cut no glorious figure; his constant insistence of the 'rights of property,' his desire to make the Senate a duplicate of the British House of Lords, in which leading 'families' should have representation, fell on unappreciative ears."[22]

Elbridge Gerry of Massachusetts had, like Madison, sought to marry a woman half his age. Unlike Madison, however, he had succeeded, and his renowned young wife, the daughter of a rich New York merchant, had been proclaimed "the most beautiful woman in America."[23] But Gerry, among the richest of the delegates, proved to be in the minority in asserting that "the evils we experience flow from the excess of democracy."[24]

Perhaps most notable was who did *not* appear at the Convention. Patrick Henry, though elected as a delegate, had "smelt a rat," and refused to attend. Thomas Jefferson was in Paris serving as the American minister to France, John Adams was being abused as the American minister in London, and John Hancock was in Boston suffering from gout.

Thus the fruit of this historic Convention, the United States Constitution, was to be the work of the younger generation.

The Convention's first order of business was to issue the Republic's first "gag order," decreeing that "nothing spoken in the House be printed, or otherwise published or communicated without leave."[25] When Jefferson heard about the order in Paris, he wrote Adams in London that "I am sorry that they began their deliberations by so abominable a precedent as that of tying up the tongues of their members. Nothing can justify this example but the innocence of their intentions and ignorance of the value of public discussions."[26] Later, however, Madison justified the order, asserting that "no Constitution would ever have been adopted by the Convention if the debates had been made in public."[27]

In any case, the gag rule appears to have been strictly adhered to, the only violation of it occurring when certain delegates felt compelled to respond to stories running in various newspapers suggesting that the Convention was considering a monarchy. The concerned delegates finally authorized a press release stating that "though we can not affirmatively tell you what we are doing; we can, negatively tell you what we are not doing—we have never once thought of a King."[28] (One can imagine how the press today might react to a four-month-long total news blackout of a Convention deciding the fate of the nation.)

Although Washington expressed the thought that any Constitution conceived by the Convention would probably not last 20 years, Madison sensed the historic nature of the convocation and resolved to take copious notes of every statement and motion made at the Convention. His diligence has since been greatly admired, for, perhaps alone of all the delegates, he attended every session on every day of the Convention. As Madison later boasted, "I was not absent a single day, nor more than a casual fraction of an hour in any day, so that I could not have lost a single speech, unless a very short one."[29] Nevertheless, he was concerned about the possible misuse of his notes by later "interpreters" of the Constitution, and he decreed that none of his notes would be made public until after his death.

Doubtless Madison was concerned that there might be attempts to extract a statement made here or there by one of the delegates to support one or another constitutional interpretation, and that there might be a failure to take into account all the circumstances of the cited assertion, such as that the assertion was made in the spirit of compromise or accommodation. His notes were finally published in 1840, four years after his death. They have since been analyzed, catalogued, and dissected more than any document except the Bible.

Although the Convention took up the some of the least controversial issues first, all knew that the critical issue on everyone's mind could not be long avoided—namely, how the small and large states would share power in both the legislative and executive branches. Rhode Island had been so sure that the rights of the small states would be disregarded that it refused to participate at all. Delaware, it will be recalled, specifically limited the authority of its delegates to preserving the principle of "one state, one vote."

Although the question had first come up as early as May 30, it was postponed when the Delaware delegation warned that any suggestion that the small states might lose their equal voting power would result in Deleware's immediate departure from the Convention.[30] The question of each state's equal voting power had, they asserted, already been debated and approved prior to forming the Confederation, and any union contemplated in violation of the principle of "one state, one vote" would have to take place without the participation of the small states. It was not until late June that the issue, which was obviously not going to go away, was again considered.[31]

In the interim, talk of a national legislature with broad powers was alarming many of the delegates, who finally realized that Madison, Hamilton, and some others had an agenda that went far beyond that authorized by the Confederation Congress. John Lansing of New York protested that "New York would never have concurred in sending deputies to the convention if she supposed the deliberations were to turn on a consolidation of the states and a national government." Both Madison and Hamilton must have looked at each other, wondering if the "jig was up," when Lansing finally demanded to know: "Is it probable that the states will adopt and ratify a scheme which they have never authorized us to propose?"[32]

Madison in particular, who had masterminded the Annapolis Convention by slipping in the addendum to the acceptance of Maryland's offer to form a four-state union, must have worried if he could get away with it again. Lansing was right. They were working on a plan that had absolutely no legal sanction from Congress.

But the Convention proceeded, inspired by a vision that transcended the Congress and all who were gathered there. On June 29 the dreaded issue of state voting power was again raised. As feared, there followed a series of emotional outbursts from delegates of both the large and small states. Rufus King was "filled with astonishment" that the small states would not be willing to sacrifice for the good of all "the phantom of state sovereignty." The Delaware delegate, Dunning Bedford, charged that the large states were seeking to have "an enormous and monstrous influence," and that

The larger states proceed as if our eyes were already perfectly blinded. Impartiality with them is already out of the question. . . . They insist that although the powers of the general government will be increased, yet it will be for the good of the whole; and although the three great states form nearly a majority of the people of America, they never will hurt or injure the lesser states. *I do not, gentlemen, trust you* (emphasis added).[33]

The Delaware delegate then went on to threaten that if the large states persisted in taking away the right of equal voting that the small states enjoyed under the Confederation, the small states "will find some foreign ally of more honor and good faith who will take them by the hand and do them justice."[34]

At this inflammatory remark threatening foreign intervention, tempers were lost and voices raised. It had been conceded by the small states that a lower House of Representatives could be based on population. But they were adamant that their interests had to be preserved by equal representation in the upper House (the Senate). Perceived to be at stake was nothing less than a choice between the "nationalist [consolidationist] Virginia Plan,"[35] favoring a strong central government, and the "New Jersey Plan or Articles of Confederation,"[36] which favored a retention of ultimate sovereignty in the states.

Some delegates sought a remedy in dissolving the states altogether, suggesting that "a map of the United States be spread out, that all existing boundaries be erased, and that a partition of the whole be made into thirteen equal parts."[37] Madison responded firmly: "Would such a scheme be practicable? The dissimilarities existing in the rules of property, as well as in the manners, habits, and prejudices of the different states, amounted to a prohibition of the attempt."[38]

Madison did not believe a national government could "extend its care to all the minute objects which fall under the cognizance of the local jurisdictions. [The objection lies] not against the probable abuse of the general power, but against the imperfect use that could be made of it throughout so great a variety of objects."[39]

Thus, the genius of Madison's vision was that he believed in a compound of the Virginia and New Jersey Plans, a compound that we have since come to know as federalism (as opposed to confederalism). Such a system of government recognized, as stated by James Wilson, that "our country is too extensive for a single government, no despot ever did govern a country so extensive."[40] The key to the success of such a system, however, lay in identifying those powers that were best exercised by the national component of the federal system, and those best exercised by the state component.

Hamilton, on the other hand, did not believe a true federal system could work: "Two sovereignties can not coexist within the same limits. . . . A compound is inherently unstable; one or the other government must swallow up the other. [The best solution would be] to extinguish the State Governments."[41]

THE GREAT COMPROMISE

On July 2 a motion to give each state an equal vote in the Senate came up for vote. The motion would have been defeated by the large states except for the fact that Daniel Jenifer of Maryland overslept on the morning of the vote (reliable alarm clocks having not been invented yet) and Abraham Baldwin of Georgia changed his vote at the last minute to support the small states. The result was a 5–5 tie on the motion.

Luther Martin of Maryland later claimed that he knew why Baldwin had changed his vote—if the small states had lost they would have stormed out of the Convention, and the hopes of a union would have been lost irretrievably. *"We were on the verge of dissolution, scarce held together by the strength of a hair"* he later wrote (emphasis added).[42] Even Washington despaired of "seeing a favorable issue to the proceedings of the Convention and do therefore repent having had any agency in the business."[43]

Although it is disconcerting to contemplate that the fate of the union rested upon the lack of a snooze alarm, the tied vote only prolonged the issue that was now dividing the Convention into two warring factions. Delegates from the large states at first pretended not to be concerned by threats of a small state walkout.

This country must be united [Morris of Pennsylvania himself threatened, and] if persuasion does not unite it, the sword will. The scene of horror attending civil commotion can not be described. The stronger party will then make traitors of the weaker, and the gallows and halter will finish the work of the sword. How far the foreign powers will be ready to take part in the confusions, I will not say. Threats [by the small states] that they will be invited here, it seems, have been thrown out.[44]

But the small states were not to be intimidated. John Rutledge declared that "the little states are fixed. They have repeatedly and solemnly declared themselves to be so. All that the larger states then have to do is to decide whether they will yield or not."[45]

In the end, however, after delegates from both large and small states had finished blowing off steam, a committee was appointed to find a compromise that would satisfy both factions. The majority of delegates were slowly coming to accept the urgency of the need for finding such a compromise. Hugh Williamson of South Carolina warned that "if no compromise should take place, what will be the consequence? A secession, I foresee, will take place. If we do not come to some agreement among ourselves, some foreign sword will probably do the work for us."[46]

The resulting "Great Compromise" contained several component parts, including the matter of counting slaves for the purpose of representation,[47] the representation by population in the lower House, and the origination of money bills in the lower House. But the key feature was the "one state, one vote" principle in the Senate, in amending the Constitution, in the Electoral College, in the contingent House election of the president, and the contingent election of the vice president in the Senate.

It was later even denied by some small states that the underlying principle of "one state, one vote" had ever even been on the negotiating table; rather it had been an absolute precondition to the participation of the small states in the union. John Dickinson, in his Fabius Letters of 1788, denied that the representation of sovereignties "was a mere compromise. It was not a mere compromise. The equal representation of each state in one branch of the legislature, was an original substantive proposition, made in convention."[48]

Madison, on the other hand, recalled that

the large states urged that as the new government was to be drawn principally from the people immediately and was to operate on them directly, not on the states; and consequently as the states would lose that importance which is not proportioned to the importance of their voluntary compliances with the requisitions of Congress, it was necessary that the representation in both Houses should be in proportion to their size. It ended in the compromise which you will see, but very much to the dissatisfaction of several members from the large states.

That the compromise (or precondition) extended to the selection of the president as well as to representation in the Senate was also made clear by Madison in arguing the case for ratification of the Constitution before the Virginia Convention in 1788. "The little states insisted on retaining their equality in both branches, unless a complete abolition of the State Governments should take place."[49]

THE ELECTION OF A PRESIDENT

The matter of a chief executive was first addressed by the Convention when a committee of the whole meeting was appointed on May 31 to discuss the Virginia Plan. This plan had proposed a government consisting of three branches (legislative, executive, and judicial).[50] When the committee reported its recommendations two weeks later, it included the election of a single executive for a term of seven years. Since it also included a plan for proportional representation in both houses of Congress, which dismayed the small states, its recommendations were tabled for later consideration.

In the weeks that followed, a series of proposals considering the chief executive and the manner in which he was to be elected were considered. Edmund Randolph proposed an executive consisting of three members, each representing a region of the country;[51] there were also proposals for a "rotating" presidency, and Hamilton proposed that an executive serve for life on good behavior.[52]

By July 16 it had been decided that there would be only one, nonrotating executive (the plural executive had been deemed to be ineffective in the states that had it), and there was tentative agreement that the term be for seven years. The most important issue remained to be resolved, however—namely, how the executive (now called the "president") would be selected.

Much of the debate centered on whether the legislature should elect the president or some institution outside the legislature. On July 17 Robert Morris of Pennsylvania proposed a popular election. Madison also initially made this proposal, but, in the words of historian Colabel House: "He was answered by the statement that a popular election would be impossible, as the small states would have no influence in it."[53] Thus, when Morris proposed direct election, his state was the only one to vote for it.[54]

It will be recalled that the final vote approving equal state representation in the Senate had been conducted on July 16. It appears that few delegates thereafter were prepared to again open up the whole question of "one state, one vote" in discussing the manner of the election of the executive. It appears to have been taken for granted after July 17 that the compromise (or concession) made to the small states in the manner of representation in the legislature (which had kept the Convention from dissolving) would be extended to the manner of the election of the executive. Thereafter, the methods discussed for electing the president were narrowed to election by Congress (including the Senate, where small states had equal representation), election by the Senate alone, by the House voting by states, or by electors chosen according to the states' representation in Congress.

Hamilton was one of the first to propose election of the president by electors chosen by the people or by the state legislatures.[55] According to House, Madison also now "spoke in favor of the electoral system, as the best substitute for election by the people at large, which could not be used."[56] Madison was already known to have vigorously opposed election by the Congress as leading to a presidency too dependent on the legislature and thus obfuscating the separation of powers between these two important branches.

Thus, the question became not *whether* the "one state, one vote" principle would be applied to the election of the executive, but rather *how* that principle would be applied. On September 4 the Committee on Postponed Matters proposed that the president be elected by electors in each state according to how many representatives to which a state was entitled in Congress, and that if any candidate failed to receive a majority of electoral votes, the election would be referred to the Senate. William Peters has explained that "by involving the Senate in the process," the Committee on Postponed Matters had attempted to "steer a political course midway between the interests of the large and small states."[57]

However, because many delegates assumed that "nineteen times out of twenty" the election of the president would be by the Senate under such a system, objection was taken to the contingency election in the Senate where he would become the "mere creature of that body."[58] One delegate noted that with only 26 members in the Senate, and a quorum of only two-thirds required, as few as eight "aristocratic" senators could elect the president. On September 6 it was proposed that the contingent election be in the

House instead, but with each state having one vote. "With what must have been an audible sigh of relief, the Convention adopted the idea."[59] In 1901 historian House analyzed this historic vote as one in which "the principle involved seems to have been the anxiety to preserve the weight of the small states."[60]

Max Farrand, whose 1913 (1987 reprint) treatise *The Framing of the Constitution of the United States* has become the standard authority on the Constitutional Convention, wrote that the central feature of the committee's report on September 4 was

the proposed method of electing the president, and that proposal was a compromise. The compromise does not appear on the surface, but it was referred to in the course of the debates, and in later years it was thus explained by several members of the convention, so that *no doubt attaches to it* (emphasis added).[61]

The substance of the compromise on the election of the executive, carried over from the compromise on legislative representation, had two component parts. First, each state's representation in the Electoral College was to be based on the number of representatives each state had in Congress, including its representation in the Senate, where each state had an equal vote. In this manner, the basic elements of the compromise on legislative representation would simply be incorporated into the plan for election of the executive. In fact, however, the perceived concession to the small states to win their approval went even further.

The original proposal by the Committee on Postponed Matters called for a contingency election in the Senate, where the small states would have an advantage far greater than in the Electoral College. In the Electoral College, the small states' votes, even in accordance with their total representation, would still be overwhelmed by electoral votes of the large states because of their greater populations. Indeed, it was only because most of the delegates assumed that most elections would finally end up in a contingency election that the compromise was accepted by the small states. In fact, however, the small states have lost the full measure of the concessions given to them, since there has been no contingent election in Congress since 1824. The small states finally agreed to shift the contingency election from the Senate to the House, apparently because of concerns about the small number of senators who would choose the president. But they insisted on keeping the same principle of "one state, one vote" in the House that they would have enjoyed in the Senate.

What has remained to the small states, therefore, is but a vestige of the total concession they thought they had obtained in return for their approval of the Committee's report on September 4. In recent years, advocates of direct election have either dismissed the compromise with the small states at the Convention as irrelevant, or denied that there was such a compromise.

With regard to their dismissal of the compromise as irrelevant, it is submitted that this historic compromise is no more irrelevant than the compromise over equal representation in the Senate is now irrelevant, or that the constitutional method for amending the Constitution is irrelevant. All of these compromises comprise the very heart of our federal system. No doubt if these advocates of direct election could carry themselves back in time to the Constitutional Convention, they might have been among those proposing, as David Brearley did, that "a map of the United States be spread out, that all existing boundaries be erased, and that a partition of the whole be made into . . . equal parts."[62]

THE CREATION OF FEDERALISM

If the delegates at Philadelphia had learned anything about America's experience with the Articles of Confederation, it was about realism. A government had to be devised that would allow the states to retain those existing local police powers reflecting local needs and customs, but to give up those powers necessary for establishing the sovereignty of a nation. In order not to vindicate Hamilton's fear (that "two sovereignties can not coexist within the same limits. . . . A compound is inherently unstable"), it was necessary to create an almost perfect balance between retained and delegated powers. Too much retained or too much delegated would destroy the balance, and with it the framework of federalism necessary for democracy to flourish. History had shown repeatedly that large countries that relied unduly on central control were inherently unstable over the long term. On the other hand, those without enough central power were soon torn by internal rivalries.

The true genius of the American Constitution was not so much its creation of a democracy. Democracy, after all, was not a new idea, having been tried (mostly unsuccessfully) at various times in human history, beginning with the Athenians. Rather it was the creation of a system of federalism within which democracy could flourish and survive that was the true historic accomplishment of the Constitutional Convention.

The states were not paper entities dreamed up by some bureaucrat on a flow chart. Upon winning independence from Great Britain, the states were sovereign, functioning governments, each with its own history and culture. Any notion that the agreements, compromises, and principles that provided the foundation for the creation of our system of federalism are irrelevant is not only anti-Madisonian and antifederalist, but also comes at least 200 years too late.

Some advocates of direct election, not prepared to dismiss considerations of federalism, have simply denied that there was any compromise at the Convention between small and large states on the question of the manner of electing the president. John Feerick, an advisor to the ABA

Commission on Electoral College Reform, has claimed that any compromise was limited to the concession to have equal state votes in the contingent House election: "The assignment of a number of electoral votes to each state in accordance with the state's representation in Congress does not appear to have been, as often is contended, a compromise of any significance between large and small states."[63]

Madison himself had explained that the "little states insisted on retaining their equality in both branches" and Max Farrand, America's foremost constitutional historian, has stated that "the proposed method of electing the President was a compromise." But it is not simply that Feerick's conclusions differ from those of the framers and constitutional historians that casts doubt on Feerick's conclusions; nor that his conclusions conveniently serve to promote the ABA proposal for direct election; rather it is a failure to appreciate the context in which the constitutional debate over presidential election took place.

Farrand himself conceded that "the compromise does not appear on the surface," but notes that "it was referred to in the course of the debates, and in later years it was explained by several members of the convention, so that *no doubt attaches to it*" (emphasis added).[64]

Recall that the debate over the manner of electing the president occurred shortly after the emotional debate over equal state representation in the Senate. That debate had almost resulted in the dissolution of the Convention ("scarce held together by the strength of a hair"), and the walking out of the small states. But the compromise of July 16 finally established the principle of "one state, one vote." The fact that the issue was not then again specifically raised as an issue in the presidential election debate that followed does not show that the small states now cared only for the adoption of the principle in the election of the legislature, and were willing to concede it in the matter of presidential election. Rather it shows that the small states had so firmly established the principle of equal state representation that there was therefore no need to reestablish it.

That this is so is clearly supported by the proposals that followed. The only proposal during the debate over presidential election that did not incorporate the principle of equal state representation was that for direct election made by Morris of Pennsylvania. It was quickly rejected on a 9–1 vote, repudiated not only by the small states, but all the other larger states as well. After having pressed their goal of proportional representation in the debate on elections to the legislature (but having compromised to save the Convention from dissolution), the large states were not about to needlessly repeat the inflammatory debate by pressing for a direct election that they knew the small states feared would enable but three large states to impose a president on the rest of the country.

As Madison later recognized, the "Great Compromise," which provided the foundation for the Constitution, went to *both the legislative and executive branches.*

THE ROLE OF ELECTORS

Advocates of direct election have justified their view that the Electoral College should be abolished by claiming that the framers never intended that electors in the Electoral College were to be agents of the will of the people, but rather were intended to exercise their own independent judgment.[65] According to this view, since the Electoral College has in fact evolved in a different way than intended (that is, reflecting the will of the people), it therefore deserves to be abolished.[66]

In fact, the specific role of the electors was never discussed at the Convention. It was doubtless envisioned that the entire process of electing electors and determining their characteristics would be an evolutionary one. In any case, in a federal system it was deemed appropriate to leave this process to each state. By giving each state not only an influence, but a stake in the electoral process itself, it was hoped that the institution of the presidency would be legitimized and capable of providing strong leadership. The confidence placed in the states in this regard has been fully vindicated, with the result that every state now provides for popular election of presidential electors.

The argument that the framers intended that electors be independent of the will of the people is based on statements made after the Convention by delegates trying to persuade the state legislatures to adopt the Constitution. These arguments of persuasion can be found in *The Federalist* (written "anonymously," but in fact written mostly by Madison and Hamilton), and in the constitutional debates in the state legislatures. Although opinions can be found supporting this view in hearings and debates that occurred many years after the ratification of the Constitution, the only authoritative source supporting the independent elector view is Hamilton, in *The Federalist* No. 68, in which he stated that it was desirable that "the immediate election should be made by men most capable of analyzing the qualities adapted to the nation."[67]

Depending upon the audience that was trying to be persuaded, many statements were made after the Convention purporting to explain why one provision or another of the Constitution would be for the good of the nation. Hamilton may very well have thought that this view of the Electoral College would persuade those who favored a parliamentary style of electing a head of state. However, he never expressed this view at the Convention during the debates. He did, however, express other views, such as that the president should be elected for life. If reformers today were to advocate a constitutional amendment extending the term of the president to life, doubtless they could also cite Hamilton's view in that regard as authoritative of a "framer's intent."

Hamilton's ideas about the construction of a national government were significant in creating the Constitution. It is well known that he favored a strong national government, and he even proposed eliminating the states as entities. But it must be recalled that these ideas were ultimately rejected by the Convention.

Although Hamilton had deep reservations about the concept of dual sovereignty inherent in Madisonian federalism, he saw in the Constitution the nation's best hope for union and a stable government, and he became the Constitution's strongest and most zealous advocate. But to cite one sentence in one of his post-Convention articles as authoritative of the "framers' intent" about the role of electors is less than persuasive.

Nevertheless, if one is to place great importance on the post-Convention views of delegates who were campaigning for ratification, the views of delegates other than Hamilton, particularly Madison, must also be taken into account.

After the Convention, Madison described the Electoral College provision of the Constitution as providing that "the President is now to be elected by the people."[68] At the Virginia ratifying convention, Madison stated that the Constitution provided that the president was to be chosen by the "people at large,"[69] and later explained to the First Congress that the president was "appointed at present by the suffrages of three million people."[70]

James Wilson told the Pennsylvania ratifying Convention that "the people may elect with only one remove."[71] Even Hamilton later expressed the view that "It was desirable that the sense of the people should operate in the choice of the person to whom so important a trust was confided."[72]

The view that the Electoral College was but a vehicle for the expression of the people was not limited to those who had actually participated in the drafting of the Constitution. In 1803 Senator Melacton Smith of Maryland stated that it was the intent of the Convention that the selection of a president should "come as immediately from the people as was practicable,"[73] and a senator from Massachusetts stated that it was the intent of the framers that "the people should elect."[74]

In his 1958 study of the Electoral College, Lucius Wilmerding asked:

Did [the framers] mean to exclude the people from all participation in the important choice [of President]? Were the Electors to "make the election according to their own will, without the slightest control from the body of the people"? It is the fashion nowadays . . . to return affirmative answers to these last two questions. The Founding Fathers would have answered them, indeed did answer them, otherwise.[75]

Despite the strongest evidence that the framers did not intend electors to exercise independent judgment, however, reformers have found the view of independent electors to be convenient, indeed irresistible, in supporting their arguments to abolish the Electoral College. As early as 1826, in a Senate committee report, reformers who had never been at the Constitutional Convention were claiming that electors "have not answered the design of their institution. They are not the independent body and superior characters which they were intended to be."[76] Such views, asserted by those who never attended the Convention, soon took on a life of their own, sometimes even creeping into judicial opinions.[77]

It may reasonably be asked how the view, however weakly supported, that the framers intended that electors exercise independent judgment supports a case for abolishing the Electoral College. (In fact, the system of electing representatives who exercise their own judgment in selecting a leader is a practice observed in most parliamentary democracies today.) The reformers' chain of logic, though not always easily followed and based on numerous dubious assumptions, apparently goes something like this: the constitutional framers were essentially propertied, antiegalitarian, and antidemocratic elitists who feared trusting the people. They therefore devised a system whereby the election of the president would be delegated to a small and elite group of electors. This system was undemocratic (almost as undemocratic as, say, Great Britain or Israel today), but the undemocratic inclinations of the Founding Fathers were foiled by the state legislatures, which initiated popular elections of electors, and by the practice of parties requiring pledges by electors to vote for the popular choice. Since the original purpose of the Electoral College was undemocratic, it should therefore now be abolished regardless of how it functions today.

It is true, of course, that the Electoral College functions differently today than when it was first established. The Convention deliberately delegated to the states the task of developing the methods and criteria for electing electors. The Electoral College is therefore the final result of 200 years of evolution and trial and error, made possible by the flexibility the Constitution so wisely provided.

This process of extraconstitutional development is the subject of the next chapter. However, it remains here to conclude the story of the development of the constitutional provisions for the election of the president and vice president.

RATIFICATION OF THE CONSTITUTION

On September 17, 1787, the Convention completed its work. Of the 52 who attended and the 73 who had been appointed, 41 delegates remained. It remained only to sign the document, and refer it to the Confederation Congress for submission to the states for ratification. However, there was still significant opposition within the Convention to the final document. Randolph demanded that the final document be open to amendments by the states in the ratification process, and that a second convention be held to address amendments. Charles Pinckney demurred, speaking for most of the rest, when he replied that "Conventions are serious things, and ought not to be repeated."[78]

All but a handful knew that it was now or never. The Constitution must be presented to the states on an "all or nothing basis." The product of that extraordinary summer in Philadelphia had been produced by the best the continent had to offer, and it was unlikely that any other group like it could ever again be assembled. The creative energies expended had been too great, the compromises arrived at too delicate, to even contemplate that such a process could again be completed. Randolph's motion was soundly defeated. The states could adopt the Constitution, or they could refuse to adopt it. But they could not change it.

It was at this point that Benjamin Franklin made his one, but enduring, contribution to the Convention. A significant number of delegates had indicated that they would not sign the final document because they did not agree with many of its provisions. Franklin rose to address them.

I confess that there are several parts of this Constitution which I do not at present approve. But I agree to this Constitution with all its faults because I think a general government necessary for us. I doubt whether any other convention we can obtain may be able to make a better constitution. For when you assemble a number of men to have the advantage of their joint wisdom, you inevitably assemble with those men all their prejudices, passions, their errors of opinion, their local interests, and their selfish views. From such an assembly can a perfect production be expected?[79]

Knowing that the refusal to sign by a significant number of delegates could greatly diminish the chances for ratification, Franklin urged even those with reservations to sign, urging that every delegate who still had reservations "doubt a little of his own infallibility, and to make manifest our unanimity, put his name to this instrument."[80] He suggested that consent be indicated by state rather than individually. The document would read "Done by Convention, by the unanimous consent of the states present," and the individual delegates would only sign as "witnesses" to the unanimous consent of the states. Thus even delegates with serious reservations would not by their signature be testifying to their agreement with its provisions, but would only be acting as witnesses to the unanimous approval of each delegation. It proved to be a masterstroke.

William Blount of North Carolina "who had not opened his mouth during the Convention, spoke now to say that while he would not have signed otherwise, he would sign in the manner proposed by Franklin."[81] In the end there were but three holdouts: Gerry, Randolph, and George Mason refused to sign.

The next hurdle was at the Confederation Congress, many of whose members were outraged at the violation of the restrictions imposed by the Congress on the Convention. Fortunately, Philadelphia delegates comprised about a third of the Congress, but it was not enough to overcome stiff resistance from others in the Congress to endorsing the Constitution. In the end, a compromise was reached under which the Congress would submit the Constitution to the states for ratification, but without comment or endorsement.

Ratification by the states was by no means assured. While Pennsylvania procrastinated, little Delaware, which had obtained its crucial concessions at the Convention, did its part by breaking the ice and becoming the first state to ratify. Pennsylvania soon followed, but only after antifederalists boycotting the assembly were physically dragged to the State House to provide a quorum to elect delegates to the ratifying convention. Even then there was strong resistance from those claiming that the Convention had "exceeded its authority"[82] by going beyond the directive of the Congress to limit the work of the Convention to amending the Articles of Confederation.

In New York ratification seemed impossible since opponents to ratification overwhelmingly outnumbered the federalists. Once again, Hamilton saved the day, threatening to join the union with New York's Southern Counties, and leaving upstate New York on its own. Even this threat produced only a narrow three-vote margin for ratification, and many of those voting for ratification demanded changes and a second convention (which of course they never got).[83]

But it was the small states that provided the momentum, as when New Hampshire ratified on June 24. Soon only North Carolina and Rhode Island remained. North Carolina, which had voted against ratification, yielded only after the union had inaugurated George Washington, and Rhode Island was induced to join only after the U.S. Senate voted to cut off all relations with it. Even then Rhode Island (which had a total population of about 37,000) voted to join by only a two vote margin.[84]

From Madison's ruse in the Virginia Assembly in August 1786, to Rhode Island's grudging ratification in May 1790, it had been a long and difficult road. And it had been by no means a sure thing.

THE TWELFTH AMENDMENT

The final constitutional chapter of the Electoral College was written in 1804, with the passage of the Twelfth Amendment. The events leading up to the passage of that amendment were associated not so much with the election of the president as with problems associated with the election of the vice president.

To say that the vice presidency was not given considerable attention at the Constitutional Convention is an understatement. Many delegates were not sure what to make of the office. On the one hand it was desired that a successor, in the event of the death of the president, should assume all the powers of the presidency. Many delegates wished to avoid the situation where an officer succeeded to the presidency without full powers. (In Great Britain, for example, a regent who governed until the heir assumed the throne had only limited powers.)

Since it was finally determined that a president would be elected to a four-year term, the delegates also wished to avoid a situation in which a successor who had no broad-based support across the nation would be asked to govern for as long as four years. The solution, therefore, was a vice president, elected nationally in the same manner as the president, who would, upon the president's death or incapacity, assume the full powers of the presidency. But such a person, who might govern the country with full powers for as long as four years, had to be a person with credentials equal to those of the president.

The problem with this solution, however, was that there was no room in the constitutional scheme for any duties or powers to be assigned to the vice president. Although the vice president was eventually assigned the role of president of the Senate, and given the power to break tie votes, he had virtually no other constitutional responsibilities. His only real job was to sit around and wait for the president to die.

The dilemma that faced the framers, therefore, was how to provide for a method that would insure the election of the highest quality person to the position of vice president when the office had very little to recommend itself to such a person. In other words, what person of the highest credentials would want a job in which there was nothing to do? As Wilmerding has described the dilemma, "one might as readily expect a theatrical player of the first magnitude to seek the role of understudy to one of his rivals as a man of presidential caliber to seek the vice presidency."[85]

The original constitutional scheme to resolve this dilemma was one of the more ingenious of the entire Convention. The fact that it didn't work does not detract from its ingenuity.

Article III of Section II of the Constitution provided that each elector shall vote for two persons. However, the purpose of providing each elector with two votes was not to vote separately for president and vice president, but rather to insure that each elector voted for at least one person who was not an inhabitant of the same state as the elector. The presumption was that electors would be inclined to vote for someone from their own state. By requiring them to vote for at least one person who was not from their own state, the hope was that the candidate with the broadest national appeal would be elected.

The scheme was also thought to have another advantage. The person who received the most votes for president would, of course, be the president. But the person who received the next most number of votes for president would be the vice president. In other words, no elector would cast a vote for vice president. Every vote cast would be for president. In this way, it was hoped that a person of the highest quality would be elected to be vice president—that is, someone who was running for president. As already noted, it was thought that no one of consequence would ever seek the office of vice president for its own sake.

Problems with this scheme were not encountered in the two elections of George Washington because the only office in contention was that of the vice president. By 1796, however, it became apparent that a party putting forth a candidate had a definite idea of which candidate it wanted for president and which candidate it wanted for vice president. It also became apparent that a minority party had ample opportunity under such a system for political mischief.

In the 1800 election, for example, the anti-Federalist party (known as the Republican and later the Democratic party) nominated Jefferson and Burr. However, the party's true choice for president was Jefferson, and its true choice for vice president was the political hack, Burr. In other words, the Republican party had not nominated two men thought worthy of the presidency (as the framers had hoped), but only one. Then, to compound their political error, they failed to instruct one of their electors to withhold one vote for Burr. Had they done so, Jefferson would have received the most electoral votes and been elected president, and Burr would have received the next most electoral votes and been elected vice president. Instead, both Jefferson and Burr received the exact same number of votes in the Electoral College, and the election was referred to the House.

In the House, the Federalists took advantage of this situation to throw their support behind Burr. This move was entirely mischievous since Jefferson was clearly the more qualified candidate for president. Presumably the Federalist strategy was to deliberately elect a Republican they thought would be ineffective and second-rate, perhaps someone who could more easily be held at bay than Jefferson.

Although Burr had been one of the two Republican candidates for president, the Republicans now "fulminated, stormed, and threatened civil war if the will of the people were thus to be defeated."[86] Two Republican governors called out the militia to "block a Federalist usurpation of the presidency."[87] Of course, the Republicans had a point: not a single elector had voted for Burr with the wish that he be elected president. On the other hand, the Federalists responded that the system had worked as it should— the majority party had put forward their two candidates, and it was only right that the minority should be permitted to choose between them. (In fact, the Federalists were only doing to the Republicans what the Republicans had done to them in 1796. In that election, the Federalists had deliberately withheld electoral votes for their true vice presidential choice, Pinckney, to insure that their true presidential choice, John Adams, would be elected. Unfortunately for the Federalists, however, they withheld too many votes, and Jefferson slipped in as the vice president.)

In the end, after 36 ballots, and lengthy political maneuvering, Jefferson was finally elected president and Burr vice president. But it was obvious that the system devised at the Convention to insure that the vice president be of equal quality to the president was not working. It simply had to be accepted as a fact of political life that parties would always put forward one candidate for president and another for vice president.

Thus a constitutional amendment was proposed by the Republicans to require a separate electoral vote for president and vice president. Unfortunately the debate that followed centered less on the merits of the proposed amendment than on which party it would favor. The Federalists, who were now clearly in the minority, saw the amendment as a ploy to deprive them of the opportunity of electing a vice president (the minimum office they thought befitting their status as the minority party). Before 1800 the Republicans had opposed such an amendment since the existing system had worked to their advantage in the 1796 election and secured them the vice presidency.

Over vigorous Federalist opposition, the Twelfth Amendment was passed by Congress and approved by three-quarters of the states in the summer of 1804—just in time for the November election, and also in time to prevent the Federalists from gaining the vice presidency. It was the death knell for the Federalists, who soon departed the American scene.

Although the most important provision of the Twelfth Amendment was the separate election of the president and vice president, there were several other changes made in the presidential election process: the number of candidates to be considered for election in the contingent House election was reduced from five to three; a majority of electoral votes was required to elect the vice president (rather than the second most number of electoral votes); the qualifications for vice president were to be the same as president; and, in case a president was not chosen by inauguration day, the newly elected vice president would become president until the new president was elected (it was presumed that the vice president would have been elected, since in the Senate the choice was limited only to the top two candidates and there was therefore no chance of any vice presidential candidate not receiving a majority of votes in the Senate).

NOTES

1. William Peters, *A More Perfect Union: The Making of the United States Constitution* (New York: Crown Publishers, 1987), 5.

2. Burton J. Hendrick, *Bulwark of the Republic: Biography of the Constitution* (Boston: Little, Brown, 1937), 35. This was because the Congress had no power to impose duties, and therefore an amendment to the articles was needed that required unanimity.

3. *Id.* at 32.

4. *Id.* at 33.

5. *Id*. at 36.

6. *Id*. at 32. (Statement of Edward Bancroft, ellipses indicating omissions have been deleted.)

7. *Id*. at 33.

8. Peters, *supra* note 1 at 9, 11.

9. Hendrick, *supra* note 2, at 55.

10. *Id*. at 63.

11. *Id*.

12. *Id*.

13. In fact, just this event could occur. Article V of the Constitution permits the convening of a new Constitutional Convention upon a call by two-thirds of the states.

14. Hendrick, *supra*, note 1, at 41.

15. *Id*.

16. Peters, *supra*, note 1, at 16.

17. *Id*. at 16.

18. *Id*.

19. *Id*. at 28.

20. Hendrick, *supra*, note 2, at 65.

21. *Id*.

22. *Id*.

23. Peters, *supra* note 1, at 43.

24. *Id*.

25. *Id*. at 30.

26. *Id*. at 31.

27. *Id*.

28. *Id*. at 135.

29. *Id*. at 31.

30. *Id*.

31. *Id*.

32. *Id*.

33. *Id*. at 97.

34. *Id*.

35. Michael Zuckert, "Federalism and the Founding: Toward a Reinterpretation of the Constitutional Convention," *The Review of Politics* (Notre Dame, 1986), 173.

36. *Id*.

37. Paul Berley, New Jersey delegate, cited in Peters, *supra* note 1, at 71.

38. M. Farrand, 321 (June 19, 1787), cited in Zuckert, *supra* note 35, at 195.

39. Farrand, 3567 (June 21, 1787), cited in *id*. at 195.

40. Farrand, 330 (June 19, 1787), cited in *Id*. at 195.

41. Farrand, 287 (June 19, 1787), cited in *Id*. at 198.

42. Cited in Peters, *supra* note 1, at 99.

43. *Id*. at 110.

44. *Id*. at 63. Ellipses indicating omissions have been deleted.

45. *Id*. at 129.

46. *Id*. at 104.

47. The delegates finally agreed that slaves would be counted as three-fifths of a person in counting population for purposes of determining a state's representation in the House.

48. Robertson, *The Debates of the Convention of Virginia 1788*, 2nd ed. (1805) 351, cited in Max Farrand, ed., *The Records of the Federal Convention of 1787*, Vol. III (New Haven: Yale University Press, 1966) at App. A, CXXXVII, 135.

49. *Id*.

50. See John Feerick, "The Electoral College: Why It Was Created," *ABA Journal* (March 1968), 249, 250.

51. Lolabel House, "A Study of the Twelfth Amendment," Ph.D. dissertation, University of Philadelphia, 1901, 58.

52. *Id*. at 60.

53. *Id*. at 15.

54. *Id*. at 11.

55. Alexander Hamilton, *Works of Hamilton* (1851), II, 393, cited in *id*. at 10.

56. *Id*. at 12.

57. Peters, *supra* note 1, at 189.

58. *Id*. at 190.

59. *Id*. at 192.

60. House, *supra* note 51, at 18.

61. Max Farrand, *The Framing of the Constitution of the United States* (New Haven: Yale University Press, 1987 [originally published in 1913]), at Chap. 11, 166.

62. Peters, *supra* note 1, at 71.

63. Feerick, *supra* note 50, at 254.

64. Farrand, *supra* note 61, at 166.

65. See, for example, John Feerick, "The Electoral College—Why It Ought to be Abolished," 37 *Fordham L. Rev.* 1 (1968).

66. *Id*.

67. Cited in *id*. at 9.

68. Cited in Lucius Wilmerding, Jr., *The Electoral College* (Boston: Beacon Press, 1958) 19.

69. *Id*.

70. *Id*. at 20.

71. *Id*.

72. *Id*.

73. *Id*.

74. *Id*.

75. *Id*. at 19.

76. Senate Select Committee on Amendments to the Constitution, Report on the Several Reservations Proposing Amendments to the Constitution, As Regarding the Election of President and Vice-President of the United States, S. Rep. 22, 19th Cong. 1st sess., 1826, 4, cited in Michael Glennon, *When No Majority Rules: The Electoral College and Presidential Succession* (Washington, D.C.: Congressional Quarterly, Inc., 1992), 8.

77. See, for example, *McPherson v. Blacker*, 146 U.S. 1 (1892), *William v. Rhodes* 393 U.S. 23 (1968).

78. Peters, *supra* note 1, at 208–209.

79. *Id*. at 210–211. Ellipses indicating omissions have been deleted.

80. *Id.* at 212.

81. *Id.* at 214.

82. *Id.* at 230.

83. *Id.* at 233.

84. *Id.* at 234.

85. Wilmerding, *supra* note 68, at 27.

86. *Id.* at 31.

87. Neal R. Peirce and Lawrence D. Longley, *The People's President: The Electoral College in American History and the Direct Vote*, rev. ed. (New Haven: Yale University Press, 1981), 41.

Chapter Four

EVOLUTION: REFINING THE ELECTORAL PROCESS

It has been noted that the constitutional contribution to the Electoral College system is minimal. The Constitution provides only that "each state shall appoint, in such manner as the legislature thereof may direct, a number of electors, equal to the whole number of Senators and Representatives to which the state may be entitled in the Congress." The Twelfth Amendment adds only that the electors will meet in their respective states, and that the candidates who receive the majority of votes as president and vice president will be elected. If no candidate receives a majority, the election is referred to the House and Senate.

The framers thus delegated to the states the primary task of refining the electoral process, and determining the details of methods to be used for electing members of the Electoral College. The task of determining whether the state refinements were consistent with the Constitution was delegated to the U.S. Supreme Court and such lower federal courts as Congress might "from time to time ordain and establish." This delegation was accomplished through Section 2 of Article III of the Constitution, which provides that the judicial power shall extend to all cases "arising under the Constitution." Subject to review by the U.S. Supreme Court, state courts also apply the Constitution, which, according to Article VI, is the "Supreme Law of the land."

Since the Constitution does not provide a means for nominating candidates to be considered by the electors for election to the presidency, political parties have formed to perform that function. There being no provision in the Constitution governing the nomination process, states have taken over the primary responsibility for regulating this process, subject, of course, to such other provisions of the Constitution as the Thirteenth, Fourteenth, and Fifteenth Amendments.

Thus state legislatures, federal and state courts, and political parties have all contributed to the task of refining the electoral process. It must therefore be acknowledged that when reformers seek to institute such changes as direct election, they are proposing not only to tamper with the Constitution, but to overturn over 200 years of legal interpretation, legislative enactments, rule-making, and custom—in short, 200 years of refining the constitutional design.

Since the nation's first presidential election in 1789, many issues have arisen in the electoral process that have required resolution. The first and most important of these is how the states "shall appoint" electors. Other issues requiring interpretation and refinement have related to the legal obligations and qualifications of electors, the qualification of voters who elect electors, ballot access, campaign spending limitations, and the applicability of the "one man, one vote" principle to the electoral process. Each will be considered separately. Although some of these issues have been briefly addressed in Chapter Two in the context of the existing electoral system, they are addressed here in more depth and detail in the context of the electoral refinement process.

APPOINTMENT OF ELECTORS

The power of the state legislatures to appoint electors was intended to be plenary. Charles Pinckney of South Carolina, a member of the Constitutional Convention, explained that "Electors of a President are to be chosen in the manner directed by the state legislatures"—that is all that is said. In case the state legislatures refuse to make these directions there is no power to compel them; there is not a single word in the Constitution that can, by the most tortured construction, be extended to give Congress a right to make or alter the state legislatures' directions on this subject. The right to make these directions is complete and conclusive and subject to no control or revision.[1]

For 50 years, it was believed by Congress that it did not even have the power to set the day for election of electors—apparently on the theory that by "determining the time of their being chosen," they would in fact also be "determining the manner of choosing."[2] For example, if Congress were to set a day when some legislatures were not in session, Congress would, in effect, be mandating appointment by popular election. When, in 1845, Congress decided to go ahead and set the day anyway (the Tuesday after the first Monday in November), at least one legislature was forced to call a special session in order to preserve its prerogative to choose the electors by legislative action.[3]

Although the eventual mode of appointment adopted by all the states was statewide popular election, it took many years of experimentation and political development for this method to be universally adopted. By 1824 about three-quarters of the states had come to prescribe appointment by popular election, but of these only about half elected electors statewide.

The others used a variety of methods, ranging from the district method to a combination of the district and general ticket methods. Those states in which the legislatures retained the privilege of appointment used an even greater variety of legislative methods, ranging from joint votes, concurrent votes, and legislative compromise with or without executive approval.

This lack of uniformity began to concern Congress. As one senator asked, in 1816, "Why should a different mode of election prevail in different states?"[4] Between 1816 and 1828 there was a flurry of proposals for constitutional amendments. Some of these, like the proposal for direct election of the president, were given little support (particularly by the small states), presumably since it would have constituted a breach of the compromises reached at the Constitutional Convention. (There were also concerns that since each state had widely differing qualifications for voters, such a system would have far different applications to each state.)

Other proposals were given more serious consideration, such as those whose purpose was not so much to favor one system over another, but to choose one uniform system whatever it might be. Thus, there were proposals to require all states to adopt, respectively, legislative appointment, popular vote by district, and popular vote by general ballot. All of these proposals would have required a constitutional amendment, and all were defeated (although the proposal for popular vote by district came the closest). One reason the district vote plan came so close to adoption was that it did not involve a betrayal of the constitutional compromise. Under this plan the small states would have retained electors equal in number to the senators and representatives to which they were entitled in Congress.

In the end the states came to adopt a universal method of appointing electors without the need for tampering with the Constitution. The universal method finally adopted was the result of two factors: the demands of the people in each state for a direct voice in the election of electors, and the necessity, acknowledged by almost all the states, to preserve their full influence in the electoral process.[5]

An example of how public clamor ultimately led to appointment by popular election was the case of the "Immortal Seventeen." These were 17 senators in the New York State Senate who in the presidential election of 1824 deliberately blocked a proposal for popular election of electors, despite an overwhelming vote for the proposal in the State House. Their ill-concealed purpose was to insure the delivery of New York's electoral vote to their mutual friend, William Crawford. Although their ploy worked only in part (the Assembly overrode the Senate, and most of New York's electoral votes went to Adams), the voters of the state were so outraged that they voted out of office the only one of the "Immortal Seventeen" who dared to run for reelection.[6] (To add to the final insult to the "Immortals," Crawford lost the election to John Adams.)

Similar popular revolts occurred in New Jersey and Pennsylvania. By 1836 every state except South Carolina appointed electors by popular election. South Carolina relented in 1868, and thereafter only two state legislatures ever chose their own electors: Florida in 1868, and a bewildered Colorado legislature in 1876 after it had just been admitted to the union.

Although public clamor soon resulted in the universal adoption of appointment by popular election, the universal adoption of the general ballot system over its rival, the district system, was delayed by political factors. The problem was that the type of system used could have a direct and immediate effect on the outcome of an election. Thus members of the majority party in a state legislature would adopt a district system if they thought it would favor the election of its party's candidate for president; the next year they might switch back to the general ticket system if that seemed to favor its candidate.

For example, in a situation where the party controlling the legislature believed its candidate was favored by a majority of all the voters in the state, it would adopt the general ticket system since that would deliver all the state's electoral votes to its candidate. If the controlling party believed that the majority of voters in the state favored an opposition candidate, however, it would adopt the district system, since that would greatly increase the likelihood that at least some of the state's electoral votes would go to its candidate. Thus, it was not unusual for a state to switch back and forth between systems.

Even Madison was not above considering the political ramifications of which system was to be adopted. According to some cynics, Madison switched his support from the district method to the general ticket method in the 1800 election because he thought it would favor Jefferson and the Republicans. Jefferson himself, who professed a preference for the district system, acknowledged that if "10 states choose . . . by general ticket, it is folly and worse than folly for the other 6 not to do it."[7]

In time, party considerations gave way to considerations of state loyalty. The theory (though challenged by some) was as follows: under a general ticket system, the state would deliver the weight of all its electoral votes to one candidate, thus giving it a significant influence on the final outcome of the election; under the district method, however, the state's electoral votes would be split (perhaps 50–50), thus effectively neutralizing that state's impact on the election.

Under this reasoning, an analogy may be found in the manner in which states vote in the contingent House election. The Twelfth Amendment provides that in the House each state has one vote. How that vote is counted is determined by majority vote within that state's delegation. Thus, if the vote is tied within a delegation, the state loses its vote and the power to affect the final choice for president. By analogy to the general election, a state like North Dakota, with only 3 electoral votes, can throw its total weight of 3 votes to its choice if it uses the general ticket system. But if California, which has 54 electoral votes, uses the district system, and splits 27–27, its net impact on the election is zero. Thus little North Dakota with its general ticket has a greater impact on the election than giant California! This is why Jefferson said that if some states adopt the general ticket, the rest are almost compelled also to adopt it.

Although political scientists and economists have often tried to prove this theory fallacious, the fact is that the legislatures of every state (except Maine and Nebraska) have adopted it and the general ticket system.

The fact that political factors have played a role in the development of the general ticket system has been emphasized by reformers as a reason why the Electoral College should be abolished. The case is made that since the Electoral College is the product of political development, it must somehow be deficient. While it is true that states have adopted the system because they think it is to their advantage, it is also true that the general ticket system has succeeded in achieving many of the goals of the framers. In every fairly conducted election but one, the winner of the majority of electoral votes has also received the most popular votes. The general ticket system has proved its worth on its own merits, and serves as a worthy product of 200 years of political legal development. It is not, however, constitutionally mandated.

In *McPherson v. Blacker* (discussed briefly in Chapter Two), it was argued that the general ticket had become so widely accepted and adopted that it had become part and parcel of the Constitution. The Court rejected this argument, reaffirming that the word "appoint" in Article II has the broadest possible application. "It has been said," observed the Supreme Court, "that the word 'appoint' is not the most appropriate word to describe the result of a popular election." Perhaps not, but it is sufficiently comprehensive to cover that mode, and was manifestly used as conveying the broadest power of determination. It was used in Article 5 of the Articles of Confederation, which provided that "delegates shall be annually appointed in such manner as the legislature of each state shall direct."[8]

Despite the important role that popular election of electors under a general ticket system has played in the electoral process, there remain two areas of concern.

First, although the popular election of electors is now the accepted mode of appointment of electors in every state, it is not constitutionally mandated. Although it is unlikely, a state legislature could, if it were so inclined, take away the vote from the people and give it back to the legislature. This could conceivably happen in a close election where it became apparent that legislative selection would favor the candidate of the party controlling the state legislature. A responsible reform would therefore be to amend the Constitution to require that all electors be chosen by popular vote. The American people have come to accept the popular election of electors as their right, and many now believe (mistakenly) that the popular election of electors is already provided for in the Constitution.

Second, although the general ticket system has proved very effective in discouraging factionalism and providing a clear electoral mandate, it too is not constitutionally mandated. Every state is free to select a different system, and two states have already done so. Uniformity in the election process is no less desirable today than it was 150 years ago. Although this reform was rejected when it was first proposed in 1826, the general ticket system was not at that time accepted by all the states. However, since today all but two states already use the general ticket system, a responsible reform would be to incorporate this system into the Constitution. This would eliminate any possible incentive for a state to switch from one system to another in the hope of favoring a particular candidate, and would make uniform each state's electoral method. It would also prevent the piecemeal dismantling of existing electoral processes by states, one by one, following the example of Maine and Nebraska, or switching back and forth between systems.

QUALIFICATIONS OF ELECTORS

The Constitution sets forth only one specific qualification of an elector: namely, that he or she not hold an "office of trust or profit under the United States." The purpose of this requirement was to insure that electors would not be under the influence of the party in power at the time the election was conducted.

How strictly this provision would be construed, however, was not made clear until the 1877 case of *In Re Corliss*.[9] In that case, George Corliss was chosen as a presidential elector by the Rhode Island electorate. However, at the time he was chosen, Corliss was the commissioner from Rhode Island of the United States Centennial Commission. The purpose of the Commission was to exhibit American artwork, and other products. Commissioners were also charged with the task of closing up the affairs of the Commission, auditing its accounts, and submitting a final report. It was to be composed of one delegate from each state. However, it was formed "under the auspices of the government of the United States."

The Court examined the three parts of the constitutional qualification requirements separately. First, was the position of commissioner an "office" of the United States? The Court stated that it was, since the Commission was created by an Act of Congress, and was not created to serve only one state or region, but "in the interest of all the States united."

Second, the Court considered the question whether the office was for "profit." The Court decided that since Corliss was to serve on the Commission without remuneration, it was not an office of "profit." However, the Constitution disqualified one who held an office of trust "or" profit.

The Court decided that Corliss' office was one of trust:

the Commissioners were to be intrusted with a large supervisory and regulative control of the property sent for exhibition; and from the time the government gave its sanction to the exhibition, and especially after the President issued his proclamation, the honor and reputation of the United States were pledged for its proper management to its own citizens. [10]

A vigorous dissenting opinion asked

what "trust" do the Commissioners receive? What power is conferred upon them? What discretion are they to exercise on behalf of the United States? They can make no contracts; they are not authorized to carry out any plan they may devise, nor can they in any way cause or compel it to be carried out. . . . There appears to be nothing in this denoting a "trust" within the meaning of the Constitution.[11]

The dissent also noted that the Constitution also provides that no person holding office may be a member of either house of Congress, yet it was a notable fact that the president of the Commission was a representative in Congress.

Other courts have not been as strict in their interpretation of the elector qualification requirements as In Re Corliss. In Commonwealth v. Binns,[12] for example, it was held that the selection of a newspaper editor to print the laws of the United States did not confer an "office" that would be disqualifying to an elector. In Sheboygan v. Parket, a commissioner appointed to issue country bonds in aid of a national railroad was held not to be an officer.[13] A Mississippi court has held that a pension agent is not an officer of the federal government.[14]

Unfortunately the courts have not been able to agree on whether an elector is a state or federal officer. In Walker v. U.S. the Eighth Circuit Court of Appeals decided in 1937 that presidential electors "are not 'federal officers' since the Federal Constitution leaves it to the state legislatures to define the method of choosing electors."[15] In 1944, however, the Supreme Court of Texas decided that a presidential elector was "not a 'state officer' " within the meaning of a state statute providing that candidates for state office should be nominated in primaries, and thus presidential electors could be nominated by party convention rather than direct election by primary.[16] If an elector is neither a state nor a federal officer, the question may be asked as to what kind of officer is an elector? In the absence of uncontroverted authority, the presidential elector appears to have fallen into some kind of constitutional crack. Many courts have held electors to be state officers, however, notably Tood v. Johnson, and Hodge v. Bryan.[17]

As discussed briefly in Chapter Two, the most important qualification for an elector is that imposed by the party that nominates him or her— namely, that he or she pledge to vote for the party's candidate for president and vice president. While it is true that the Constitution does not require electors to pledge their votes as a condition for qualification, it is also true that it does not forbid a party from imposing such a qualification. The Constitution simply does not say one way or the other. But, absent a prohibition, there appears to be no reason why a party can not set its own standards and qualification for the electors it chooses to nominate.

Thus far, the courts have agreed with this contention. In 1952 the Supreme Court held that it is not violative of the Constitution for a party to require a candidate for the office of elector to take a pledge to vote for the party's nominee.[18] The Court observed that "as is well known, political parties in the modern sense were not born with the Republic. They were created by necessity, by the need to organize the rapidly increasing population, scattered over our land, so as to coordinate efforts to secure needed legislation and oppose that deemed undesirable."[19] It also noted that "the party conventions of locally chosen delegates, from the county to the national level, succeeded the caucuses of self-appointed legislators or other interested individuals. Dissatisfaction with the manipulation of conventions caused that system to be largely superseded by the direct primary."[20]

Nevertheless this view prevailed only against vigorous opposition. The Supreme Court of Alabama, before being overruled by the U.S. Supreme Court, had previously stated:

We appreciate the argument that from time immemorial, the electors selected to vote in the college have voted in accordance with the wishes of the party. But in doing so, the effective compulsion theory has generally been taken for granted, so that the voting for a president and vice president has been usually formal merely, but the Twelfth Amendment does not make it so. The nominees of the party for president and vice president may have become disqualified, or peculiarly offensive not only to the electors, but their constituents also. They should be free to vote for another, as contemplated by the Twelfth Amendment.[21]

It is also notable that both Supreme Court Justices Williiam O. Douglas and Robert Jackson dissented vigorously from the view that electors could be bound by pledges exacted prior to their nomination. Justice Douglas conceded that a law requiring electors to vote in accordance with their pledge

does no more than to make a legal obligation of what has been a voluntary general practice. If custom were sufficient authority for amendment of the Constitution by Court decree, the decision in the matter would be warranted. Usage may sometimes import changed content to constitutional generalities, such as "due process of law," "equal protection," or "commerce among the states." But I do not think powers or discretion granted to federal officials by the federal Constitution can be forfeited by the court for disuse. A political practice which has its origin in custom must rely upon custom for its sanctions.[22]

Jackson too found fault with required pledges:

The Court is sanctioning a new instrument of power in the hands of any faction that can get control of the Democratic National Convention. . . . This device of pre-pledged and oath-bound electors imposes upon the party within the state an oath-bound regularity and loyalty to the controlling element in the national party. It centralizes party control and, instead of securing for the locality a share in the central management, it secures the central management in dominance of the local vote in the Electoral College. If we desire free elections, we should not add to the leverage over local party representatives always possessed by those who enjoy the prestige and dispense the patronage of a national administration.[23]

Finally, both dissenters characterized a party pledge requirement as effectively stating: "All who are not ready to follow blindly anyone chosen by the national convention are excluded from the primary, and that, in practice, means also from the election."[24]

The views of Douglas and Jackson were rightly overruled by the majority. First, the dissenters' view of the role of the presidential elector relied heavily, indeed exclusively, on *The Federalist* No. 68. Although its author (Hamilton) was not named by the justices in their dissent, it will be recalled that Hamilton was virtually alone is his view that electors were expected to exercise their individual judgment, and that Madison and others saw the Electoral College as a means of reflecting the will of the people (see Chapter Three). Second, the dissenters may have had another purpose in espousing a view that, if enacted, would have seriously dedemocratized the electoral process. If electors were truly permitted, and even encouraged, to cast votes of their own choosing without regard to the presidential choice of those who nominated and elected them, it would have caused serious, perhaps irreparable, damage to the institution of the Electoral College. It would certainly have given momentum to movements to reform the College and amend the Constitution.

A hint of this motive can be found in Justice Douglas' comment in his dissent that

the demise of the entire electoral system would not impress me as a disaster. At its best it is a mystifying and distorting factor in presidential elections which may resolve a popular defeat into an electoral victory. . . . To abolish it and substitute direct election of the President, so that every vote wherever cast would have equal weight in calculating the result, would seem to me a gain for simplicity and integrity of our governmental processes.[25]

In view of this espousal of democracy in the electoral process, it is difficult to reconcile his opinion to allow electors to cast views in defiance of the popular will, other than to see his opinion as a means of deliberately undermining the institution of the Electoral College so as to trigger demands for a Constitutional overhaul.

In fact, the majority opinion carries into effect not only the letter but also the spirit of the framers' intent. As Madison made clear, the electors were expected to reflect the will of the people, and a pledge required of electors does no more than insure that this reflection takes place. A pledge does not force electors to vote in any particular manner.[26] It only requires them to *promise* that they will vote in a particular manner. They are free not to make the pledge, in which case the party has a right to nominate others who are willing to make the pledge.

Although many states have passed criminal laws forbidding electors from breaking their pledges, no such law has ever been enforced, and the constitutionality of enforcement would be questionable. Since 1820, only seven electors have betrayed their party loyalty or their pledges. None of these wayward votes has ever come close to affecting an election, and those who cast them appear to have been seeking notoriety or to become some kind of footnote in the history books. Responsible reform, however, should address the problem of the "faithless elector" (see Chapter Seven).

VOTER QUALIFICATIONS

Section 2 of Article II of the Constitution does not provide that all U.S. citizens may vote for presidential electors. Rather, it provides only that the electors shall be appointed as the state legislatures direct. Once a state determines that electors shall be chosen by popular vote (as all states have done), it has wide latitude to determine eligibility to vote. It may not, however, determine eligibility in a way that would violate the Fourteenth Amendment (guaranteeing equal protection of the laws),[27] the Fifteenth (forbidding abridgement of the right to vote based on race or color), the Nineteenth (forbidding abridgement of the right to vote based on sex), the Twenty-fourth (striking the poll tax), and the Twenty-sixth (forbidding restrictions based on age for voters 18 years or older).

Until the Twenty-third Amendment, voters residing in the District of Columbia were not given the right to vote for a presidential elector because the District had no representatives in Congress, and the Constitution only provided for electors equal to the number of representatives in Congress. The Twenty-third Amendment resolved this by allocating to the District not less than the electoral votes awarded to the least populous state (now three).

In *Oregon v. Mitchell*,[28] the Supreme Court struck down state "durational residency" provisions that had effectively disenfranchised many American citizens who had only recently moved to a state but had not yet met the state residency requirements to vote. In that case the Court approved congressional legislation that substituted uniform residency requirements for voting for electors in every state.

In 1976 Congress passed the Overseas Citizens Voting Rights Act,[29] which provided that American citizens residing outside the United States could vote by absentee ballot in their last state of residency. This act was based on prevailing law, which stated that one retains citizenship in a state until new legal domicile or state citizenship is obtained. A House Report on the act stated its purpose:

The Committee believes that a U.S. citizen residing outside the United States remains a citizen of his last state of residence and domicile for purposes of voting in Federal Elections under this bill, as long as he has not become a citizen of another state and has not otherwise relinquished his citizenship in such prior state.[30]

However, neither the Constitution, case law, nor the Citizens Voting Rights Act provides for U.S. citizens who are not citizens of any state. In the case of *The Attorney General of the Territory of Guam on Behalf of All U.S. Citizens Residing in Guam Qualified to Vote Pursuant to the Organic Act*,[31] the Ninth Circuit Court of Appeals held that the rights of American citizens on Guam were not violated by prohibiting their voting in the U.S. presidential and vice presidential elections.

Thus U.S. citizens who can not claim state citizenship have truly fallen through a constitutional crack. There are several solutions that should be considered as part of a package of responsible reform. The purpose of the Twenty-third Amendment was to enfranchise citizens in the District of Columbia who had long been denied the right to vote for presidential electors. Since the District is a purely federal jurisdiction that has already been given more electoral votes per person than many states, all U.S. citizens who are not also citizens of a state should be permitted by absentee ballot to vote for the three electors allocated to the District of Columbia.

BALLOT ACCESS

Other U.S. citizens who have claimed disenfranchisement are those supporters of small or third parties that are unable to meet the requirements to have their electors placed on the ballot. The Supreme Court has held that if a state makes it too difficult for a third party to get on the ballot, such restrictions may violate the Fourteenth Amendment (see Chapter Two).[32] In general, states can limit access to the ballot in order to insure that its electoral purpose is fulfilled.[33]

Unfortunately, however, the Supreme Court has not been precise in setting forth standards for determining when state election laws are too strict to pass muster. In *Illinois Board of Elections v. Socialist Workers Party*,[34] for example, the standard suggested by the Court was very strict—namely, that the state must use the "least drastic means" of restricting access to the ballot by third parties, and must avoid restrictions that are "overbroad." In *Anderson v. Celebreeze*,[35] on the other hand, the Court suggested a more lenient standard—that the "state's important regulatory interests are generally sufficient to justify reasonable, nondiscriminatory restrictions."[36] The

Court also suggested that there was no one standard that could be applied: "Constitutional challenges to specific provisions of a state's election laws therefore can not be resolved by any 'litmus-paper' test that will separate valid from invalid restrictions."[37]

In 1988 a state court interpreted these rather vague Supreme Court guidelines as follows:

> To determine the validity of ballot access restrictions, a court must first consider the character and magnitude of the asserted injury to the rights protected by the First and Fourteenth Amendments that the plaintiff seeks to vindicate. It then must identify and evaluate the precise interests put forward by the State as justifications for the burden imposed by the rule. In passing judgment, the court must not only determine the legitimacy and strength of each of those interests, it must also consider the extent to which those interests make it necessary to burden the plaintiff's rights. Only after weighing all these factors is the reviewing court in a position to decide whether the challenged provision is unconstitutional.[38]

The courts have had difficulty, therefore, in applying these standards. A state's requirement that a party get signatures of 15% of the electorate has been judged unreasonable.[39] In *McLain v. Meier*[40] a 5% requirement was upheld where a viable write-in alternative was provided. A number of Courts have upheld at least a 3% requirement, depending upon such variables as the time permitted for obtaining the signatures, the size of the electorate, whether signatures are required of the entire electorate or registered voters, and whether write-in votes are permitted.[41] In *Gus Hall (Communist Party) v. Simcox*, the Seventh Circuit struggled through volumes of case precedent before finally upholding Indiana's 2% requirement.[42] Constitutional scholar Lawrence Tribe has suggested that a 5% requirement marks the dividing line between reasonable and unreasonable ballot restrictions.[43]

LIMITATIONS ON CAMPAIGN CONTRIBUTIONS AND SPENDING

Section 1 of Article II of the Constitution gives Congress the power to determine the time of choosing electors. It does not specifically give Congress the power to affect the process of electing electors in the states. Attempts by Congress to in any way regulate the process of electing electors have therefore been challenged.

In 1884, however, federal power to regulate the election of electors for president and vice president was upheld in the case of *Ex Parte Yarbrough*.[44] According to the Supreme Court, the power to regulate includes the authority to protect the electoral process against the two great natural and historical enemies of all republics, open violence and insidious corruption. [For] if this government is anything more than a mere aggregation of delegated agents of other states and governments, each of which is superior to the general government, it must have the power to protect the elections on which its existence depends from violence and corruption [including] the free use of money in elections, arising from the vast growth of recent wealth.[45]

In 1925 Congress passed the Federal Corrupt Practices Act,[46] which provided that any political committee that accepted campaign contributions for the purpose of influencing the election of presidential electors was required to register the names of all contributors, keep detailed accounts, and comply with a variety of other accounting requirements. In *Burroughs and Canon v. U.S.*,[47] defendants charged with violating the act claimed that the act was unconstitutional because it purported to regulate the election of electors beyond that permitted by Section 1 of Article II of the Constitution.

The Supreme Court rejected this contention, stating that

So narrow a view of the powers of Congress is without warrant. The Congressional Act under review seeks to preserve the purity of presidential and vice presidential elections. Neither in purpose nor in effect does it interfere with the power of a state to appoint electors or the manner in which their appointment shall be made. It deals with political committees organized for the purpose of influencing elections in two or more states. . . . Its operation is confined to situations which, if not beyond the power of the state to deal with at all, are beyond its power to deal with adequately. It in no sense invades any exclusive state power.[48]

In 1971 Congress passed the Federal Election Campaign Act (amended in 1974),[49] which, among other provisions, limited political contributions to candidates for federal elective office, limited expenditures by groups "relative to a clearly identified candidate" to $1,000 per candidate per election, and provided for public financing of political parties. The amount of funding was to depend upon the percentage of votes a party received in a prior election.

Between 1952 and 1972 the amount of money spent on federal election campaigns rose by a staggering 300% at a time when the consumer price index rose but 58%. The avowed purpose of the Campaign Act was to help control these spiraling costs of campaigning, but its more important purpose was to equalize the financial resources of candidates. It was hoped that by imposing such limitations on campaign spending, candidates would be elected on their qualities and merits rather than on how much money they had or could raise. In addition, it would increase the opportunities of well-qualified candidates who did not have access to substantial financial resources. Had the act been upheld, it would have gone far toward democratizing the electoral process.

In a 300-page opinion, the Supreme Court in *Buckley v. Valeo*[50] held the contribution limitations to be constitutional, but struck down the expenditure limitations as unconstitutional. It struck down the expenditure limitations not on grounds that it was beyond federal power to regulate presidential elections, but rather on grounds that any such limitations violated the First Amendment!

"The First Amendment," the Court declared, "denies government the power to determine that spending to promote one's political views is wasteful, excessive, or unwise. In the free society ordained by our Constitution it is not the government but the people who must retain control over the quantity and range of debate on public issues in a political campaign."[51]

Justice Byron White's vigorous dissent pointed out the incongruity of upholding limitations on contributions without also upholding limitations on campaign expenditures:

It would make little sense to me, and apparently made none to Congress, to limit the amounts an individual may give to a candidate or spend with his approval but fail to limit the amounts that could be spent on his behalf. Yet the Court permits the former while striking down the latter provision. No more than $1000 may be given to a candidate or spent at his request or with his approval; but otherwise, apparently, a contributor is to be constitutionally protected in spending unlimited amounts of money in support of his chosen candidate.[52]

Justice White gave the example of two brothers, each of whom

spends $1 million on TV announcements in which he appears, urging the election of the above named candidate in identical words. One brother has sought and obtained the approval of the candidate; the other has not. The former may be prosecuted [under the Act], and the latter may not, even though the candidate could scarcely help knowing about and appreciating the expensive favor. For constitutional purposes, it is difficult to see the difference between the two situations. I would take the words of those who know—that limiting independent expenditures is essential to prevent transparent and widespread evasion of the contribution limits.[53]

Finally, White takes the majority to task for equating money with First Amendment freedoms:

Proceeding from the maxim that "money talks" the [majority] finds that the expenditure limitations will seriously curtail political expression by candidates and interfere substantially with their chances for election. As an initial matter, the argument that money is speech and that limiting the flow of money to the speaker violates the First Amendment proves entirely too much.[54]

White points out that taxes on newspapers deprive those papers of money that might be spent on larger newspapers, but no one would suggest that newspaper companies are immune from taxation under the First

Amendment simply because they must comply with the law as does everyone else. White continued:

In any event, money is not always equivalent to or used for speech, even in the context of political campaigns. Expenditure ceilings reinforce the contribution limits and help eradicate the hazard of corruption. There is nothing objectionable in the attempt to insulate the political expression of federal candidates from the influence of large sums of money. I regret that the Court has returned them all to the treadmill.[55]

White's arguments were rejected by the Court, and there is at present no limit to the amounts of money that political action committees or other groups may spend to promote a candidate's election by the presidential electors—at least as long as the candidate does not give official sanction to the committee. This decision is indeed unfortunate. Reformers who are truly dedicated to democratizing the electoral process would do well to concentrate on seeking a remedy to the problem of the corrupting influence of money on presidential campaigns, rather than attempting to alter the federalist structure of the Electoral College.[56]

APPLYING THE "ONE MAN, ONE VOTE" PRINCIPLE TO THE ELECTORAL PROCESS

It will be recalled that the "One Man, One Vote" principle was specifically rejected by the framers at the Constitutional Convention in at least five areas: representation in the Senate, representation in the Electoral College, selection of the president in a contingent House election, selection of the vice president in a contingent Senate election, and ratification of constitutional amendments. As a result of the "Great Compromise," and in the interest of creating a truly federal Republic, the principle of equal state representation was adopted instead (see Chapter Three).

Despite the obvious intent of the framers, the historical context in which the principle of equal state representation was adopted, and the specific design of the Electoral College as set forth in the Constitution, serious efforts have been made to challenge the Electoral College, and specifically its general ballot feature, on grounds that it violates the Equal Protection Clause of the Fourteenth Amendment.[57]

Prior to the precedent-shattering Supreme Court case of *Baker v. Carr* in 1962,[58] no such challenge could conceivably have been entertained. In the 1946 case of *Colgrove v. Green*,[59] the Supreme Court had held that the question of the constitutionality of apportionment of voting districts was nonjusticiable under the long-established "political question" doctrine, which the Court later found to be "one of the rules basic to the federal system and this Court's place within that structure."[60] Under this doctrine, it was considered beyond the constitutional role of the judiciary to supervise, veto, or otherwise intervene in matters concerning the structure and organization of the political institutions of the states. Even the task of guaranteeing a republican form of government to the states under Article IV of the Constitution has been assigned to Congress, not the judiciary.[61]

As early as 1849, the Supreme Court had stated that "it rests with Congress to decide what government is the established one in a state. [The] right to decide is placed there, and not in the courts."[62] Later in *Pacific States Telephone v. Oregon*,[63] the Court asked whether Article IV authorizes the

judiciary to substitute its judgment as to a matter purely political for the judgment of congress on a subject committed to it and thus overthrow the Constitution upon the ground that thereby the guarantee to the States of a government republican in form may be secured, a question which after all rests upon the assumption that the states are to be guaranteed a government republican in form by destroying the very existence of a government republican in form in the Nation?[64]

Nevertheless, in the 1964 case of *Baker v. Carr*, [65] the Supreme Court held for the first time that a claim that a state's apportionment statute was violative of the Fourteenth Amendment was within reach of judicial protection and not nonjusticiable as a political question.

Justices Felix Frankfurter and John Harlan valiantly protested what they saw as the disregard of both precedent and the fundamentals of federalism. Characterizing the Court's ruling as a "massive repudiation of the experience of our whole past in asserting destructively novel judicial power," Justice Frankfurter warned that the ruling would "impair the Court's position as the ultimate organ of the 'Supreme Law of the Land.'"[66] The plaintiff's claim that the apportionment of representatives for the Tennessee General Assembly among that state's counties was, according to Frankfurter, a "hypothetical claim resting on abstract assumptions [being] made for affording illusory relief for a particular evil even though it foreshadows deeper and more pervasive difficulties in consequence . . . the Framers carefully and with deliberate forethought refused to so enthrone the judiciary."[67]

The dissenters finally concluded that

the notion that representation proportioned to the geographic spread of population is so universally accepted as a necessary element of equality between man and man that it must be taken to be the standard of a political equality preserved by the Fourteenth Amendment is, to put it bluntly, not true. [It] has never been generally practiced, today or in the past. It was not the English system, it was not the colonial system, it was not the system chosen for the national government by the Constitution, it was not the system predominantly practiced by the states at the time of the adoption of the 14th Amendment. Unless the judges of this Court are to make their private views of political wisdom the measure of the Constitution, the 14th Amendment provides no guide for judicial oversight of the representative problem.[68]

The decision in *Baker v. Carr* was followed by a series of decisions rigidly imposing the "one man, one vote" standard to states employing a county unit system,[69] the apportionment of congressional districts,[70] apportionment of seats to a state house,[71] and even to delegates chosen for a national party convention.[72]

In the case of *Gray v. Sanders,* in which the Supreme Court struck down an electoral system giving rural counties weighed votes, Justice Harlan responded:

The majority says the conception of political equality from the Declaration of Independence, to Lincoln's Gettyburg Address, to the 15th, 17th, and 19th Amendments can mean only one thing—one person, one vote. [But according the this Court's precedent], "to assume that political power is a function exclusively of numbers is to disregard the practicalities of government. Thus, the Constitution protects the interests of the smaller against the greater by giving in the Senate entirely unequal representation to populations."[73]

What may be most important about *Gray v. Sanders,* however, is what Justice Douglas, writing for the majority, said about an issue that was not even litigated in the case. In *dictum,* Douglas acknowledged that *"the only weighing of votes sanctioned by the Constitution concerns matters of representation such as . . . the use of the Electoral College in the choice of the President"*[74] (emphasis added).

In *Westbury v. Sanders,*[75] the Court declared that congressional districts must be nearly equal in size. In this case, Justice Potter Stewart joined the dissenters, and Justice Harlan again demurred in what was to prove a losing cause. Harlan disputed the majority's contention that the framers intended each congressional district to be exactly the same size by pointing out that the framers guaranteed the smaller states one representative regardless of their population. Thus inequality in the size of congressional districts is virtually locked into the Constitution. Harlan noted, perhaps with exasperation over the hopelessness of his cause, that the majority had "declared constitutionally defective the very composition of a coordinate branch of the Federal Government."[76]

Westbury was followed by *Kirkpatrick v. Preisler,*[77] in which the Court declared that each state must seek to "achieve precise mathematical equality"[78] in Congressional districts.

Justice Harlan's last opportunity to stem the tide came in the 1964 case of *Reynolds v. Sims,*[79] in which the Court intervened, under authority of the Fourteenth Amendment, to order states to equalize districts represented in their own legislatures. In an exhaustive 45-page dissenting opinion, Harlan summarized the history of the Fourteenth Amendment, revealing that the authors of this amendement were from states with unequal voting districts, and that there was legislative intent, as stated by the Fourteenth Amendment's leading proponent in Congress, that "the exercise of the elective franchise is exclusively under the control of the states."[80]

Harlan's last words on this issue were that

these decisions cut deeply into the fabric of our federalism. No thinking person can fail to recognize that the aftermath of these cases will have been achieved at the cost of a radical alteration in the relationship between the States and the Federal Government, more particularly the Federal Judiciary. The Constitution is not a panacea for every blot on the public welfare, nor should this Court be thought of as a general haven for reform movements. The Constitution is an instrument of government, fundamental to which is the premise that in a diffusion of governmental authority lies the greatest promise that this nation will realize liberty for all its citizens.[81]

In 1975 the Court of Appeals for the D.C. Circuit, following the precedent of *Sanders*, *Westbury*, and *Gray*, sustained a Fourteenth Amendment challenge to the manner of electing delegates to the 1976 Republican Convention.[82] Although the Fourteenth Amendment applies only to state, as opposed to private, action, the Court found "state action" in the fact that "the states and the federal government have served to institutionalize the major parties and by implication the narrowing process through protection of incumbents in reapportionment and . . . through financing of both primary and general election campaigns of major party candidates."[83]

The most recent Supreme Court decision in this area was the case of *Department of Commerce v. Montana*, decided in 1992.[84] In that case, the Court retreated slightly from its prior rigid holdings under the Fourteenth Amendment, and upheld a congressional reapportionment plan (known as the "Hill" method), which resulted in the loss of a representative by Montana. The Court conceded that if Montana had kept its seat, "each district would have been closer to the ideal size of a Congressional District than the reapportioned single district."[85] Recognizing that none of the reapportionment plans considered by Congress could have procured the goal of "one man, one vote," the Court used language more reminiscent of the words of Justice Harlan than Justice Douglas in stating that the goal of mathematical equality is

rendered illusory for the Nation as a whole by the constraints imposed by Article I, Section 2: the guarantee of a minimum of one representative for each state and the need to allocate a fixed number of indivisible representatives among 50 states of varying populations. The constitutional framework that generated the need for a compromise between the interests of the larger and smaller states must also delegate to Congress a measure of discretion broader than that accorded to the states, and Congress' apparently good-faith decision to adopt the Hill Method commands far more deference, particularly as it was made after decades of experience, experimentation, and debate, and was supported by independent scholars, and has been accepted for half a century.[86]

The Supreme Court's application of the Fourteenth Amendment to state and congressional reapportionment was made possible by the fact that there is no specific constitutional scheme for such apportionment. That the Electoral College provides such a scheme would seem, therefore, to immunize it from the same kind of constitutional attack. In 1966, however, a group of academics and electoral "reformers," apparently stymied in their efforts to amend the Constitution, joined forces with 12 states to challenge the unit voting feature of the Electoral College, claiming that this feature "unconstitutionally deprived voters of equal representation in the electoral college."[87] The petitioners claimed that " the state unit voting laws deny the voting rights of minority voters within each state by totally canceling their effects when the state's entire electoral vote is awarded to the winner of a bare plurality of the popular vote."[88]

The Supreme Court refused to hear the case on its merits, choosing instead to decline to hear the claim by "exercising its discretion not to hear suits brought between two or more states."[89] It is difficult to imagine, however, that even if the Court had chosen to decide this case on the merits, it would not have upheld the Electoral College and the unit voting procedures adopted by each state pursuant to Article II, which specifically gives each state the authority to "appoint [electors] in such manner as the legislature may direct." Nevertheless, while Baker v. Carr and its progeny give some cause for concern, it is comforting to reflect that even Justice Douglas, who was at the forefront of the Baker v. Carr revolution, specifically conceded in Gray that "the only weighing of votes sanctioned by the constitution concerns matters of representation such as the use of the Electoral College in the choice of a President."[90] It is also difficult to imagine that the Court would have overturned 100 years of precedent lodged in McPherson v. Blacker, which stated unequivocally that "the appointment of electors is placed absolutely and wholly within the legislatures of the several states."[91]

In any case, a number of state and lower federal courts have determined that neither the Electoral College nor the unit voting procedure adopted by the states violates either the Fourteenth or Fifteenth Amendments.[92]

ELECTION DAY

In Maddox v. Board of State Canvassers,[93] the Supreme Court of Montana held that "the legislature cannot constitutionally extend beyond that statutory election day the time for depositing ballots, so far as presidential electors are concerned."[94]

NOTES

1. 10 Annals, 128–129, cited in Lucius Wilmerding, Jr., The Electoral College (Boston: Beacon Press, 1958), 44. Re Opinion of the Justices, 107 A. 705 (Supreme

Court of Maine 1919); *Re State Question No. 137*, 244 Pac. 806 (Supreme Court of Oklahoma 1926); *Todd v. Johnson*, 99 Ky. 548 (1896); *Donclan v. Bird*, 118 Ky. 178 (1904); *Hodge v. Bryan*, 149 Ky. 110 (1912); *Marshall v. Dillon*, 149 Ky. 115 (1912). See also *In re Absentee Voters Law* 80 N.H. 595 (1921); Electoral College Case, 8 Fed. Cas. (D. of South Carolina) 4336; *Vertrees v. State Board of Elections*, 141 Tenn. 645 (1919); *Fineran v. Bailey*, 2 F.2d 363 (5th Circuit 1924).

2. 2 Annals, 1868 (1791), cited Wilmerding, *supra* note 1, at 45.

3. *Id.*

4. 29 Annals, 224 (Senator Elgius Fromentin of Louisiana, 1816), cited in *Id.* at 53.

5. *Id.*

6. *Id.* at 52.

7. Jefferson to Monroe, January 12, 1800 (Jefferson, *Works*, IX, 90), cited in *Id.* at 60.

8. 13 Sup. Ct. Reptr. 3, 8 (1892).

9. *In Re Corliss*, 11 R.I. 639 (1876).

10. *Id.* at 642.

11. *Id.* at 647.

12. 17 S&R 219, cited in *In Re Corlis*, 11 R.I. 639, 649.

13. 70 U.S. 93, 3 Wall. 93 (1865).

14. *Id.*

15. *Walker v. U.S.* 93 F.2d 383.

16. *Stanford v. Butler*, 181 S.W. 2d 269 (Tex. 1944). See also *Spreckels v. Graham*, 194 Cal. 516, 228 P. 1040 (1924).

17. 19 Ky. 548, 36 S.W. 987. See also *In Re State Question No. 137*, 118 Ky. 178; *McCreary v. Williams* 153 Ky. 49; *Eagle v. Cox*, 268 Ky. 58.

18. *Ray v. Blair*, 343 U.S. 214 (1952). See also *Lett v. Dennis*, 221 Ala. 432; *Steve v. McQueen*, 166 So. 788 (1936) *Ray v. Garner*, 57 So. 2d 824 (1952).

19. 343 U.S. 214, at 220.

20. *Id.*

21. *Ray v. Blair*, 57 So. 2nd at 398 (Ala. 1952). See also *Adair v. Drexel*, 74 Neb. 776; *Morrow v. Wipf*, 225 D. 146; *Ladd v. Holmes*, 40 Or. 167; *Seay v. Latham*, 143 Tex. 1; *Carter v. Tomlinson*, 149 Tex. 7 (discussed in 29 Tex. L. Rev. 378).

22. 343 U.S. at 232.

23. *Id.* at 234.

24. *Id.*

25. *Id.* at 232.

26. See *State v. Albritton*, 37 So. 2d 640 (the Supreme Court of Alabama refused to enjoin presidential electors from voting to confirm the instruction of their party).

27. *William v. Rhodes*, 393 U.S. 23 (1968).

28. 400 U.S. 112 (1970).

29. 42 U.S.C. §1973(d)(1976 & Sup. 1981).

30. H.R. Rep. No. 649, 94th Cong. 1st. sess. 7, cited in 1975 U.S. Code Cong. & Ad. News, 2358, 2364.

31. *Attorney General v. U.S.*, 738 F.2d 1017 (1984).

32. *Williams v. Rhodes*, *supra* note 27; *Anderson v. Celebrezze*, 460 U.S. 780 (1983). See *Illinois State Bd. of Elections v. Socialist Workers Party*, 440 U.S. 173 (1979); See

also *Kamins v. Board of Elections*, D.C., 324 A.2d 187 (1974) (statutes providing for nomination of candidates for presidential electors by executive committees of major parties and by petition properly provide an exclusive means under which candidates may have their names printed on the ballots); *Hawke v. Myers*, 4 N.E. 2d 397 (Ohio, 1936) (state statute directing that names of candidates for presidential electors shall not be printed upon ballots but that names for president shall be printed on ballot with the statement that a vote for the candidate named would be a vote for their elector. Held constitutional).

33. *Georges v. Carney*, 691 F.2d 297, 300 (7th Cir. 1972). See also *Labor's Educational and Political & Club Independent v. Danforth*, 561 S.W. 2d 339 (Mo. 1978); *Moore v. Ogilvie*, 394 U.S. 814 (1969); *Hadnott v. Amos*, 393 U.S. 904 (1968); *Seay v. Latham*, 143 Tex. 1 (1944); *Spreckels v. Graham, supra* note 16.

34. *Ill. St. Brd* 440 U.S. 173, 185–186 (1979).

35. 460 U.S. 780 (1983). See also *Dant v. Brown*, 717 F.2d 1491 (5th Cir. 1983).

36. *Anderson*, 460 U.S. 780.

37. *Id*. at 789.

38. *National Prohibition Party v. Colorado*, 752 P.2d 80 (1988) at 83.

39. *Williams v. Rhodes, supra* note 27.

40. 637 F.2d 1159 (9th Cir. 1980). See also *Wallace v. Thornton*, 251 S.C. 319 (1968); *American Independent Party v. Wallace*, 92 Idaho 336 (1968); *Anderson v. Polythress*, 246 Ga. 435 (1980); *Canaan v. Abdelnout*, 710 P.2d 268 (CA. 1985).

41. *Populist Party v. Herschler*, 746 F.2d 656, 660 (10th Cir. 1984) (per curiam); *Libertarian Party v. Florida*, 710 F.2d 790 (11th Cir. 1983) (3%); *Arutonuff v. Oklahoma State Election Bd.*, 687 F.2d 1375 (10th Cir. 1982) (5%); *Beller v. Kirk*, 328 F.Supp. 485 (S.D. Fla. 1970) (three-judge panel) (per curiam), aff'd without opinion under the name of *Beller v. Askew*, 403 U.S. 925 (1971) (3%); *Wood v. Putterman*, 316 F.Supp. 646 (D.Md.) (three-judge panel), aff'd without opinion in 400 U.S. 859 (3%); *Populist Party v. Orr*, 595 F.Supp. 760 (S.D.Ind. 1984) (upholding Indiana's 2% requirement).

42. 766 F.2d 117 (1985).

43. Laurence H. Tribe, *American Constitutional Law* (Mineola, N.Y.: Foundation Press, 1978), 783. See also Comment, Thomas S. Chase, "Deadline Unconstitutional: A Trend Toward Strict Scrutiny in Ballot Access Cases—Anderson v. Celebrezze 103 S.Ct. 1564 (1983)" 18 *Suffolk U.L. Rev.* 24 (1984); Comment, "Legal Obstacles to Minority Party Success," 57 *Yale L.J.* 1276, 1286 (1948); Frampton, "Challenging Restrictive Ballot Access Law on Behalf of the Independent Candidate," 10 *Rev. Law & Social Change* 131 (1980).

44. 110 U.S. 651 (1884).

45. *Id*. at 657–658 (66%).

46. Title III, 43 Stat. 1053, 2 U.S.C. 241 et seq. (1925).

47. 290 U.S. 534 (1934).

48. *Id*. at 534.

49. 83 Stat. 3, Amended by 88 Stat. 1263.

50. 424 U.S. 1 (1976).

51. *Id*. at 57.

52. *Id*. at 260.

53. *Id*.

54. *Id*. at 263–264. Ellipses indicating deletions have been omitted.

55. *Id*. Ellipses indicating deletions have been omitted.

56. In light of the decision in *Buckley v. Valeo*, 424 U.S. 1 (1976), any such reform would probably be a unique constitutional amendment.

57. See Michael O'Sullivan, "Artificial Unit Voting and the Electoral College," 65 *So. Cal. L. Rev.* 2421 (1992); *Delaware v. New York*, 385 U.S. 895 (1966).

58. 369 U.S. 186, 202 (1962) Justice Williiam Brennan interpreted *Colgrove v. Green* to nevertheless permit the granting of jurisdiction.

59. 328 U.S. 549 (1946).

60. *Rescue Army v. Municipal Court*, 331 U.S. 549.

61. *Pacific States Telephone v. Oregon*, 223 U.S. 118 (1912).

62. 7 How. 1 (1849).

63. 223 U.S. 118 (1912).

64. *Id.*

65. *Id.* at 260.

66. *Id.*

67. *Id.* at 269–270.

68. *Id.* af 301. Ellipses indicating deletions have been omitted to avoid clutter not affecting the substance of the cited passage.

69. *Gray v. Sanders*, 372 U.S. 368 (1963).

70. *Westberry v. Sanders*, 376 U.S. 1 (1964).

71. *Reynolds v. Sims*, 377 U.S. 533 (1964).

72. *Ripon Society v. National Republican Party* 525 F.2d 548 (1975).

73. *Id.* at 385, citing *McDougal v. Green*, 335 U.S. 281.

74. *Id.* at 380.

75. 376 U.S. 1 (1964).

76. *Id.* at 22.

77. 394 U.S. 526. See also *Karcher v. Daggett*, 462 U.S. at 730.

78. *Id.* at 530–531.

79. 388 I/S/ 533 (1964).

80. *Id.* at 599 (citing Mr. Bingham; ellipses indicating deletions have been omitted.)

81. *Id.* at 624–625. Ellipses indicating deletions have been omitted.

82. *Ripon Society v. National Republican Party*, *supra* note 72.

83. *Id.* at 553. The challenged method for selecting delegates was the employment by the party of a "victory bonus," awarding extra delegates to states that had voted Republican in the prior election.

84. 112 S. Ct. 1415 (1992).

85. *Id.*

86. *Id.*

87. O'Sullivan, *supra* note 57, at 2440.

88. Richard Claud, *The Supreme Court and the Electoral Process* (Baltimore: Johns Hopkins University Press, 1970), citing brief for Plaintiff at 82, *Delaware v. New York*, *supra* note 57. Also cited in O'Sullivan, *supra* note 57 at 2441, fn. 136.

89. O'Sullivan, *supra* note 57 at 244, fn. 139, citing *Texas v. New Mexico*, 462 U.S. 554 (1983).

90. 372 U.S. at 379.

91. 146 U.S. 1, at 34.

92. See, for example, *Penton v. Humphrey*, 264 F. Supp. 250 (S.P. Miss. 1967), *Williams v. Virginia State Board of Elections*, 288 F. Supp. 622; *Hitson v. Baggett*, 446 F. Supp. 674 (M.D. Ala. 1978); cited and discussed in Sullivan, *supra* note 57, at 2442.

93. 149 P.2d 112 Mont. (1994).

94. *Id.*

Chapter Five

ELECTIONS: ELECTORAL
EFFECTS AND APPLICATIONS

Many reformers have made reference to past presidential elections as examples of how the Electoral College has failed to serve the best interests of the American people. However, since there has been only one fairly conducted presidential election in American history in which the winner of the majority of electoral votes failed to also obtain the most popular votes (the election of 1888), reformers have taken to creating "what-if" scenarios by playing statistical games with past elections. They have tried to show that, in a particular election, if a few thousand votes had gone the other way in one state, a few hundred a different way in another state, and so on, a popular vote winner might have failed to gain a majority of electoral votes, and a "wrong president" could have been elected. As already discussed in Chapter One, there are several reasons why such scenarios contribute little to a responsible discussion about the merits of the Electoral College system.

First, the Electoral College was conceived as a compromise in our federal system, as was equal state representation in the Senate and in the ratification of amendments. A winner in the Electoral College who fails to win the most popular votes is no more a "wrong president" than legislation passed by the Senate is the "wrong legislation," or an amendment passed by the States (and not by popular vote), is the "wrong amendment."

Second, it must be remembered that campaigns are conducted by those who are well aware of the rules of the game. Strategies in past elections have been based on winning a majority of the electoral votes, not on winning the most popular votes or achieving some kind of ill-conceived moral victory. Thus, even in the election of 1888, when Benjamin Harrison won the election with a majority of electoral votes but did not (by a narrow margin) win the most popular votes, there is no way to know if he might have won a majority of popular votes if his campaign had been geared to doing so. Thus, instead of campaigning in close but critical states, Harrison might have rationed his limited time campaigning to win more popular votes in states he already considered safe in the electoral column. The same might be noted in response to the numerous "what-if" scenarios concocted by reformers.

Third, the case for preserving federalism in the Electoral College does not rest on a denial that, once in every 200 years or so, a president might be elected with an electoral majority and popular vote minority, just as the case for preserving equal state representation in the Senate does not rest on a denial that legislation might be passed that would not be passed if senators were elected on a strictly proportional basis.

It has already been noted that in the opinion of many political scientists, a direct election would, as in most parliamentary democracies, produce a multiparty system. In such a system, two parties, totally unacceptable to the majority of voters, might frequently be the top two plurality winners, thus forcing a runoff between the two parties rejected by the majority. The "winner" of such a "popular vote" election would surely provide a far better example of a "minority president" than anything the Electoral College has ever produced, and would certainly be far more likely to occur more than once in every 200 years.

Defenders of the Electoral College system can create some what-if scenarios of their own. If a popular vote system had been in effect in past American presidential elections, there would surely have been an incentive for more parties to seriously contend for the presidency, and the likelihood of a minority president being elected would have been very high. But even if we assume that there would not have been more parties splitting the vote, what-if scenarios can be created from the actual statistical data of past elections showing that a minority president would have been chosen under a direct election system.[1]

In fact, however, the creation of what-if scenarios is about as enlightening as the musings of the hungry man who wanted a peanut butter and jelly sandwich: "If I had some peanut butter, I could have a peanut butter and jelly sandwich, if I had some jelly, and if I had some bread."

Ultimately, the case for preserving federalism must rest on the merits of the Electoral College system itself. But since reformers persist in using the results of past elections to support their arguments for direct election,[2] this chapter includes a short review of past presidential elections with an analysis of how the Electoral College system has affected their outcome. Details of elections already referred to in previous chapters are summarized here only briefly.

PRESIDENTIAL ELECTIONS PRIOR TO 1824

Prior to 1824 there is no record of a total popular vote for any presidential candidate. It will be recalled that the method of electing electors was delegated to the states. In the first presidential election (1789) there were only a few months between the time New York ratified the Constitution and the date for the first presidential election. With little election infrastructure in place, and time of the essence, most state legislatures elected the electors. The few states that attempted a popular election had a hard time. New Hampshire, for example, conducted a popular election of electors, but no electors received a majority and the legislature ended up having to make the selection.

Only once before 1824 did a candidate fail to win a majority of electoral votes. In 1800 Jefferson and Burr, both Republicans, each received 73 electoral votes. Even in this election, there would have been no problem if the Republicans had simply instructed one Republican elector to withhold a vote for Burr (the intended vice presidential candidate). Adams and Pinckney, the Federalist candidates, each received 65 and 64 electoral votes. Since no candidate received a majority of electoral votes, the election was referred to the House, where Jefferson was eventually elected. There would appear to be nothing about this election that would be grist for the reformer's mill, since there was no popular vote tally conducted, and Jefferson, the ultimate winner in the House, was the obvious choice for president. It will be recalled, however, that this election did reveal the need to reform the electoral system to provide for separate electoral ballots for president and vice president. This was subsequently accomplished by the Twelfth Amendment in 1804.

THE PRESIDENTIAL ELECTION OF 1824

The election of 1824 is often cited by reformers as an example of a defect in the Electoral College system. In fact, it is an example of how well the system worked.

By 1824 records of popular vote totals began to be tabulated.[3] However, those tabulations are of limited usefulness to the historian because, even in 1824, about a quarter of the states did not provide for popular election of electors.

The electors in that election gave Andrew Jackson 99 electoral votes, John Quincy Adams 84, William H. Crawford 41, and Henry Clay 37. Thus none of the four major candidates received a majority of electoral votes, and the election was referred to the House. Adams was promptly elected in the House by a majority of 13 states. Adams did not receive a majority of electoral votes or a majority of popular votes as recorded from those states providing for popular election. Because of this, reformers have cited this election as an example of how the will of the people was thwarted by the electoral process in 1824.

Before responding to this contention, two characteristics of this election should be noted. First, the general ballot system had not yet been universally adopted. Second, the two-party system had not yet fully developed, and the election was conducted more in the manner of a primary than a general election, since each of the four candidates was of the same party (the Democratic, formerly called the Republican). Third, the popular vote tallies came only from some of the states, and therefore cannot be considered as an accurate measure of the popular vote of the country at large.

In fact, this election provides an excellent example as to why the general ballot system should be retained as an essential feature of the Electoral College. Had all the states appointing electors by popular election in 1824 used the general ticket system, it is likely that one of the candidates (probably Jackson) would have received an electoral majority. Jackson would have needed only 13 more electoral votes to claim a majority, and he lost at least that many in states employing the district system of electing electors. Thus, had the Electoral College system as it works today been the system in the election of 1824, Jackson almost certainly would have been a clear electoral vote winner.

By 1824 the Federalists had faded from the American scene, but no new party had yet come to establish the role of the opposition. Today, the system of primaries and conventions would have reduced the field of major candidates and thereby also reduced the likelihood that no candidate would receive an electoral majority. In this regard, it must be emphasized that the Electoral College system was still in its earliest days of development, and had not yet achieved the creation of a two-party system. This would take place only later, after the general ticket system came to be adopted as an essential feature of the Electoral College, and primaries and conventions came to replace caucuses as the means of nominating candidates.

Thus, far from being an example of a distortion of the electoral process, the presidential election of 1824 serves as an example of why it is important that the Electoral College system generally, and the general ticket system in particular, be retained.

A final observation of the election of 1824 concerns the fact that it was the last election in which a presidential candidate did not receive a majority of electoral votes, and the election was referred to the House. The election of 1824 was therefore conducted in the manner in which most democracies of the world now elect their leaders—that is, by legislative choice. Nevertheless, this election still falls into the category of elections that reformers claim should cause "an atmosphere of crisis." It may be recalled that an advisor to the ABA Commission on Electoral Reform has claimed that "if a popular vote winner were to lose a presidential election, or if the House of Representatives were required to select the President, resentment, unrest, public clamor for reform and an atmosphere of crisis would probably ensue."[4] Abbott and Levine likened the election of a president with a minority of popular votes to the "Great San Andreas Earthquake."[5]

The election of 1824 did indeed take place in a time of violence and upheaval: the "economic depression of 1819, delayed aftermath of the War of 1812, the Missouri question, and dramatic flare-up of the latent sectional conflict over slavery."[6] If ever there was a time ripe for an atmosphere of crisis, 1824 would have been that time. Perhaps the best response to the fears expressed by the ABA and Abbott and Levine is to cite the following passage from Samuel Flagg Bemis' authoritative work, *John Quincy Adams and the Union*, in which is described the final chapter of the election of John Quincy Adams: "General Andrew Jackson stepped forth and grasped the President's hand. Men marveled that a question notoriously menacing republics throughout history . . . had been settled so peaceably, and . . . with such good will."[7]

But perhaps this scene should not be described as the final chapter. In 1832 Jackson came back to win the presidency over Adams by the highest electoral vote majority since Washington, and with a popular vote majority not equaled until the election of Theodore Roosevelt in 1904.[8]

PRESIDENTIAL ELECTIONS AFTER 1824

Since the almost universal adoption of the general ticket ballot after 1832, there have been few viable third-party candidates, and presidents have most often been elected by an overwhelming electoral majority and a comfortable popular vote majority or plurality. In 1836 Martin van Buren won by 97 electoral votes and a 51% popular vote majority, and in 1840 Harrison won by 174 electoral votes and 53% popular vote.

There were also substantial electoral vote margins and popular vote percentages in the following elections: 1844, Polk 65 (50%); 1848, Taylor 36 (47%); 1852, Pierce 212 (51%); 1856, Buchanan 60 (46%); 1860–64, Lincoln 108 & 191 (40 & 55%); 1868–72, Grant, 134 & 286 (53 & 56%); 1892, Cleveland 132 (46%); 1896, McKinley 95 (51%); 1900, McKinley 137 (52%); 1904, T. Roosevelt 197 (56%); 1908, Taft 159 (52%); 1912–16, Wilson 347 & 23 (42 & 49%); 1920, Harding 277 (60%); 1924, Coolidge 246 (54%); 1928, Hoover 357 (58%); 1932–44, F. Roosevelt, 413, 515, 367 & 433 (57, 61, 55 & 53%); 1948, Truman 114 (50%); 1952–56, Eisenhower 353 & 384 (55 & 57%); 1964, Johnson 434 (61%); 1968–72, Nixon 110 & 503 (43 & 61%); 1976, Carter 57 (50%); 1980, Reagan 440 (51%).[9]

The overwhelming electoral and popular vote majorities and pluralities in the above elections would not have been possible in a multiparty system. Most reformers, however, are unwilling to credit the Electoral College and the general ticket ballot for the two-party system, despite evidence that most democracies that lack an election method comparable to the Electoral College have multiparty systems.

In several of the elections noted above, the narrowing effects of the Electoral College may be specifically noted. It will be recalled that the election of 1860 was unusual in that the Democrats were split between two nominees, Stephen Douglas and John Breckinridge. Since electoral votes are awarded to plurality winners within states, Abraham Lincoln won by an overwhelming 108-vote electoral vote margin despite winning less than 40% of the popular vote. The lesson of the Electoral College to parties or factions unwilling to compromise and work within a two-party system was as follows: a party that makes the compromises necessary to unite behind a single candidate will have the best chance of winning the election.

Some reformers have claimed that similar lessons are given in a direct election system. In fact, however, a direct election system encourages factionalism. In many parliamentary democracies, parties deliberately refuse to compromise or join with other parties, in the hope that in multiparty races they will end up with the balance of power, or even win with a small plurality of the vote. In such a manner, small parties can exact concessions or exercise leverage out of all proportion to their overall support from the electorate, which may be very small.

The 40% runoff provision proposed by some direct election advocates would make the tendency toward factionalism even more extreme. In the first phase of a multiparty election, a small party with little broad support could hope to become one of the final two in a runoff. Such a party might then become a nationally recognized party almost overnight, despite gaining only a small plurality of the overall number of popular votes. The lure of such a prize would greatly increase the incentive to participate in the first phase of the election, thus encouraging even more factionalism.

Every generation or so, however, the disciplinary effects of the Electoral College must be learned anew. In 1912 Theodore Roosevelt and other renegade Republicans refused to reach a compromise with their party. Their "Progressive" party accomplished little except to provide Woodrow Wilson with an electoral tidal wave.

Unfortunately, the very success of the Electoral College in discouraging factionalism and fostering the two-party system leaves little direct proof in its wake of disciplinary effects. It is impossible to prove, for example, exactly how many third parties and their candidates have been discouraged from creating factions, and have thereby been encouraged to make compromises and accommodations within the two-party system. Reformers often refuse to be persuaded by the example of other democracies in which factionalism is endemic, or even by congressional testimony of third party representatives. It will be recalled that a former Socialist party official testified before Senator Bayh's committee on electoral reform that "One thing we all had in common was an absolute detestation of the Electoral College. . . . It was one of the chief barriers to the success of minor parties. . . . Under direct election we would have made hay."[10]

Thus, reformers purport to believe that the two-party system, most untypical in the world's democracies, would naturally have developed in the United States without the Electoral College. That they could be (and almost certainly are) wrong in this regard, however, has not deterred them from their continuing efforts to destroy the Electoral College and mobilize public opinion against it.

CLOSE ELECTIONS

If one defines a "close" election as one in which the two top candidates receive a popular vote percentage within 1% of each other, there have been five such elections in American history: In 1880 James Garfield won with a .05% popular vote margin, Grover Cleveland won with a .2% margin in 1884, John Kennedy with .2% in 1960, and Richard Nixon with .7% in 1968. In only one of these close elections did the popular vote winner lose in the Electoral College—the election of Benjamin Harrison in 1888 despite losing by .8% in the popular vote.

Although the latter election falls into the reformers' "wrong president" category of elections, the Electoral College in fact performed exactly as it was intended in each of these five elections.

The 1880 election of Garfield was the closest (in terms of popular votes) in American history. After the election debacle of 1876 (discussed later), the last thing the country needed in 1880 was an election in which there was no clear winner. As the election returns dribbled in from far-flung rural areas in 1880, it was apparent that it would be a long time before a clear-cut popular vote winner would emerge. Fortunately for the country, however, there was no need to wait, or recount each and every popular vote in each and every county and hamlet in the United States to determine who would be the president (a task that might have taken months). Instead the Electoral College presented the country with a clear winner, and the electoral margin was so substantial that even the outcome of the popular votes in a few close states would not have affected the outcome.

The nation was saved again in 1884 from the effects of an ambiguous outcome. The popular vote was again extremely close, within .2%, but the Electoral College gave a clear electoral majority to Cleveland.

In the election of 1888 the country was yet again spared a constitutional crisis that might have arisen had there been a direct election system in effect. Again, the popular vote was extremely close, the candidates being within .8% of each other. Unlike in 1876, however, there was no constitutional crisis because once again the Electoral College provided a clear winner—in this case Benjamin Harrison by a 65 electoral vote margin. Because Harrison was not the popular vote winner, this election is one of those that Feerick and others say should have produced "an atmosphere of crisis." Instead, as one historian has observed, in the aftermath of this election "the country didn't turn a hair. They just elected [Cleveland] the next time, and we had good, solid, stable, tranquil, and legitimate government."[11]

The election of 1960 was discussed in some detail in Chapter One, and that discussion will not be repeated here, except to note that the 1960 election was so close that the country would surely have been thrown into a constitutional abyss had there been a direct election system. A claim of fraudulent voting in Illinois and a dispute about how the popular vote in Alabama should be counted would very probably have brought a repeat of the 1876 election debacle in which a commission finally had to be created to resolve the question of disputed votes.

Fortunately the Electoral College system once again spared the nation such a crisis by producing a clear winner the day after the election, and the issue of fraudulent votes in Illinois and miscounted votes in Alabama never required a lengthy resolution, since the outcome of such a resolution would not have affected the result in the Electoral College. Nevertheless, if any election were to meet the reformers' definition of a "wrong winner" it would be this one, since pursuant to the most rational method of counting Alabama's popular votes (as set forth in the Congressional Quarterly), Nixon received the most "popular" votes. (The official count of a plurality of popular votes for Kennedy was achieved only by using a method that counted the votes for Democratic electors in Alabama twice.)[12]

THE PRESIDENTIAL ELECTION OF 1876

There has probably been more written about the presidential election of 1876 than all the other American presidential elections combined. It is probably the most analyzed, examined, scrutinized, and dissected election of all time. It is also probably the most misunderstood. Even in the modern press and journals, the election continues to be the subject of impassioned opinion. Just in the past few years, journals have published articles entitled "The Stolen Election,"[13] "The Master Fraud of the Century,"[14] and claimed that "the theft of the 1876 election . . . was an act scripted in the editorial offices of the New York Times."[15]

More important, from the standpoint of the present discussion, it is the election most often quoted and cited by reformers as an example of an Electoral College malfunction, and the election of a "wrong winner."[16] Reformers have blamed this one election, and by implication the Electoral College system, for a wide range of ills including racial strife.[17] Others have claimed that the "1876 election demonstrated a grave defect in the Consti-tution . . . so that the resolution of the entire presidential election can swing on the intrigues and maneuvers in a partisanly motivated Congress."[18] Still others have chosen to give the election even more cosmic proportions, asserting that "the cost of Rutherford B. Hayes' electoral victory then, was tremendous in terms of subsequent history—a cost still being paid today."[19]

In fact, as it will be shown, the problems that arose in the election of 1876 had little to do with the Electoral College. That there was massive fraud on a widespread scale at the local and state levels has never been in doubt. But the frauds were of the kind that could afflict any election and any election system. Although this election was discussed briefly in Chapter One, it is necessary to take a closer look at what really happened in 1876 because of the great emphasis and attention this election has been given by reformers seeking to support their argument for direct election.

As Ulysses Grant's second term drew to a close, it became apparent to many observers that the scandals of his administration would prevent Grant from running for a third term. Grant's vice president, Schuyler Colfax, had been implicated in the Credit Mobilier scandal, Grant's personal secretary had been indicted, the secretary of war had been impeached, and Grant's brother had been implicated in the selling of Indian trading posts. There were additional scandals involving the Pacific Mail, the Whiskey Ring, and the Emma Mine Swindle.[20]

As recently as May 1875, Grant had indicated a willingness to run for a third term, and the practice of extracting 2% of a civil service employee's salary for campaign contributions gave an incumbent an enormous advantage. But the scandals, new details of which seemed to be breaking by the day, were making a third term less and less likely. Then in December 1875 the House of Representatives passed a resolution by a 233–18 margin "reaffirming the two term tradition 'as part of our republican system of government, and that any departure' from this time honored custom would be unwise, unpatriotic, and fraught with peril to our free institutions."[21] (A constitutional amendment to this effect would not be ratified until 1947, when the shoe was on the other political foot, and Republicans pushed through the Twenty-second Amendment limiting presidential terms to two. Democrats called this amendment a direct slap at the memory of Franklin Roosevelt and a "pitiful victory over a great man sleeping on the bank of the Hudson.")[22]

A mad scramble was now launched in both parties to select a nominee for president in 1876. Republicans pushed aside the front-runner for the nomination, James G. Blaine, who had been tainted by scandals of his own, and chose Rutherford B. Hayes, who was untainted by scandal and who had a solid and honest record as governor of Ohio. The Republican platform reaffirmed the constitutional rights of all citizens, particularly the rights of suffrage of African Americans, the need for a common public school system, the separation of church and state, reform of the civil service, equal rights for women, protection of immigrants, and conservation of public lands.

But the Democrats, who had slowly gathered momentum during the scandal-ridden years of the Grant administration, chose a strong candidate of their own, Samuel Tilden, who as a strong reform governor of New York had relentlessly cracked down on corruption, prosecuted the Tweed Ring, and brought standards of frugality and strict financial accountability to the state. The Democratic platform called for fidelity to the union, support for the Fourteenth and Fifteenth Amendments, a demand for civil over military authority in the South and a denunciation of the excesses of Republican Reconstruction policy, and finally a call for honesty and economy in government.

In an age of greed and corruption, both candidates probably represented the most honest and able the two major parties could have found within their ranks. But the gains of the Democrats in Congress and the state legislatures, and the strong candidacy of Tilden soon had the "Republicans running scared." In eight southern states, "redeemers"(a term equated by Republicans with white supremacy) dedicated to restoring home rule had taken power from Reconstruction governments.[23] There was a growing clamor in the South to remove all military forces in the South, and there was far less assurance than in 1868 and 1872 that the Southern states could be held in any presidential election, particularly if the suffrage of African Americans could not be guaranteed.

Aware of what was at stake in the upcoming election, and perhaps sensing how close it might be, both parties began to appeal to the basest instincts of the electorate. Typical of the campaign rhetoric was that heard at a Republican rally in which the speaker railed that

Every enemy this great republic has had for twenty years has been a Democrat. Every man that shot Union Soldiers . . . was a Democrat. Every man that loves slavery better than liberty was a Democrat. The man that assassinated Lincoln was a Democrat . . . Every scar you have got on your heroic bodies was given to you by a Democrat. . . . Every arm that is lacking, every limb that is gone . . . is a souvenir of a Democrat.[24]

A campaign issue became "Shall the Rebels have the government?"[25]

Tilden was personally assailed, and his tax returns were dissected amid charges by the Republican press that he had underpaid his 1862 taxes. Tilden continued to be hounded by Republican prosecutors, until, after having spent $45,000 in legal expenses, the case against him was dropped.[26] Despite a creditable war record that showed consistent support for the Union during the Civil War, Tilden was accused of "a cowardly and double-faced attitude during the war"[27] and was even accused of collusion with the Tweed Ring he had prosecuted, apparently based on the fact that he had once "concluded a letter to Tweed with the salutation 'very truly your friend.' "[28]

Democrats were put on the defensive by a charge that Tilden would favor reparations to the South for war damage,[29] and only occasionally managed to go on the offensive, as when they accused Hayes of income tax derelictions.[30]

The events taking place on election day 1876 have been recorded by historians: "Whites used threats, floggings, and outright murder to keep blacks away from the polls. The success of the so-called 'Mississippi Revolution of 1875' emboldened some whites to step up their attacks," and the Ku Klux Klan was active.[31] Southern politicians countered with allegations of military intimidation at the polls.

As the returns came in on election day, November 7, there was little doubt that Tilden was the winner. By evening it was clear that Tilden had taken Connecticut, New Jersey, Indiana, and, most important, New York. There was activity and excitement at Democratic headquarters in New York, and deep gloom at Republican headquarters, which was almost deserted by late evening.

The next morning, most newspapers indicated a clear Democratic victory. Hayes wrote his son "I bow cheerfully to the result. We are all well. You will talk discreetly and exhibit no ill temper about adversaries."[32] In an interview with a Cincinnati newspaper, Hayes stated that "I think we are defeated. . . . I am of the opinion that the Democrats have carried the country and elected Tilden."[33] President Grant stated that he believed Tilden had been elected.[34] The Republican House leader wrote "It now appears we are defeated by the combined power of rebellion, Catholicism and whiskey, a trinity very hard to conquer. [The Presidency has] gone down in the general wreck."[35]

But then there occurred the first of two extraordinary events in this notorious election. Unfortunately for the Democrats, both of these events can now be classified among the most monumental political blunders of all time.

In the early hours of November 8, Democratic headquarters sent two telegrams to the *New York Times*. The first read "Please give your estimate of the electoral votes for Tilden. Answer at once."[36] The second asked specifically for the results from Florida, Louisiana, and South Carolina.

Without realizing it, the Democratic leaders at headquarters had committed their first egregious blunder. Not only had they revealed their uncertainty about the results from the three states mentioned, but they had tipped off this fact to the nation's most influential newspaper—which just happened to be dominated by fiercely partisan Republicans. The managing editor of the *Times*, John Reid, had spent time in a brutal Confederate prison and was known to have a "fanatical hatred"[37] for the Democratic party.

Immediately, the *Times* political writers did some quick calculations. If the three states mentioned in the telegram from Democratic headquarters could somehow be held for the Republicans, Hayes could win by exactly one electoral vote—185 to 184. However, such a victory would require every single elector from those states. Not even a single elector from those states could go to Tilden.

A two-pronged counterattack was immediately launched. First, *Times* political editor Edward Cary wrote an editorial claiming that "the election is still in doubt,"[38] and explaining how it was that Hayes could be a one-vote electoral winner. Reid, meanwhile, went over to the Fifth Avenue Hotel to inform Zach Chandler, the Republican party chairman. Chandler instantly recognized the possibilities, and ordered the suppression of telegrams from his Republican chairmen in Florida and Louisiana conceding those states to Tilden. He then immediately sent out a telegram to the Republican state organizations in the states needed for a Hayes victory. The telegram simply stated: "(c)laim Louisiana, Florida, and South Carolina at all hazards, through thick and thin."[39] Then Chandler released a public statement, declaring that "Hayes has 185 votes and is elected."[40] The *Times* dutifully followed up with a headline proclaiming "The Battle Won."[41]

There was only one minor problem with the Republican scheme at this point: returns showed Tilden the winner in all three states. However, none of the popular vote returns in the three states had yet been "certified" by local boards and officials.

Within days, lawyers, representatives, and "statesmen" from both parties converged on the election boards on each of the contested states. However, the Republicans had one overwhelming advantage—in all of the contested states the Republicans controlled the certifying election boards.

What happened in Louisiana was not untypical of what happened in Florida, South Carolina, and Oregon (which had by now been added to the list of contested states). Louisiana's certifying board consisted of "an undertaker, a saloon-keeper, and two thoroughly disreputable carpetbaggers—all of whom would be indicted for fraud within the year."[42] Hearings were held, at which were revealed "shocking discrepancies in population figures, voter registration, and ballots cast."[43] Although the returns showed "comfortable" majorities of Democratic votes cast, the Republican board retired to the seclusion of an executive session and decided to throw out all the votes in two counties with Democratic majorities. The result, to no one's surprise, was a razor-thin majority for the Republican slate, which was duly "certified" and signed by the incumbent Republican governor. (Two years later, the "Potter Committee" would reveal that the elector signatures had actually been forged.)

Not to be outdone, however, a Democratic Election Board conducted its own canvass of returns, and found there to be an overwhelming majority for the Tilden ticket. This set of returns was duly "certified" by the Democratic "governor-elect," and also sent to Washington.

A Louisiana senator observing these events, and listening to "bloodcurdling accounts of election-eve atrocities," wrote to Hayes that the hearings seemed "more like the history of hell than of civilized communities."[44]

Similar events in the other contested states resulted in conflicting sets of returns being sent to Washington. In Florida, three sets of returns were certified—two by governors, and one by the attorney general. The governor stated that "it is terrible to see the extent to which all classes go in their determination to win. Conscience offers no restraint." (That governor, Lew Wallace, later wrote the novel *Ben-Hur*.)[45]

In Oregon there were allegations of a "vote-buying foray to win a Republican elector,"[46] and the sum of $8,000 allegedly changed hands (a sum the receiver claimed was for "expenses.")

With the election outcome hanging on these disputed and conflicting state returns, it was obvious that Congress would have to sort out the mess. But how, and according to what procedures? Historian Sydney Pomerantz has described the situation at this point as follows:

As Congress got under way, [it remained now for the Republicans] to consolidate the gains achieved thus far, to calm everything, concede nothing, and to hold the Democratic majority in the House in check by divisive tactics played out in the halls of Congress and behind the scenes. Alert, aggressive, resourceful, the seasoned veterans of the party in power prepared to pursue the great game of politics with a grim determination and deadly earnestness that allowed for no retreat. The Democrats, for their part, confident that right was on their side, trusted in the moral sense of the people to insure an equitable solution of the dispute.[47]

John Goode, a congressman at the time, later wrote that

notwithstanding the opinion prevalent throughout the country . . . that Mr. Tilden had been elected, certain able, astute and resourceful leaders in the Republican party, being unwilling to surrender the enormous power and patronage belonging to the presidential office, determined that they would contest every inch of ground, and, if possible, would snatch victory from the jaws of defeat.[48]

Several scenarios now became possible. The Republican president of the Senate (Thomas Ferry) could assert, under the constitutional duty delegated to him to "count" the votes, the power also to choose between conflicting certified returns of votes. For a time, the Republicans appeared to be pursuing this plan. However, this assertion was constitutionally dubious, and, in any case, Ferry himself, to the consternation of his colleagues, later agreed to the appointment of an electoral commission. Another alternative was that neither candidate would be certified as elected, in which case the election would be referred to the House, where the Democrats had the advantage. For obvious reasons, the Republicans fiercely rejected this alternative. The final alternative, a compromise, was the congressional appointment of an electoral commission to which resolution of all disputed electoral slates would be referred.

Amid talk of compromises and deals, the latter alternative was finally agreed to by both parties. Under this proposal, an electoral commission would decide which disputed state returns to count. However, under the final congressional resolution the commission's decision was not to be truly final, but rather subject, upon objection by five senators and congressmen, to concurrent action of both houses. Both parties purported to support the appointment of a commission "whose authority none can question and whose decision all will accept."[49]

It was by now apparent that the Republican strategy was to hunker down and wait for the Democrats to make another mistake. Obligingly, the Democrats now committed their second monumental blunder.

The commission agreed to was to be bipartisan, consisting of five members each from the Supreme Court, the House, and the Senate. Representatives from the House and Senate were equally divided between Republicans and Democrats. Four of the five representatives from the Supreme Court were also equally split between the two parties. However, the crucial fifth member of the Supreme Court delegation was to be selected jointly by the other four. The fifth member chosen was Justice David Davis, who was considered by all to be objective and nonpartisan.

Although many Democrats had serious reservations about the commission, many were persuaded to support it because they anticipated that Justice Davis would be on it. Then, on January 25, a surprise event occurred—Davis was unexpectedly elected to the Senate by the Illinois legislature, and had to resign from the commission. It was at this point that the Democrats made the blunder that has left historians shaking their heads ever since. For reasons never understood by objective observers, the Democrats agreed to the selection of a Republican justice, Joseph Bradley, as the fifteenth member. It was later explained that this concession was made because Bradley, despite his partisanship, had previously shown his objectivity by voting in a judicial opinion to strike certain provisions of the hated Enforcement Act passed by the Republicans in Congress. In addition, others had reassured the Democrats that Bradley would be impartial. It was, however, to prove a fatal concession to Republican forces fiercely determined to press every point of advantage.

On February 1, 1877, Congress convened to count the electoral votes. When the name of Florida was called, the three sets of elector votes were opened. There were objections, and the slates were referred to the commission. The critical vote was to be that of Bradley, who was now besieged with lobbyists from all sides. Although at first he teased the Democrats with hints he might vote for the Tilden electors, in the end he voted Republican, and the votes of Florida were awarded to Hayes on a vote of 8–7. Although the House voted to overturn the decision, the Senate did not, and the commission's decision was thereby sustained.

This process was repeated when Louisiana's two slates were submitted, and was to be repeated yet again with North Carolina and Oregon. By now, many Democrats were beginning to see the handwriting on the wall. Although it was unlikely they could reverse the process, they still possessed the power to delay the inevitable outcome by filibustering and other procedural delays. A delay beyond March 4, the date of the inauguration, might open up a whole new set of problems for the Republicans.

It was at this stage that certain Southern congressmen began pressing for concessions in an attempt to at least salvage something from their impressive showing at the ballot box. An accommodation was reached between representatives of the two parties, which historian Pomerantz has described as "committing Hayes to self-determination for the people of South Carolina and Louisiana subject to the Constitution of the United States and the laws made in pursuance thereof." In return, Democrats promised to "guarantee political and civil rights under the new dispensation, and to refrain from partisan reprisals against the local Republicans."[50]

Nevertheless, some filibustering continued, as did the political maneuvering. In the end, with less than 48 hours remaining before the scheduled inauguration, the president of the Senate, his voice quivering, formally announced that Hayes was president of the United States pursuant to an electoral count of 185–184.

The nation's press now had a field day, calling the election of Hayes an "injustice and a fraud," and "a confidence game."[51] Democratic Speaker of the House Randall stated that although the Democrats had won at the ballot box, they had "yielded temporary possession of the administration" in order to "save the nation from civil commotion."[52] Indeed, Tilden's personal restraint, and his discouragement of all talk of asserting the will of the people by force or demonstrations, may very well have saved the republic from "civil commotion." Hayes sneaked into the White House on March 3, and immediately took the oath of office in a private ceremony.

But the Democrats were not about to let the Republicans off the hook. Although demands for Congress to request a Supreme Court review of the electoral decision got nowhere, a proposal by Clarkson Potter for a congressional inquiry was approved over strenuous Republican opposition. This inquiry soon became a national spectacle, as experts and professors of mathematics were paraded before the committee to "decipher" hundreds of "coded" telegrams. Hundreds of witnesses, in over 3,000 pages of testimony, were called upon to give their shocking accounts of all the events leading to the electoral debacle. But this airing of the nation's dirty laundry did not stop with the Republicans, and soon the Democrats too were being "denounced for frauds, violence, and intimidation, with Tilden himself being compelled to answer before the bar of public opinion and the committee the charges of attempted vote-buying by his party managers."[53]

This, then, is the election that reformers have sought to blame on the Electoral College system—not the corruption, not the vote-buying, and not the intimidation, but the Electoral College! In fact, not only did the Electoral College system not contribute to the debacle, but the crisis could have been much worse without it.

The election of 1876 took place during a critical turning point in the nation's history. During the period after the ratification of the Fifteenth Amendment, the franchise of African Americans had been assured only by military and Reconstruction governments in the Southern states. By 1876, however, "redeemer" governments had begun to take power in many Southern states, and military authority was giving way to civilian authority. That African Americans, a strong source of Republican support, were concentrated in these Southern states created a situation not before faced by the nation. Historian Paul Haworth has asserted that if there had been fair and free elections in the Southern states, many of these states would have voted Republican, and the "much vaunted Democratic majority of the popular vote which after all, stood for absolutely nothing—would have been overcome."[54]

If Haworth is correct, it may be that the final decision in favor of Hayes was the just one. However, it will never really be possible to determine whether the Republican votes lost due to intimidation of African Americans exceeded the Democratic votes lost due to unfair Republican certification of returns in Florida, South Carolina, and Louisiana. By all accounts the conduct of both parties was inexcusable and shameful. But such conduct would have called into question the results of any close elections, including a direct election.

The difference is that in an Electoral College system the problems become isolated and easier and more practical to deal with. In 1876 the focus of the dispute was on only four states. While there may have been problems in other states, these problems were moot since they did not rise to the level of affecting who won the electoral vote in those states. Had there been a direct election system in effect, however, the votes in every state would have been the subject of automatic dispute. Every vote lost in Florida could be made up by a vote found in Ohio, or New York, or New Jersey. It has been observed what the country went through in trying to audit the returns in just four states. Imagine for the moment this task multiplied sixfold, with returns in every state being challenged, and having to be audited and recertified.

In all elections except 1876, the Electoral College has succeeded in protecting the nation from the crisis of a disputed election. In the election of 1960, for example, we saw how a dispute over fraudulent votes in Illinois and a miscounting of the popular votes in Alabama created no crisis whatsoever because, even if the frauds had been pursued and a recount demanded, the Electoral College result would not have been affected. Had there been a direct election in 1960, there would very likely have been a demand for a recount of the votes in Illinois. No doubt recriminations and demands for commissions and congressional action would have abounded. In a close direct election where each vote would, literally, be critical, this would in turn have triggered demands for recounts in many other states, as both parties scrounged for votes in every nook and cranny of the Republic. Such a spectacle would have made the election of 1876 look like a community civics class.

The only reason the Electoral College was unable to provide this protection in 1876 was that the fraud and intimidation were spread over an entire region. The electoral votes of the states involved were, combined, sufficient to bring the candidates within one electoral vote of each other. In all other elections in which electors have been elected by popular vote, the Electoral College has provided a comfortable cushion to the winning candidate, even when the popular vote has been uncomfortably close.

Under a direct election system, a constitutional crisis could easily arise in any close election. Under the Electoral College system, such a crisis can arise only when there is widespread corruption across an entire region. Since the former is far more likely to occur than the latter (as history reveals), the Electoral College system devised by the framers clearly provides the best assurance of an orderly transfer of power in the Republic.

NOTES

1. For example: in the election of 1860, if in the first phase of a popular election, only 2.5% of Lincoln's vote had gone to both Douglas and Breckinridge, the latter two Democrats would have squeezed out Lincoln in a runoff. It is doubtful if either Douglas or Breckinridge would have been the "majority" choice in a face-to-face contest with Lincoln. (In the actual election Lincoln and Bell of the Constitutional Union party together were the popular choice of the majority.)

2. See, for example, Neal R. Peirce and Lawrence D. Longley, *The People's President: The Electoral College in American History and the Direct Vote Alternative*, rev. ed. (New Haven: Yale University Press, 1981); David W. Abbott and James P. Levine, *Wrong Winner: The Coming Debacle in the Electoral College* (New York: Praeger, 1991).

3. Sources for the popular vote may be found in Svend Peterson, *A Statistical Study of American Presidential Elections* (New York, 1963); Richard Scammon, *America at the Polls* (Pittsburgh, 1965); and The Congressional Quarterly, *Guide to 1976 Elections* (Washington, D.C., 1975), cited and tallied in Peirce and Longley, *supra* note 2, App. A, 239–246.

4. John D. Feerick, "The Electoral College—Why It Ought to be Abolished," *Fordham Law Review* 37 (1968): 1.

5. Abbott and Levine, *supra* note 2, at 1.

6. Samuel Flagg Bemis, *John Quincy Adams and the Union* (New York: Alfred A. Knopf, 1956), 11.

7. *Id.* at 53.

8. In 1832 Jackson won by an electoral majority of 178–83 and a popular vote majority of 56%. In 1904 Theodore Roosevelt was elected by a 56.9% popular vote majority.

9. Extrapolated from election data set forth in App. A of Peirce and Longley, *supra* note 2, at 240–245. All popular vote percentages are rounded to the nearest percentage point.

10. Hearings on S.J. Res. 1, 8, and 18 before the Subcommittee on the Constitution of the Committee of the Judiciary, U.S. Senate, 95th Cong., 1st sess. (July 22, 1977); transcription set forth in Martin Diamond, "The Electoral College and the Idea of Federal Democracy," *The Journal of Federalism* (Winter 1978): 75–76.

11. *Id.* at 72.

12. The Democratic slate of electors in Alabama consisted of five electors pledged to Kennedy, and six who were unpledged. The "official" tally counted the popular votes for Democratic electors twice—once for the unpledged, and once for Kennedy. The more fair method, proposed by the Congressional Quarterly, would have awarded Kennedy only five-elevenths of the total Democratic vote for electors. Under this more reasonable method, Nixon would have received 237,981 votes, Kennedy 147,295, and unpledged (Byrd) 176,755, and Nixon would have been credited with a national popular vote margin of 58,181 votes. Fortunately, this entire problem was mooted by Kennedy's overwhelming electoral majority. (Discussed and analyzed in Peirce and Longley, *supra* note 2, at 66–68.)

13. Michael J. Glennon, *When No Majority Rules: The Electoral College and Presidential Succession* (Washington, D.C.: Congressional Quarterly, Inc., 1992), 18.

14. Roy Morris, Jr., "Master Fraud of the Century: The Disputed Election of 1876." *American History Illustrated* 23 (July 1988): 28.

15. Mark D. Harmon, "The *New York Times* and the Theft of the 1876 Presidential Election," *Journal of American Culture* 10 (1987): 25.

16. Abbott and Levine, *supra* note 2, at 25.

17. *Id.* at 59; see also Lawrence D. Longley and Alan G. Braun, *The Politics of Electoral College Reform*, Foreword by U.S. Senator Birch Bayh. (New Haven: Yale University Press, 1972), 35. "The results [of this election] were even more sordid. . . . This deal—the compromise of 1877—became one crucial element of a new willingness to give the south carte blanche to go its own way in its own affairs, including the development of its own peculiar institutions, such as Jim Crow segregation."

18. Peirce and Longley, *supra* note 2, at 56–57.

19. Longley and Braun, *supra* note 17, at 35.

20. Many of the facts related here pertaining to the election of 1876 may be found in Sidney I. Pommerantz, "Election of 1876," in *The Coming to Power: Critical Presidential Elections in American History*, Arthur M. Schlesinger, Jr. and William P. Hansen, eds. (New York: Chelsea House Publishers in association with McGraw-Hill, 1972). See also A. M. Gibson, *A Political Crime: The History of the Great Fraud*, (New York: William S. Gottsberger, 1969); John Goode, "The Electoral Commission of 1877," *The American Law Review* 38 (January and February 1904): 1.; Bernard A. Weisberger, "The Stolen Election," *American Heritage* 41 (July/August 1990): 18; Morris, *supra* note 14; and Harmon, *supra* note 15.

21. Schlesinger, *supra* note 20, at 180.

22. *Id.*

23. Morris, *supra* note 14, at 32.

24. *Id.* at 31.

25. Schlesinger, *supra* note 20, at 189.

26. Harmon, *supra* note 15, at 36.

27. *Id*.

28. *Id*.

29. Schlesinger, *supra* note 20, at 191.

30. *Id*. at 192.

31. Morris, *supra* note 14, at 32.

32. Schlesinger, *supra* note 20, at 194.

33. John Goode, speech delivered at Hot Springs, Va., August 24, 1903.

34. *Id*.

35. Schlesinger, *supra* note 20, at 194.

36. Harmon, *supra* note 15, at 38.

37. *Id*. at 37.

38. *Id*. at 38.

39. *Id*.

40. Morris, *supra* note 14, at 32.

41. *Id*.

42. Morris, *supra* note 14, at 32.

43. Schlesinger, *supra* note 20, at 196.

44. Morris, *supra* note 14, at 32.

45. *Id*.

46. Schlesinger, *supra* note 20, at 199.

47. Pommerantz, in *Id*. at 199.

48. Goode, *supra* note 33.

49. Schlesinger, *supra* note 20, at 202.

50. Pommerantz, in *id*. at 209.

51. *Id*. at 213.

52. *Id*.

53. *Id*. at 219.

54. Paul Haworth, *The Hayes-Tilden Disputed Presidential Election of 1876* (Cleveland: Burrows Brothers, 1906).

Chapter Six

REFORM: PROPOSALS AND ALTERNATIVES

There is no exact account of the number of proposals and alternatives for electoral reform that have been introduced in Congress since the time of the Constitutional Convention. Estimates range from no less than 500 to over 700. These proposals range from the labyrinthine and the bizarre to the simplistic.

An example of the former was a proposal by Senator James Hillhouse in 1808 to have retiring senators choose a president by drawing colored balls from a box.[1] A plan introduced by Senator Lazarus Powell in 1864 proposed that electors meet in groups of six and select the president by lot from among another group of six electors.[2] The most simplistic of all the plans, of course, is the proposal for direct election, despite its obvious danger of selecting a minority president (see Chapters One and Five). In between these two extremes has been a variety of other schemes, many of which have been seriously considered. Some have even come close to being adopted and proposed by Congress.

One plan or another has been fashionable at various times in the nation's history, depending on whose interests the proposed plan would favor. In the 1820s the district plan was popular, and was proposed as a means of reducing the "present weight of the large states."[3] The plan enjoyed a revival in the 1950s by conservative and rural interests. It was finally killed by opponents who recognized, as stated by Senator Paul Douglas, that the plan was an obvious attempt to "deliver the cities bound hand and foot, into the power of the rural sections of the country."[4] Professor John Dixon warned that the district plan played into the hands of those seeking to entangle the judiciary into presidential elections and that if the plan were adopted "we shall have gerrymandered the Presidency."[5]

The proportional plan has enjoyed periods of high fashion during several periods in the nation's history, the most recent being during the 1950s when it was introduced in the form of the Lodge-Gossett Plan. Most of the electoral reforms in Congress have been supported by high-sounding rhetoric claiming that the proposed reform would be in the best interests of the country as a whole. Fortunately for the Republic, the sponsors of the Lodge-Gossett plan were not very discreet in giving their candid views of what interest groups the plan would favor and whom the plan would harm. On July 17, 1950, Representative Ed Gossett supported his proposed reform in a speech on the House floor in which he asked whether it was right for the present Electoral College system to place a premium on "labor votes, or Italian votes, or Irish votes, or Negro votes, or Jewish votes," claiming that the present system permitted undue influence on Middle East policy because "there are 2.5 million Jews in the city of New York alone."[6] Gossett also claimed that the power the Electoral College gave to African Americans was what had led to the hated fair-employment platforms of the major parties.

No opponent to the proposed reform could have asked for a better speech, and support for the proposal quickly evaporated. Since then, most reformers, particularly advocates of direct election, have been much more circumspect about giving their true reasons as to why they want to tamper with the Constitution, since all the arguments in favor of the proportional plan also apply to direct election.

The real problem with proposing a constitutional amendment based on a perceived advantage it will give to one group or another is that demographics and political views change over time. A plan that may favor one group in 1860, for example, may not do so in 1994. The Republic is indeed fortunate that a precedent was not set in the earliest days of amending the constitutional plan for electing a president every time there was a perceived political advantage to be gained by doing so. Protected thus far by the formidable constitutional barrier to amending the Constitution, the Electoral College has endured as an impartial arbiter of the presidential election process. One major reason for its long endurance is that it has, thus far, been impervious to political tampering. It was not adopted by the framers to favor Democrats or Republicans, conservatives or liberals, cities or towns. Rather it was adopted as a critical cornerstone of federalism in which a stable democracy could flourish.

Had the earliest reformers been able to amend the Constitution to suit their perceived political goals, numerous other changes would doubtless have followed over the years. The process of electing a president might have switched back and forth from direct election, to district, to proportional, depending upon the prevailing mood. Parties in power would have had every incentive to "change the rules of the game" to their own benefit. Had an early proposal for direct election been adopted, the proliferation of small parties, the factionalization of the political process, and the election of minority presidents would surely have brought demands for reform. The process would doubtless have been changed periodically to accommodate the fashion or political agenda of the day.

It has been claimed, at various times, that the Electoral College favors the Republican party (i.e., in the 1980s when the Republicans had an alleged electoral lock in the South and Mid-West); or the Democratic party (in the 1930s when Roosevelt had the alleged electoral lock). The fact is that over time the Electoral College favors no one. Indeed, the only time when it could possibly have favored any one group was in the election of 1888, the only fairly conducted election in which the electoral vote winner did not match the popular vote winner. To claim that the Electoral College has favored any particular group in any election other than 1888 is to claim that direct election would have favored the same groups.

But the Electoral College has not endured only because of its long acceptance and impartiality. It has also endured because of its success in meeting the needs of the nation. It remains, however, to examine a few of the many hundreds of proposals that have been made to amend the Constitutional plan for electing the president.

THE DISTRICT SYSTEM

There are several varieties of district systems that have been proposed. A common type of district plan would superimpose presidential districts on existing congressional districts. Each district in the nation would elect not only one representative to the House, but also elect exactly one presidential elector. In addition, two electors (representing the two senators to which each state is entitled) would be elected statewide.[7]

A subvariety of the district plan would not superimpose presidential districts on existing congressional districts, but rather create a whole new map of presidential districts by dividing each state into districts equal in number to the total number of senators and representatives to which the state is entitled.

The sole redeeming feature of either type of district system is that it retains the essential feature of federalism agreed to at the Constitutional Convention. That is, each state would continue to have electors equal in number to the total number of senators and representatives to which it is entitled. But it retains this feature at the expense of every other desirable feature of the existing Electoral College system.

All but two states now employ the general ticket system to elect electors to the Electoral College. That is, electors are chosen statewide, rather than by district. The general ticket system is thus immune from political attempts to gerrymander districts to the advantage of one party or the other—that is, to alter the geographic boundaries of the area in which a candidate is to be elected. Under the Constitution, state boundaries are simply not subject to political tampering.[8]

The practice of gerrymandering may be illustrated by the following example: assume that a state has within it ten districts. About 48% of the state's electorate supports Party A, and 52% supports party B. Unfortunately for Party A, however, its support is concentrated in 3 districts where it has 90% support. In the remaining 7 districts, it enjoys an average of only 30% support. Pursuant to elections held in districts with the existing geographical boundaries, therefore, it will elect 3 representatives out of 10. If party B is in power, however, it may attempt to redraw the geographic boundaries so that in each district Party A has only 48% support. In such a manner, Party A can be deprived of any representatives (despite its 48% statewide support), and Party B will get all 10. In the same manner, if party A can gain control, it may be able to draw the boundaries so that it has 60% support in 6 counties, but only 20% support in the remaining 4. Thus, despite having only 48% statewide support, it may elect 6 of the 10 representatives.

The practice of redrawing the geographic boundaries of a district to gain such political advantage has become known as the practice of "gerrymandering." The enormous incentive to engage in its practice should be apparent from the above example. It is not surprising, therefore, to learn that its practice has plagued congressional elections since the very earliest time of the Republic. It was noted in Chapter Four that the judiciary began to get heavily involved in this area when it decided *Baker v. Carr*[9] and *Gray v. Sanders*.[10] Fortunately, the Electoral College system and the general ticket ballot have spared the presidential election process from the problems associated with gerrymandering.

It is apparent that there would be enormous incentives for gerrymandering under the district system for electing a president. The incentives for redrawing district boundaries to affect a presidential election would be equal or even greater to the incentives for redrawing boundaries to affect congressional elections. Doubtless the courts would be drawn in, as they already have been in the area of congressional elections.

The district system would also not have the discouraging effect on third and extremist parties that the Electoral College has under the general ticket ballot. The chances of an extremist party winning an entire state are relatively small. Its chances of winning a particular district, however, would be substantially greater.

Finally, the district system does not provide the same unambiguous result as the general ticket ballot. By splitting each state's electoral vote, the impact of each state is proportionately decreased. If an election is extremely close in the popular vote, it is likely to be extremely close in the electoral vote as well. Each district might become critical, creating an incentive to recount each challenge and every vote within the close district districts. In close elections it would be unlikely that there would be a clear winner, and the final result could be delayed for a long period, thus bringing uncertainty to the entire political process.

So what is gained from using a district system? The only real claim of its supporters is that such a system would lessen the possibility of electing a "wrong" president—that is, a president who wins a majority of electoral votes without winning the most popular votes. Without conceding that such a president would in any way be "wrong" in our federal system, it should be noted that had the district system been in effect in other elections, "the district plan would have had their outcomes reversed."[11] In 1960, for example, John Kennedy would have lost the election under the district plan despite having received the most popular votes according to the official tally.

The district system is not prohibited by the Constitution, and any state is free to adopt it. Maine and Nebraska have already done so. If more states were to follow, the nation could return to the situation that existed in the early 1800s, in which states switched back and forth between systems depending upon which party a system favored. Responsible reform would make uniform the general ticket system, which has been adopted by 48 of the 50 states. In the nuclear age the Republic can no longer risk the delays, uncertainties, and incentives for political intrigue that are inherent in the district system.

THE PROPORTIONAL SYSTEM

> Even the cleverest surgeon cannot divide one man up—proportionately or otherwise—and expect him to live.
>
> Henry Cabot Lodge[12]

The proportional system would attempt to award electoral votes in the same proportion as the popular vote. Like the district system, it has the redeeming feature that it would retain the federalist allocation of electoral votes to each state. Unlike the district system, however, there would not be the political incentive to practice gerrymandering. The earliest proposals for a proportional system were introduced in Congress in the late 1800s. They provided that electoral votes would be awarded in the same percentage as the popular vote, with each electoral vote rounded off to the nearest one electoral vote. Thus, if a candidate received 59% of the popular vote of a state that was entitled to 10 electoral votes, he or she would be awarded six votes; if he or she received 66%, 7 electoral votes.

Later proposals provided for rounding each elector off to the nearest thousandth of a percentage point. Thus a candidate could receive a fraction of electoral votes, such as 2.308 electoral votes. A proportional plan introduced in Congress in 1950 would have combined the system with the automatic plan, whereby the actual electors would be abolished and each state would automatically be awarded the electoral votes of a state in the same percentage as the popular vote the candidates received.

The proportional plan was supported and opposed—for mostly the wrong reasons. Supporters such as Gossett felt it would lessen the influence of minorities, particularly that of African Americans and Jews. In this one respect Gossett's interpretation coincided with the views of Clarence Mitchell, the Washington director of the National Association for the Advancement of Colored People, who stated that the proportional plan would

effectively draw the political eye teeth of all independent votes, including the Negro voter, as far as Presidential elections are concerned. . . . If the Gossett proposal goes through, the Negro vote and the vote of any other minority, national and religious group will no longer be important. . . . The Gossett proposal is antiurban, antinorthern, and antiliberal.[13]

Democrat Paul Douglas observed that

Some of the [proponents of proportional representation] have been frank enough to admit that they are talking about Negroes, Jews, Catholics . . . but to others [they refer] to farmers . . . veterans, the aged. . . . If the Republican Party succeeds in having the Gossett resolution adopted that will put an end to . . . the civil rights issue from national politics. . . . No surer method of introducing confusion and lack of confidence in our electoral system could be devised.[14]

Democratic Senator John Kennedy observed that the proportional plan

has been discredited in the past and promises only doubt and danger for the future. . . . No minority Presidents have been elected in the 20th century; no breakdown in the electoral system, or even widespread lack of confidence in it can be shown. . . . There is obviously little to gain—but much to lose by tampering with the Constitution.[15]

Although both supporters and opponents perceived that one group or another was harmed or favored by proportional representation, for every view that one group was favored by the Electoral College there was a political scientist who claimed that same group was disadvantaged. (It will be recalled that Abbott and Levine claim that the Electoral College disadvantages African Americans, Mormons, and homosexuals.)[16]

The real problem with the proportional plan is the same as that of direct election—namely, that it would encourage factionalism, discourage compromise, and magnify the problems of ambiguity and delay in cases of close elections. A few senators chose not to base their opposition on perceived political grounds, but instead recognized that it would "weaken the two party system."[17]

The only nonpolitical reason given in support of the plan was that it would reduce the chances of a wrong president elected without a majority of the popular vote. Even by this misguided standard, however, the proportional plan fails. Had it been in effect in the elections of 1880, 1896, and 1960, it would have elected popular-vote losers Hancock, Bryan, and Nixon.

Indeed, even under this misguided standard put forward by reformers, the Electoral College has proven superior to either the direct or proportional plans.

THE AUTOMATIC PLAN

At first blush the automatic plan would appear to have none of the evils associated with direct election, the district system, or the proportional plan. The automatic plan would go no further than to eliminate the actual office of elector, and would continue to award electoral votes in the present manner. That is, there would no longer be electors who would actually be elected and subsequently meet to cast their votes. Instead, the popular vote winner of a state would simply be automatically credited on the computer with the number of electoral votes allocated to that state.

Ironically, it is the very modesty of this plan that makes it unlikely to be adopted. More radical reformers fear that the adoption of such a plan would "be worse than having no reform at all. Not only would it write into the Constitution the evils of the unit vote system, but its adoption would undoubtedly preclude meaningful reform indefinitely."[18] Others have asserted that "it is hardly worth cranking up the complex and protracted amendment process to accomplish so little—it would be almost like chasing a fly with an elephant gun."[19]

Some opponents of the automatic plan have claimed that it would harm the two-party system by making it easier for splinter parties to get on the ballot.[20] This claim does not appear particularly persuasive in light of the many other factors that are involved in being placed on the ballot.[21]

However, the radical reformers do have a point about whether it is worth going through the process of amending the Constitution for so insignificant a reform. The automatic plan addresses only one small aspect of the Electoral College—the problem of the faithless elector. Despite the fact that faithless electors have cast only 7 out of 17,000 votes cast in the past 150 years, and have never come close to affecting an election, it would nevertheless ease anxieties if this problem were addressed.

As will be explained in the final chapter, there are a number of areas in which the Electoral College could use some fine tuning. The faithless elector is only one of those areas. If the amendment process is to be utilized, all areas should be addressed in one package.

There are several ways in which the faithless elector problem can be dealt with, and the automatic plan is not the only way. It can be argued, of course, that the actual office of elector is unnecessary, and that computers can do the job once performed by electors. There is some truth to the claim that the meeting of human electors is an old and archaic ceremony. There is, perhaps, no conceptual or political rationale for its retention. But the same could be said for many ceremonies of state that commemorate a past tradition. There is certainly no political or conceptual rationale for retaining the tradition of the inaugural address or parade. New presidents could simply put their remarks on a disc and electronically transfer them to a computer network and the parade itself could certainly be dispensed with.

Doubtless the tradition of the president's State of the Union Address could be dispensed with and put on videotape. The day may even come when meetings of the Senate and House in the Capitol are considered archaic, and it is suggested that their work can be conducted more efficiently on an electronic computer network. But many Americans would consider that something would be lost in such an arrangement. It may well be that some electors consider their appointment and meeting to be a useless exercise. But others consider the office to be an honor and appreciate that their meeting is part of a tradition that began when the first Electoral College met to elect George Washington. If the only real concern is that of the faithless elector, this can be dealt in with in other ways. For example, a package of responsible reform could provide that a vote cast by an elector in violation of his or her pledge could be changed to a vote in compliance with the elector's pledge by a majority vote of either House of Congress. It would be rare that such a remedy would be required (perhaps once or twice a century), but its constitutional availability might ease the anxieties of some reformers.

In any case, at least the automatic plan would not tamper with the essential characteristics of the presidential election process that were devised by the framers and have been refined and developed over 200 years.

LEGISLATIVE ELECTION

It will be recalled that the Constitution delegates to each state the appointment of electors. With but one or two minor exceptions all states had, by the 1830s, provided for appointment of electors by popular election. The most recent election in which a legislature chose electors was in 1944, when the Mississippi legislature chose electors to oppose all the other party slates.[22]

It has been proposed by William Martin, writing for the *American Bar Association Journal*,[23] that state legislatures should again begin selecting electors. Martin has expressed the view that the election of a president has become too centralized and nationalized, and that the only way to return to the scheme envisioned by the framers is to let the state legislatures choose the electors. "Have we the courage" Martin has asked, "to bring this plan out in the open and elect legislatures which will carry it out? It has been tested in our early history and electors then selected their best and most patriotic citizens for President. It is valid. It is Constitutional."[24]

Martin is correct in stating that such a plan would be constitutional. But he is incorrect in suggesting that any particular plan for appointing legislators was envisioned by the framers. Rather, what the framers envisioned was a process of development as each state determined what was the best way of selecting electors. The framers' faith and confidence in the state legislators has been fully vindicated as each state has chosen popular election as the most democratic and fair method of selecting electors. Indeed, popular election of electors has now become such an integral part of the Electoral College that a responsible reform would enshrine this process in the Constitution.

HYBRIDS

A few of the more bizarre proposals for electoral reform have already been mentioned, but most others are not worthy of serious attention. In 1861 Representative Clement Vallendigham of Ohio proposed an electoral reform that he hoped might avert the Civil War. Under his plan, the country would be divided into four large regional districts, one of which would include the South. In order to be elected president, a candidate would have to receive a majority of electors in each of the four regional districts.[25] Other than its general impracticability, this plan's obvious deficiency was that it would be rare for any president to be elected under such a system, and a subsequent election by the Congress would defeat the purposes of the plan.

Other hybrids have included plans to elect presidents alternately from North and South,[26] to require a plurality of popular votes and a majority of electoral votes,[27] and a wide variety of combinations of popular vote, majority vote of electors, pluralities in a majority of states, or pluralities in states having the majority of voters.[28] One hybrid plan, known as the bonus plan, is worthy of special attention.

THE BONUS PLAN

In 1978 the Twentieth Century Fund enlisted the contributions of a distinguished panel of Americans to study the Electoral College and make recommendations.[29] Members of the Task Force included historian Authur Schlesinger, Jeane Kirkpatrick (later to be the U.S. representative at the United Nations), and other distinguished historians, lawyers, journalists, political scientists, and educators.[30] The final recommendation of that group was the bonus plan. Although the plan itself proved to be just another inconsequential and ultimately ignored hybrid, the Twentieth Century Fund study is nevertheless notable for its having conducted the most in-depth study of the Electoral College system.

Although the members of the Task Force represented no political constituency, and thus had no federalist interest to protect, they nevertheless represented some of the brightest and most independent thinkers that could have been brought together. Although, in the end, their study made a recommendation of the bonus plan, the study they produced stands as perhaps the most persuasive defense of the Electoral College system.

The preface to the study states:

The Electoral College has weathered great changes—demographic and technological as well as political—in the nature of presidential elections, and more than once in the nation's history, has been challenged. Yet it has endured, in part because it stands for some important and cherished principles, in part because proposals for replacing it have threatened those principles.[31]

In explaining how it reached its final recommendations, the Task Force stated that

initially, the Task Force saw no way of reconciling what was apparently irreconcilable. Several members [noted] that the probable consequences, some necessarily unforeseen, of changing the system might amount to a cure that was worse than the disease. Others supported direct election. Faced with these opposing choices, the Task Force appeared to be merely replaying the inconclusive data that had gone on for so long. Nevertheless the Task Force's discussions revealed a remarkable degree of consensus on critical issues and on the values to be preserved.

Included on the Task Force were some hard-core advocates of direct election.[32] In order to achieve any kind of consensus, it was necessary to address their overriding concern of the once-every-two-century possibility of a president being elected without a popular majority. For the rest of the Task Force, however, it was essential to retain the basic federalist values of the Electoral College as well as preserve those aspects that nurtured the two-party system and provided for a conclusive result.

The necessity of satisfying the advocates of direct election resulted in the "bonus" factor of the Task Force's plan. Under this plan, virtually all the essential characteristics of the Electoral College would be retained. That is, each state would continue to be entitled to electors equal in number to its senators and representatives. However, electoral votes would be automatically awarded to the winner of each state's popular votes (the automatic plan), and the winner of the national popular vote would get an extra 102 electoral votes (the bonus).

The sole claimed redeeming feature of the bonus plan (other than retaining the basic apparatus of the Electoral College) appeared to be that it would have provided for the election of Grover Cleveland in 1888. That is, in every election conducted in the United States, the plan would have selected the popular vote winner as the winner in the Electoral College. (According to mathematician Samuel Merrill, however, it would still be possible to elect a popular vote loser under the bonus plan.)[33]

However, the concession to the direct election advocates was greater than was perhaps apparent to those who wished to preserve the basic values of the Electoral College. By giving a bonus of 102 electoral votes to the winner of the popular vote, a presidential election was made subject to the same kind of uncertainties and delays that would accompany a close direct election. Thus, in return for giving up the once-every-two-century possibility of a popular vote loser, the bonus plan gave up obtaining a decisive result in close popular vote elections.

For example, if the bonus plan had been in effect in 1960, the winner of the election would have been determined by who received the popular vote bonus of 102 electoral votes. That is because without the bonus, Kennedy received 303 electoral votes, and Nixon received 219. Therefore, whichever candidate received the most popular votes (and the 102 bonus electors) would be the winner.

It will be recalled, however, that there was a serious dispute as to which candidate was entitled to claim the most popular votes in Alabama. Although only five of the Democratic electors were pledged to Kennedy, the official count nevertheless awarded to Kennedy the popular votes of the unpledged Democratic electors, and the electors pledged to Byrd. Under the method of counting popular votes recommended by the Congressional Quarterly, however, Kennedy should have been awarded only five-elevenths of the popular votes cast for Democratic electors. Under this calculation, Nixon would have won the popular vote both in Alabama and nationwide, and would have been entitled to the 102 bonus points and the presidency.

There were strong arguments both for and against the method used by the wire services that awarded to Kennedy the popular votes cast for all the Democratic electors. The basic weakness of this method, however, was that it counted the popular votes for the unpledged electors twice—once for the unpledged electors, and once for Kennedy! In many respects, the Congressional Quarterly method of counting the votes would have been far more fair.

Fortunately, the nation was spared a divisive argument over which candidate should have been credited with the popular vote majority in Alabama. The dispute faded into a footnote in history, because, under the Electoral College system, there was a clear winner regardless of who won the popular vote in Alabama or nationwide. It was for this reason that Nixon did not challenge the popular vote allocation in Alabama. Had the bonus plan been in effect, however, the question would have been absolutely critical to the outcome of the election.

With the entire election hanging on which method was used to count Alabama's popular votes, Congress would probably have been obliged to appoint an electoral commission to resolve the dispute. The nation would very likely have had to endure a prolonged period of uncertainty, as both parties pressed to have their representatives appointed to the commission. In short, the process would have been very similar to that which the nation endured in 1876, with one very important exception.

In 1876 the law provided that the president was not to be inaugurated until March 4 of the following year. Even so, the long process of appointing commissions, listening to testimony, and making decisions took until March 2. In 1960 the law provided that the president was to be inaugurated on January 20. Despite the greater demands for "procedural due process" that Americans in 1960 would doubtless have demanded, an electoral commission would have had to act even more swifty than the one appointed in 1876. It should also be recalled that in the cold war year of 1960, a period of uncertainty and ambiguity in the election of the president would have had far graver consequences than in 1876.

Members of the Twentieth Century Fund Task Force who favored retention of the Electoral College apparently acceded to the bonus plan as the price of retaining the basic apparatus of the Electoral College. Doubtless they did so in order to reach a consensus and head off a more radical demand for popular election. But in doing so they conceded one of the most important features of the Electoral College system—the production of a clear-cut and unambiguous winner. They also proposed to burden the present system with one of the worst features of direct election.

It may be that no one on the Task Force seriously considered the bonus plan to be a viable alternative to the present system, and reached its compromise only to avoid an absolute deadlock. Nevertheless, the distinguished Task Force's acknowledgment of the basic principles and advantages of the Electoral College system would have been sufficient to justify its hard work.

For example, the Task Force recognized that "under the direct election, the states would be deprived of their constitutional role in the election of the President. This might weaken not only state political parties but also the influence of state and local issues in presidential campaigns."[34] In reviewing the track record of the Electoral College in past national elections, it acknowledged that "the election of 1888 is the only undisputed example of a runner-up victory,"[35] thus rejecting the claims of some radical reformers that the elections of 1824 and 1876 provide examples of electoral malfunction. It also acknowledges that in the 1960 election, the Congressional Quarterly's method of allocating Kennedy only five-elevenths of the Alabama Democratic popular vote would have been a "seemingly fairer method."[36]

Most important, however, the Task Force rejects the simplistic notion that direct elections result in electing the majority candidate. When "the candidate with the most votes among multiple candidates wins less than 50%," he will not necessarily be "the most preferred candidate because, if given another choice, more than half the people may prefer one of his opponents."[37] The study concludes that by "majoritarian standards," the "direct popular vote is somewhat arbitrary."[38] More important, "direct election does not guarantee that the candidate with the most support wins if there are more than two candidates."[39]

On the question of whether a direct election would encourage factionalism and multiple parties, the Task Force cited a contemporary study conducted by Bradley Canon. According to Canon, the Task Force states,

the possibility of a runoff [in a direct election] has a striking effect; it reduces the proportion of votes going to the top candidates and lowers the number of candidates receiving significant numbers of votes. [Canon's analysis] generates support for the idea that the existence of run-offs actively encourages more candidates to enter, thus reducing the proportion of the vote going to the top candidates.[40]

Canon's study concludes that direct elections that provide for a runoff encourage more minor parties than even a direct election without a runoff.[41]

The Task Force concluded that

under direct election, state boundaries would become irrelevant in counting votes, and the position of state parties in national campaigns might therefore be weakened. State political parties, once the most vital element of the national structure of party organization, have already seen their position eroded by the reform of the national nominating process and by the changing nature of political campaigns; direct election might continue that erosion.[42]

But perhaps the most important of the Task Force's conclusions was that

the one point on which the case for direct election seems to be weakest and the case for the Electoral College seems to be strongest is in yielding a clear result.... [W]hlie no one would create the Electoral College de novo today, it is defended with a vigor that derives from decades of results that are considered satisfactory.[43]

THE CONTINGENCY ELECTION

There have been many proposals over the years to reform the provision for election of the president by the House where no candidate has received a majority of electoral votes in the general election. Many of these proposals have been attached to other proposals, such as the ABA proposal for a runoff election where no candidate receives 40% of the votes in a popular election. Other plans have proposed to retain the House election, but allow each representative to have one vote or to have a vote by a joint session of Congress.[44] Peirce and Longley have claimed that the contingency election has been "almost universally condemned."[45]

The proposals for reform of the contingency election fall into two categories: those that would continue to have Congress elect the president if no candidate receives a majority of electoral votes, and those that would bypass Congress and provide for a runoff election. Since the arguments are different for both these categories of reform, they will be dealt with separately.

Most arguments for a runoff in lieu of an election by Congress are based on the assumption that any election by Congress would be inherently undemocratic. In fact, it should be noted that most of the world's democracies provide for the election of their chief of state in exactly this manner. Nevertheless, the constitutional provision for a contingency election in the House should be examined on its own merits.

The problems with any kind of a runoff election have been noted by Judith Best. In her study of runoff elections in other countries, she has noted that such elections result in additional "expense, voter fatigue, and a drop-off in participation."[46] She has also suggested that the uncertainty created during the period between the first and second election would "foster political intrigue" and "shorten the time available for an orderly transition of power." In addition it would "necessitate a national recount, and weaken or alter the two party system."[47] It has already been noted that runoffs can reduce the possibility of electing a true majority candidate.

Although such reasons provide a practical reason not to adopt a runoff system, there are more fundamental reasons to reject it. It will be recalled that the manner of electing the president was included in the Great Compromise (see Chapter Three). Indeed, it was the promise of equal state representation in the contingent House election that finally resolved the dispute between small and large states. When it was finally proposed as a means of breaking the deadlock, the Convention adopted the idea "with what must have been an audible sigh of relief"[48] that a walkout by the small states had been averted and a final compromise achieved.

It will also be recalled that the small states believed that their right to equal state representation in the House would prove to be a significant concession. Because the Electoral College process has worked so much better than any convention delegate had ever dreamed, the small states have already been deprived of most of the benefits of their bargain. The small states anticipated that many, if not most, elections would be referred to the House, where the small states would have equal representation. In fact, no election has been referred to the House since 1824.

In short, the contingent election in the House is part of the "whole solar system of government power."[49] If this part of the solar system is to be tampered with, then the other parts of the federalist system must also be looked at, such as the equal representation of the states in the Senate, and the equal power of states to ratify constitutional amendments.

Nevertheless, betrayals of federalist principles might be justified in the extreme situation where a constitutional provision has caused or threatens to cause great harm. So far, the only potential harm that reformers can point to is that, once every 200 years or so, this nation might have to employ the method used by most of the world's democracies to elect their heads of state.

In fact, not only has the contingent election not caused or threatened to cause any harm to the Republic, it has been a very positive force in the development of the presidential election process. Next to the general ticket ballot, this feature of the electoral process has probably contributed more to the creation of the two-party system and the discouragement of faction-alism than any other one feature.

Remember that early in the 1992 presidential election, Ross Perot dropped out of the race, despite placing very competitively in the national polls. One of the reasons he gave was that the most he could hope for in the election was to deprive the other two candidates of an electoral majority, thus sending the election into the House, where he would certainly lose. Had the ABA provision for a runoff election been in effect, Perot would have had every reason to stay in the race, hoping for a narrow second-place finish in the general election that would have qualified him for the runoff. In short, it was the provision for a House contingency election that narrowed the field down to two candidates, making it possible for the voters to elect a majority, or large plurality, president.

Perhaps the most attractive feature of the contingent House election is that it has the effect of reinforcing the two-party system without actually having to be implemented. The mere knowledge that this contingency provision exists is usually enough to narrow the field to a number that will permit the election of a president with a majority or large plurality of the popular vote. Without this provision, the country would probably have had by now a large number of presidents who received neither a majority nor large plurality of the popular votes.

Proposals to elect the president in a joint session of Congress or to give each representative a separate vote would only serve to further diminish the value of the federalist bargain made to the small states. It would also create the possibility most feared by the small states—that the vast armies of representatives of just a few large states could overwhelm the election process and dictate a choice to the rest of the country. Federalism was simply not founded on such a basis, and our union would never have existed had such a plan been insisted upon at the Constitutional Convention.

But in the final measure, the contingent House election should be re-tained because it has so faithfully served the cause of democracy and federalism within which democracy has flourished for 200 years.

DIRECT ELECTION

The simplest of all the proposed alternatives to the Electoral College is, of course, the direct election. It was first advocated as early as the Constitutional Convention, but was voted down by a vote of 1 state in favor, 9 states against. It was first proposed in Congress as a constitutional amendment in 1816. However, it was soundly defeated by senators led by Maryland Senator Robert Harper, who stated that direct election "threw out of view altogether the federal principle which the states are represented. . . . It would destroy that influence of the smaller states...and thus destroy a very important principle of the Constitution."[50]

Over 100 proposals for direct election have been introduced in Congress since 1816. None have been successful. In 1956 a direct election proposal was defeated by a Senate vote of 28–63. The opposition was led by Senator John Kennedy of Massachusetts, who stated that "I should hate to see the abolition of state lines. . . . The Presidential election is determined on the basis of 48 separate units. I think the election should be decided in each one of them."[51]

The most ambitious assault on the Electoral College was launched in Congress in 1969 under an umbrella of relentless invective. One representative called the Electoral College "barbarous" and "dangerous."[52] In 1970 the assault was continued, but was stemmed in part by the testimony of such experts as Theodore White and assistants to former presidents.[53] In the end, however, it was the runoff feature of the direct election plan that caused many members of Congress to pause. "Everyone is much scared of the runoff feature" explained one legislative aide.[54] In 1979 representatives of minority groups testified against a proposal for direct election, claiming that it would "have a disastrous impact . . . on black people."[55]

Although the 1969 proposal came closest to being adopted, all were ultimately defeated. Apparently many members have felt as historian Clinton Rossiter did, that "we should hesitate a long time before replacing a Humpty-dumpty system that works for a neat one that will blow up in our faces."[56]

Nevertheless, the quest to abolish the Electoral College continues today. Proposals for direct election constitute the most direct threat, for several reasons. First, unlike most of the other proposed reforms, direct election is simplistic and easy for the man and woman in the street to understand. Pollsters find it easy to ask voters whether they would favor "direct popular election of the president" instead of the Electoral College, which is not generally understood by the average voter. Often the question is simply asked "do you believe that the presidential candidate who receives the most popular votes should be elected?"

Second, the very term "direct popular election" has an aura of "democracy" about it. It simply sounds more democratic. Reformers have encouraged this view by perpetuating myths, such as that the framers were antidemocratic elitists who proposed the Electoral College as a means of insulating the presidency from the people. (In fact they left the selection of electors to the legislatures, all of which subsequently provided for popular election of electors.)

However, many of those who profess to favor direct election state that they are unaware of the federalist origins of the Electoral College; the role the College played in the Great Compromise, which included equal state representation in the Senate; and the fact that direct election may encourage factionalism and produce a minority president. Others are not aware of the delays and ambiguities inherent in the direct election process. Most have heard only arguments in favor of direct election, and have heard few if any defenses of federalism.

Advocates of direct election have dismissed virtually all of the concerns of those who favor retention of the Electoral College. Evidence of the Electoral College's contribution to the creation of the two-party system is dismissed—apparently on the theory that the two-party system is a natural state of political affairs.

Despite the specific statements of Madison that "the little states insisted on retaining their equality in both branches,"[57] and the findings by constitutional historian Max Farrand that "the proposed method of electing the President was a compromise,"[58] advocates of direct election persist in taking the view that there was no such compromise.

On the one hand, Peirce and Longley simply assert that the "Great Compromise was devised to settle the dispute over representation in Congress, not the Electoral College."[59] Although acknowledging the many references to the presidential compromise in *The Federalist* papers and in ratifying conventions, they nevertheless conclude that Madison and the constitutional experts must be wrong, and that the argument that the Electoral College was "central to the institution of the presidency . . . is simply false."[60]

On the other hand, Peirce and Longley describe the subject of the "big versus small state interests" at the Constitutional Convention as the "Great Irrelevancy."[61] If it is so irrelevant, one may wonder why the fact that a compromise occurred is so vigorously denied.

Nevertheless, the reformers' vehement rejection of the view that the Electoral College was part of the Great Compromise is intriguing as it suggests that even the reformers believe such a compromise, if it existed, would be relevant as revealing a significant aspect of federalism. If such reformers could be convinced that such a compromise did exist, one wonders if they would remain undeterred, or whether they would then concede that direct election would be a betrayal of an important federalist principle.

Reformers rarely address the objection, stated by John Kennedy, that "direct election would break down the federal system under which most states entered the union, which provides a system of checks and balances to insure that no area or group shall obtain too much power."[62] Kennedy's observation that the Electoral College is but one aspect of the "solar system of government power" is dismissed on grounds that such other parts of the solar system have changed—citing the rise of political parties and the primary system. It is clear, however, that Kennedy was not speaking of parties or primaries, but the essential ingredients of federalism agreed to as part of the Great Compromise at the Federal Convention—that is, the equal representation of states in the Senate and in the ratification of constitutional amendments. Neither of these two latter aspects of federalism has changed in the past 200 years.

In 1977, renowned historian Arthur Schlesinger wrote that "should an abstract standard of equity require the abolition of large-state advantages in presidential elections, then surely it requires the abolition of the small state advantage in the Senate."[63] Reformers Peirce and Longley dismissed this idea as a "red herring" on grounds that, under the Constitution, deprivation of equal representation in the Senate requires unanimous consent of all the states.[64] It is true that at the Constitutional Convention the small states did not trust the large states and were prudent enough to insist upon their right to veto any proposal to deprive them of their right to equal suffrage in the Senate. It now appears that their lack of prudence in protecting those same rights in the executive branch is to be used against them. But this does not make Schlesinger's point a red herring.

Reformers put much stock in the fact that some representatives from the small states are willing to forsake the Electoral College birthright won by their forbears at the Constitutional Convention. Presumably the point to be made is that small states are now willing to give up whatever rights were once given to them in the presidential election process. If such a willingness is to be found to forsake suffrage rights in the Electoral College, why not also in the Senate? It would take the consent of all the states, to be sure (rather than just 34 to abolish the Electoral College), but it could be done if all the small states were to recognize the "undemocratic" constitution of the U.S. Senate.

Honest reformers have at least been willing to concede that the direct election poses severe problems in close elections. Peirce and Longley, for example, have conceded that

many states are unable to report an official account until several weeks after election day, as local boards of elections languidly carry out their duties. If recounts are necessary or challenges reach the courts, the process of establishing an official count can drag on well into the term of the official who has been elected. It is in this area of the speed in the count and challenge procedure, rather than in obtaining, finally, a conclusive national count, that the direct vote for president raises the most serious problems.[65]

In addressing such problems in a direct election, Peirce and Longley appear to put much faith in a federal takeover of the election process,[66] and in "automatic, mandatory retallys." A federal takeover, of course, presents its own problems of federalism. More important, however, it must be recognized that mandatory retallys and technological advances in vote-counting will not solve the problem of delays and challenges. First, there are many delays that can not be eliminated simply by advanced computers. Absentee votes cast by Americans overseas must still be tabulated and fed into a computer or vote-counting machine. Allegations of fraud are frequently based on intimidation, denial of access, and other matters totally unrelated to the accuracy of machines. Even total nationwide computerization, which would help somewhat, is a long way off. Even if advanced machines had been available in 1876, it is doubtful that they would have helped very much in resolving the kinds of problems encountered in that election.[67]

An example of the kinds of delays that are encountered with a direct election system was illustrated in the Twentieth Century Fund's 1978 study of the Electoral College: in the 1974 New Hampshire Senate election, official returns showed that the Republican had won by 355 votes. A recount, however, showed that the Democrat had won by 10 votes. An appeal was had to an electoral commission, which ended up having to scrutinize each individual vote. After this scrutiny, the commission determined that the Republican had actually won by a margin of 2 votes out of a quarter of a million cast. This decision was in turn referred to the Senate Rules Committee, which, after considerable deliberation, determined that it was unable to reach a conclusion. Party politics soon reared its ugly head, and a proposal to hold a new election was filibustered by party opponents. The matter was settled only when the candidates themselves agreed to a new election. But the entire process took up almost a year (or about one-sixth of the senatorial term).[68]

The consequences of this delay in seating a senator were not particularly severe (except perhaps for New Hampshire), since no matters of national security or nuclear responsibility were at stake. Had this been a presidential election, such a delay could have created a constitutional crisis of catastrophic proportions. Fortunately, when this country has had presidential elections that have been as close as the New Hampshire election (as in 1880), the Electoral College has provided an instant clear-cut winner. The sole exception was in 1876, when massive fraud across an entire region put the popular vote counts in so many states at issue that a favorable Republican resolution in each of four entire states would give the Republican an electoral majority of exactly one vote.

It is true that if there were another election involving massive regionwide fraud, a recount might be necessary even under the Electoral College system. This has occurred only once in our history, and is unlikely to occur again. However, the delay and uncertainty created in the New Hampshire election is likely to occur in any close presidential election. Close elections in American history have occurred frequently, and are likely to occur again. It therefore follows that the chances of a constitutional crisis arising are far more likely under a state of direct election than under the Electoral College.

Under a direct election system, any close election would require the recounting of virtually *every vote*. Under the Electoral College system, a recount would be required only in that state in which the vote is very close, or in which there are challenges to the votes. Votes in states that are not in doubt do not need to be counted.

Historian Theodore White has explained that the Electoral College is

like a vessel. We have a vessel now with 50 separate containers. They slosh around a bit, but they are contained. If you have this whole pack of 75 million votes cascading in all at once, the sloshing and the temptation to stall here or there will, I think be enormous. This is such a gamble . . . that it appalls me to think of it.[69]

Historians, constitutional scholars, and political scientists have carefully set forth the dangers involved in tampering with the Constitution in the manner of selecting the president. However, as long as direct election is simplistically espoused as a more democratic alternative, without explaining the inherent dangers, it will continue to be a threat to the system that has served our nation so well for 200 years. In the end, only education and dedication to the principles for which this nation stands can save this grand American institution.

NOTES

1. Final Report of the Commission on National Elections, Georgetown University, *Electing the President: A Program for Reform*. Robert E. Hunter, ed. (Washington, D.C.: The Center for Strategic and International Studies, 1986).

2. *Id.*

3. *Id.* at 138.

4. Statement of Democratic Senator Paul Douglas of Illinois, cited in Neal Peirce and Lawrence D. Longley, *The People's President: The Electoral College in American History and the Direct Vote Alternative*, rev. ed. (New Haven: Yale University Press, 1981), 173.

5. *Id.*

6. *Id.* at 149.

7. See, for example, Thomas M. Durbin, "The Electoral College Method of Electing the President and Vice President and Proposals for Reform," *Congressional Research Service* (August 8, 1988), 22.

8. Section III of Article IV of the Constitution states that no "state shall be formed or erected within the jurisdiction of any state; nor any state be formed by the junction of two or more states, or parts of states, without the consent of the Legislators of the States concerned as well as of the Congress."

9. 369 U.S. 186 (1962).

10. 372 U.S. 368 (1963).

11. David W. Abbott, and James P. Levine, *Wrong Winner: The Coming Debacle in the Electoral College* (New York: Praeger, 1991), 127.

12. Congressional Record, 1950, p. 886, cited in Peirce and Longley, *supra* note 4, at 148.

13. Congressional Record, 1956, 5644–5646, cited in *id.* at 152.

14. *Id.* at 156.

15. *Id.*

16. Abbott and Levine, *supra* note 11, at 90–95.

17. Congressional Record, 1956, 5644–5646; Peirce and Longley, *supra* note 4, at 152.

18. Testimonial of Donald Scott, chairman of the Chamber Study Group on Electorial College Reform, March 6, 1966, cited in *id.* at 160.

19. Congressional Record, 1966, 3764 (daily ed.), cited in *id.* at 160.

20. View of Arthur Vandenburg of Michigan, Congressional Record, 1934, 8944–8945, 9127, cited in *id.* at 158.

21. See Chapter Five.

22. Act of November 4, Ex. Sess. ch. 2 (Miss. 1944).

23. William Logan Martin, "Let the State Legislators Choose Them," *American Bar Association Journal*, 44 (December 1958): 1182.

24. *Id.* at 1185.

25. Charles A. O'Neill, *The American Electorial System* (New York, 1887), 257–258, cited in Peirce and Longley, *supra* note 4, at 173.

26. *Id.*

27. *Id.*

28. *Id.*

29. Report of the Twentieth Century Fund Task Force on Reform of the Presidential Election Process, *Winner Take All*, background paper by William R. Keech (New York: Holmes and Meier, 1978).

30. *Id.* at 3.

31. *Id.* at 38. Ellipses indicating deletions have been indicated.

32. For example, Neil R. Peirce, journalist, *The National Journal*, Washington, D.C.

33. Samuel See Merrill, "Imperial Estimates for the Likelihood of a Directed Verdict in a Presidential Election," *Publics Choice* 33, no. 2, 127–133 (1978); cited in Peirce and Longley, *supra* note 4, at 176–177.

34. *Winner Take All*, *supra* note 29, at 11.

35. *Id.*

36. *Id.* at 43.

37. *Id.* at 45.

38. *Id.*

39. *Id.*

40. *Id.* at 63.

41. *Id.* at 64.

42. *Id.* at 66.

43. *Id.* at 69.

44. Peirce and Longley, *supra* note 4, at 178.

45. *Id.* at 177.

46. Judith Best, 9 cited in *Winner Take All*, *supra* note 29, at 53.

47. *Id.*

48. William Peters, *A More Perfect Union: The Making of the United States Constitution* (New York: Crown Publishers, 1987), 192.

49. Michael J. Glennon, *When No Majority Rules: The Electoral College and Presidential Succession* (Washington, D.C.: Congressional Quarterly, Inc., 1992), 76, citing Congressional Record, Senate Bill 150, 84th Cong., 2nd sess., March 20, 1956.

50. Peirce and Longley, *supra* note 4, at 161–162.

51. *Id.* at 165.

52. Representative Celler, cited in *id.* at 185.

53. *Id.* at 189.

54. *Id.*

55. *Id.* at 203.

56. *Id.* at 205.

57. Robertson, *The Debates of the Convention of Virginia, 1788* (2nd ed., 1805) 351, cited in Max Farrand, ed., *The Records of the Federal Convention of 1787*, Vol. I (New Haven: Yale University Press, 1966), 135.

58. *Id.*

59. Peirce and Longley, *supra* note 4, at 215.

60. *Id.*

61. *Id.* at 215.

62. Cited in Glennon, *supra* note 49, at 76.

63. Peirce and Longley, *supra* note 4, at 172.

64. Article V of the Constitution provides that "no state shall, without its consent," be deprived of its equal suffrage in the Senate.

65. Peirce and Longley, *supra* note 4, at 231.

66. Peirce and Longley (*id.*) cite, with approval, the work by Kinvin Wroth "Election Contests and the Electoral Vote," *Dickenson L. Rev.* 65 (October 1960–June 1961): 321, in which Wroth suggests, in Longley's words, that "federal courts be given exclusive jurisdiction in the event of contested presidential vote returns" *Id.* at 232.

67. Citing *Winner Take All, supra* note 29, 231, recommending that "federal law require an automatic, mandatory retally of all votes cast."

68. *Id.* at 59.

69. 1979 Senate Hearing, p.347, cited in Peirce and Longley *supra* note 4, at 202.

Chapter Seven

CONCLUSION: THE CASE FOR PRESERVING FEDERALISM

The district system, the proportional plan, direct election, and a variety of hybrid plans have been proposed hundreds of times since the Constitutional Convention of 1787. For the reasons set forth in the previous chapters, none of these plans has been found to be acceptable. None preserves the basic elements of federalism and the constitutional compact; and none would preserve the two-party system, discourage factionalism, and still produce, at the lowest possible risk of a constitutional crisis, a clear result in a presidential election.

In light of their failure to amend the constitution, frustrated reformers have focused mostly on theoretical dangers and problems that might occur. The danger most cited is that, once every two centuries or so, a president might be elected with a minority of popular votes. In return, they are willing to sacrifice not only the basic principles of federalism, but the asset that is priceless in a free and peaceful society—a clear and prompt result in the election of the national leader. Far from being a danger, the Electoral College and the general ticket ballot are the two most important features of the unique American system for electing a chief of state.

The other dangers cited by reformers are truly minimal and theoretical—that is, that electors might break their pledges, thus frustrating the popular will, and that state legislatures might reassert their right to elect the electors. In fact, only 7 electors out of 17,000 who have cast their votes in American elections have broken their pledge. Since 1876, no state has even hinted at depriving state voters of their right to elect electors.

Nevertheless, the reformers have a point with regard to faithless electors and the right of legislatures under the Constitution to appoint electors. These two problems should be addressed as part of any package of responsible reform. But to many reformers, these potential problems provide a convenient fig leaf for their true agenda: to abolish the Electoral College and undermine the principles of federalism. Indeed, many reformers have actively resisted efforts to specifically address these particular problems, for fear that any such minor reform would jeopardize their agenda for a radical change in the electoral process. This is indeed unfortunate, for the Electoral College system has already been refined to the limits permitted outside the Constitution. A constitutional amendment would be required to specifically address the potential problems of the faithless elector and legislative appointment of electors.

In addition, there are other aspects of the electoral process that should be addressed, such as the disenfranchisement of American citizens who are not citizens of a state.

Retaining the Electoral College, even with its present minor potential problems, would be preferable to the adoption of any of the major radical reforms that have been proposed. It may be that a package of responsible reform will be impossible as long as radical reformers consider such a package to be a threat to their own agenda. Nevertheless, what follows is the outline of a package of six responsible reforms that specifically address the real potential problems and that, if implemented, would neither undermine federalism nor the basic structure of the electoral process.

1. Enfranchising All American Citizens

Under the Constitution, only states and the District of Columbia may appoint electors. This provision effectively disenfranchises American citizens who are not citizens of a particular state or the District of Columbia. It is proposed that the District of Columbia be designated as the electoral repository for all citizens of the United States who are not citizens of states, and the number of electors from the District of Columbia should reflect the total population of such citizens according to the constitutional formula for awarding electoral votes.

2. Legislative Appointment of Electors

Although the Constitution provides that each state shall have plenary power to determine the manner in which electors are chosen, all states have now adopted popular election as the method of choosing electors. Although it is highly unlikely that a state would ever revert to legislative or executive appointment of electors, it is theoretically possible, in a critical election, that a state might be tempted to revert to direct legislative appointment. Therefore, the Constitution should be amended to provide that state electors shall be chosen by popular election in each state.

3. The General Ticket Ballot

All states but two have long adopted the general ticket ballot (unit rule) as the means of casting electoral votes. The two states that have reverted to the district method, Maine and Nebraska, have not been a major factor in recent elections. (Maine, despite its theoretical adoption of the district system, has not ever cast its votes except as a bloc.) The general ticket ballot, developed over two centuries and now adopted by almost all the states, has provided the Electoral College with its most important tool for nurturing and sustaining the two-party system, discouraging factionalism, and producing a clear-cut winner the day after each election. Although the threat to uniformity created by the district systems adopted by Maine and Nebraska is very small and theoretical, the potential danger of a state being able to manipulate the electoral process for political ends should be eliminated. The Constitution should be amended to require each state to adopt the general ticket ballot.

4. The Faithless Elector

The automatic plan, which eliminates the office of elector, automatically awards electoral votes to candidates receiving a plurality of votes within a state. It is an acceptable means of insuring that electors, by breaking their pledges, do not thereby frustrate the will of the people who elected them. However, there is an alternative method that would not dehumanize the electoral process, or unnecessarily bring to a halt the 200-year tradition of electors meeting in their respective states to cast their votes for president—a uniquely American tradition that has ocurred like clockwork, every four years, since Washington was elected president.

Rather, an amendment could give Congress the right to change any vote cast by a faithless elector to a vote for the candidate to whom the elector was pledged. Such a vote should be limited only to changing the unpledged vote to the candidate to whom the elector was pledged, and no other disposal of the vote should be permitted. The requirement for making this change should be minimal, such as a majority vote of either house of Congress.

It will be recalled that when elector Lloyd Bailey cast his vote for George Wallace rather than Richard Nixon in 1968, Congress attempted to challenge the vote as not having been "regularly given" in accordance with 3 United States Code 15. This challenge was not successful, primarily because many members of Congress believed that the Constitution gave an elector the right to vote for any candidate, even in violation of a pledge. Thus, in the view of many members of Congress, Bailey's vote was nevertheless "regularly given." The amendment proposed would eliminate this uncertainty, and would specifically give Congress the right to reverse any vote cast by an elector in violation of a pledge to the electorate.

5. Congressional Certification of Electoral Votes

It will be recalled that 3 U.S.C. 15 states that

if there shall have been any final determination in a state in the manner provided for by law of a controversy or contest concerning the appointment of all or any of the electors of such state, it shall be the duty of the executive of such states . . . to communicate under the seal of such state to the archivist of the United States a certificate of such determination.

3 U.S.C. 15 then provides that such a certification shall be accepted by Congress unless both houses concurrently determine that such certified electoral votes were nevertheless not "regularly given."

There are three problems with these provisions. First, each state should be required to provide a method for resolving electoral controversies, although most states certainly now do so.

Second, a specific statutory choice should be made as to whether the incumbent governor or the governor-elect has the power and duty to certify the electoral slate. It will be recalled that in the election of 1876, the imcumbent governor and governor-elect of several states certified different electoral returns to Congress, thereby throwing the entire presidential election into doubt. To avoid delay, the imcumbent governor should probably be designated.

Third, the electoral slate as certified by the governor should be absolutely final. The U.S. Code provision permitting Congress to overturn even certified returns if they are found to have not been "regularly given" is ambiguous and vulnerable to both political intrigue and mischief, which could cause delays and political upheaval similar to what the nation endured in 1876. Congress' power to overturn any electoral vote should be limited to the narrowly defined power to change a specific elector's vote cast in violation of a pledge to the candidate to whom an elector was originally pledged.

It is doubtful that any commission or other body appointed by Congress to "second-guess" a governor's certification would be any more legitimate than that of a sitting elected state governor. Remember that in 1876 the election appointed by Congress was, by necessity, split along strictly party lines, and the one supposedly nonpartisan member effectively ended up choosing the president. Any advantages in accuracy or procedural due process that might be gained by allowing a lengthy and partisan federal electoral commission to second-guess a properly certified state electoral slate would be more than outweighed by the delay and uncertainty created by such a commission, not to mention the dangers of conflict and upheaval.

This change in the law would not require a constitutional amendment, but could be accomplished by amending sections 6 and 15 of Chapter 3 of the U.S. Code.

6. The Contingent House Election

The importance of retaining the contingent House election has been noted in previous chapters. The contingent election reinforces the Electoral College in nurturing the two-party system and discouraging factionalism, and has proved critical in insuring the election of a president favored by a majority or large plurality of the American people.

However, the procedures for this election should be more specifically set forth. First, a determination should be made as to whether the incumbent House or the new House should elect the president. There is at present no agreement on which House would elect the president. Although it has been argued in Chapter One that the incumbent House should elect the president, the most important provision would be to make a clear-cut choice between the old or the new House.

Second, there should be a specific provision clarifying whether the votes within each state delegation should be by majority or plurality vote. Although a majority would be preferred, the best option would be to reduce the number of eligible candidates in the House to the two top electoral vote-getters in the Electoral College. In this case, all votes within a delegation would either be a majority, or a tie vote, in which case a state's vote would still be lost. Reducing the number of candidates in the House to two would also reduce considerably the possibility that a vice president would be chosen in the Senate who was of a different party than the candidate chosen to be president by the House.

Third, the quorum requirements in both the contingent House and Senate elections should be eliminated. This would reduce the incentive for political mischief by one party deliberately refusing to attend the election, in the hope that the election would thereby be delayed for some ulterior political purpose. With no quorum requirement, it is assumed that few if any members of Congress would choose not to attend a House election of the president or Senate election of the vice president.

Fourth, a specific date should be chosen for both the contingent House election of the president and the contingent Senate election of the vice president. This date should be no more than one, or at the most two, weeks after the general election. The House election should preferably be held first. Such a provision would limit delay and uncertainty and inhibit political mischief that might be caused by delaying tactics of either party.

Fifth, it should be provided that all votes in a House election should be by open, rather than secret, ballot. Although the proposed changes with regard to the contingent House and Senate elections could be made by statute, incorporation of the changes in a constitutional amendment would be preferable.

None of these six proposed changes would alter the basic federalist structure of the electoral process, or reduce the substantial advantages the present system provides. They would, however, eliminate the possibility of conflict and uncertainty in the event of unusual and unanticipated occurrences in the electoral process. It is submitted that all of the proposed changes would further refine the electoral process; and it is hoped that the fear of preventing a radical resturcturing would not prevent the adoption of such reforms. Even without such reforms, the plan of the constitutional framers remains far superior to the hundreds of plans that have been proposed since the Constitutional Convention.

Longley, Lawrence D., and Alan G. Braun. *The Politics of Electoral College Reform.* Foreword by U.S. Senator Birch Bayh. New Haven: Yale University Press, 1972.

MacBride, Roger Lea. *The American Electoral College.* Caldwell, Id.: Caxton Printers, 1963.

Madison, James, Alexander Hamilton, and John Jay. *Federalist Papers: A Commentary on the Constitution of the United States, Being a Collection of Essays.* New York: M. Walter Dunne, Publisher, 1901.

Memoirs of John Quincy Adams: Comprising Portions of His Diary from 1795 to 1848, Charles Francis, ed. New York: J. B. Lippincott, 1875.

Michener, James A. *Presidential Lottery: The Reckless Gamble in Our Electoral System.* New York: Random House, 1969.

Nevins, Allan. *Letters of Grover Cleveland.* New York: Houghton Mifflin, 1933.

Peirce, Neal R., and Lawrence D. Longley. *The People's President: The Electoral College in American History and the Direct Vote Alternative,* rev. ed. New Haven: Yale University Press, 1981.

Peters, William. *A More Perfect Union: The Making of the United States Constitution.* New York: Crown Publishers, 1987.

Polsby, Nelson W., and Aaron Wildavsky. *Elections: Strategies of American Electoral Politics.* New York: Charles Scribner's Sons, 1964.

Pommerantz, Sidney I. *The Coming to Power: Critical Presidential Elections in American History,* Arthur M. Schlesinger, Jr. and William P. Hansen, eds. New York: Chelsea House Publishers, in association with McGraw-Hill, 1972.

The Records of the Federal Convention of 1787, Vols. I–IV. Max Farrand, ed. New Haven: Yale University Press, 1966.

Report of the Twentieth Century Fund Task Force on Reform of the Presidential Election Process, *Winner Take All.* Background paper by William R. Keech. New York: Holmes and Meier, 1978.

Schlesinger, Arthur M. *The Age of Jackson.* Boston: Little, Brown, 1945.

Wells, Gideon. *The Diary of Gideon Wells,* Vol. III. New York: Houghton Mifflin, 1911.

Wilmerding, Lucius, Jr. *The Electoral College.* Boston: Beacon Press, 1958.

Woodward, C. Vann. *The Compromise of 1877 and the End of Reconstruction.* Boston: Little, Brown, 1951.

Yunker, John H., and Lawrence D. Longley. *The Electoral College: Its Biases Newly Measured for the 1960s and 1970s,* Randall B. Ripley, ed. Beverly Hills, Calif.: Sage Publications, 1976.

PERIODICALS

"ABC's of How America Chooses a President." *U.S. News & World Report.* 96 (February 20, 1984): 39.

Amar, Vik, and Reed Akhil. "Split Decision." *Washington Monthly.* 24 (November 1992): 22.

American Law Division, Congressional Research Service. "Majority or Plurality Vote Within State Delegations When House of Representatives Votes for the President." Washington, D.C.: Library of Congress (unpublished document) (June 10, 1980).

BIBLIOGRAPHY

BOOKS

Abbott, David W., and James P. Levine. *Wrong Winner: The Coming Debacle in the Electoral College*. New York: Praeger Publishers, 1991.

Bemis, Samuel Flagg. *John Quincy Adams and the Union*. New York: Alfred A. Knopf, 1956.

Best, Judith. *The Case Against Direct Election of the President: A Defense of the Electoral College*. Ithaca, N.Y.: Cornell University Press, 1975.

Brams, Steven J. *The Presidential Election Game*. New Haven: Yale University Press, 1978.

Claud, Richard. *The Supreme Court and the Electoral Process*. Baltimore: Johns Hopkins University Press, 1970.

Dougherty, John Hampden. *The Electoral System of The United States: Its History, Together With a Study of The Perils That Have Attended its Operations, an Analysis of The Several Efforts by Legislation to Avert These Perils, and a Proposed Remedy by Amendment of the Constitution*. New York: Putnam, 1906.

Farrand, Max. *The Framing of the Constitution of the United States*. New Haven: Yale University Press, 1987 (originally published in 1913).

Final Report of the Commission on National Elections, Georgetown University. *Electing the President: A Program for Reform*, Robert E. Hunter, ed. Washington, D.C.: The Center for Strategic and International Studies, 1986.

Gibson, A. M. *A Political Crime: The History of the Great Fraud*. New York: William S. Gottsberger, Publisher, 1969.

Glennon, Michael J. *When No Majority Rules: The Electoral College and Presidential Succession*. Washington, D.C.: Congressional Quarterly, Inc., 1992.

Hargrove, Erwin C., Donald R. Mathews, and others. *Choosing the President*, James David Barber, ed. Englewood Cliffs, N.J.: Prentice-Hall, 1974.

Hendrick, Burton J. *Bulwark of the Republic: Biography of the Constitution*. Boston: Little, Brown, 1937.

Archer, J. Clark, Fred M. Shelly, Peter J. Taylor, and Ellen R. White. "The Geography of U.S. Presidential Elections: Enduring Geographic Cleavages Divide the Electorate. They Weigh Heavily in the Electoral College System and Demand That a Winning Candidate Build a Geographic Coalition. *Scientific American*. 259 (July 1988): 44.

Banzhaf, John F., III. "Multi-Member Electoral Districts—Do They Violate the "One Man, One Vote" Principle?" *The Yale Law Journal*. 75 (1960): 1309.

Banzhaf, John F. "One Man, 3.312 Votes: A Mathematical Analysis of the Electoral College." *Villanova Law Review*. With Comments by The Honorable Birch Bayh, The Honorable Karl E. Mundt, The Honorable John J. Sparkman, and Neal R. Peirce. 13 (Winter 1968): 304.

Banzhaf, John F., III. "Weighted Voting Doesn't Work: A Mathematical Analysis." *Rutgers Law Review*. 19 (1965): 317.

Barnes, Fred. "College Counseling." *New Republic*. 199 (July 18, 1988): 13.

Barnes, Fred. "A Donkey's Year: All the Signs Point to a Democratic Victory in November." *New Republic*. (February 29, 1988): 16.

Bates, Stephen. "How Dukakis Can Still Be President; and You Thought Dan Quayle Was Next in Line." *Washington Monthly*. 20 (December 1988): 34.

Bayh, Birch. "Electing a President—The Case for Direct Popular Election." *Harvard Journal on Legislation*. 6 (January 1969): 127.

Bickel, Alexander M. "Is Electoral Reform the Answer?" *Commentary*. 46 (December 1968): 41.

Corn, David. "Beltway Bandits." *Nation*. 254 (June 29, 1992): 884.

Cusak, Michael. "Eight Elections That Made Political History." *Scholastic Update*. 117 (October 5, 1984): 22.

Diamond, Martin. "The Electoral College and the Idea of Federal Democracy." *The Journal of Federalism*. (Winter 1978): 63.

Dolan, Joseph, and Frank Chmelik. "Role of the Courts in Election '80: A 3-Ring Circus for a 3-Way Race." *National Law Journal*. (August 18, 1980): 24.

Duffy, Michael. "The 34% Solution." *Time*. 139 (June 1, 1992): 34.

Dunn, Katheryn A. "Time for Fairness in the Presidential Electoral Process: Major and Minor Party Candidates in Competition." *The Journal of Law & Politics*. 6 (Spring 1990): 625.

Durbin, Thomas M. "The Anachronistic Electoral College." *Federal Bar News & Journal*. 39 (October 1992): 510.

Durbin, Thomas M. "The Electoral College Method of Electing the President and Vice President and Proposals for Reform." *Congressional Research Service*. (August 8, 1988).

Durbin, Thomas. "Presidential Primaries: Proposals Before Congress to Reform Them and Congressional Authority to Regulate Them." *The Journal of Law & Politics*. 1 (Spring 1984): 381.

"Electing the President: Recommendations of the American Bar Association's Commission on Electoral College Reform." *American Bar Association Journal*. 53 (March 1967): 219.

"The Electoral Battle Map." *Scholastic Update*. 125 (October 9, 1992): 8.

Evans, Michael K. "Democrats Are Boxed in Wrong Electoral Corner." *Industry Week*. 223 (December 10, 1984): 112.

Fallows, James. "Plains Talk: What Jimmy Carter's First Bid for Public Office Tells Us About Politics Today." *Washington Monthly*. 24 (November 1992): 43.

Feerick, John D. "The Electoral College—Why It Ought to be Abolished." *Fordham Law Review*. 37 (1968): 1.

Feerick, John D. "The Electoral College: Why It Was Created." *American Bar Association Journal*. 54 (March 1968): 249.

Forbes, Malcolm S., Jr. "Election Prediction: Michael Dukakis Will Win." *Forbes*. 142 (November 14, 1988): 33.

Forbes, Malcolm S., Jr. "Helpful, Useful Antique." *Forbes*. 143 (February 6, 1989): 27.

Forbes, Malcolm S., Jr. "Politically Paralyzing Ploy." *Forbes*. 150 (July 6, 1992): 26.

Forbes, Malcolm S., Jr. "Talking About Politics." *Forbes*. 136 (September 16, 1985): 31.

Gewirtz, Paul. "House Party: How Not to Elect a President." *New Republic*. 207 (July 27, 1992): 38.

Gewirtz, Paul. "Jackson's Hole." *The New Republic*. 207 (July 27, 1992): 40.

Goode, John. "The Electoral Commission of 1877." *The American Law Review*. 38 (January and February 1904): 1.

Gossett, William T. "Electing the President." *Detroit College of Law Review*. 4 (1983): 1283.

Gossett, William T. "Electing the President: New Hope for an Old Ideal." *American Bar Association Journal*. 53 (December 1967): 1103.

Harmon, Mark D. "The *New York Times* and the Theft of the 1876 Presidential Election." *Journal of American Culture*. 10 (1987): 35.

House, Lolabel. "A Study of the Twelfth Amendment." Ph.D. dissertation, University of Philadelphia, 1901.

Kefauver, Estes. "The Electoral College: Old Reforms Take on a New Look." *Law and Contemporary Problems*. 27 (Spring 1962): 188.

Kirby, James C., Jr. "Limitations on the Power of State Legislatures Over Presidential Elections." *Law and Contemporary Problems*. 27 (Summer 1962): 495.

Kirkpatrick, Jeane J. "Martin Diamond and the American Idea of Democracy." *The Journal of Federalism*. (Summer 1978): 7.

Kleber, Louis C. "The Presidential Election of 1876." *History Today*. 20 (1970): 806.

Levinson, Sanford. "Gerrymandering and the Brooding Omnipresence of Proportional Representation: Why Won't It Go Away." *UCLA Law Review*. 33: 257.

Marshman, D. M., Jr. "Who Really Elects the Presidents?" *American Heritage*. 24 (February 1973): 103.

Martin, William Logan. "Let the State Legislator Choose Them." *American Bar Association Journal*. 44 (December 1958): 1182.

Mayhew, David, and Bruce Russett. "How the Democrats Can Win in '92." *New Leader*. 72 (January 9, 1989): 13.

McKay, Robert B. "Reapportionment: Success Story of the Warren Court." *Michigan Law Review*. 67 (December 1968): 223.

McLaughlin, John. "The Electoral-Vote Lock." *National Review*. 40 (August 5, 1988): 26.

Mikva, Abner J. "The Electoral College: How Democratic Was—and Is—the Constitution?" *Prologue*. 19 (Fall 1987): 177.

Millus, Albert J. "The Electoral College—Should Anything Be Done About It?" *New York State Bar Journal.* (February 1982): 84.

Morris, Roy Jr. "Master Fraud of the Century: The Disputed Election of 1876." *American History Illustrated.* 23 (July 1988): 28.

Nelson, Michael C. "Partisan Bias in the Electoral College." *The Journal of Politics.* 37 (November 1974): 1033.

"No Margin for Error (An American Survey)." *Economist.* 325 (November 7, 1992): 27.

O'Sullivan, Michael J. "Artificial Unit Voting and the Electoral College." *Southern California Law Review.* 65 (July 1992): 5.

Parshall, Gerald. "The Feuding Fathers." *U.S. News & World Report.* 114 (February 1, 1993): 54.

"Population Shifts Could Increase Democratic Woes in 1992 Election." *National Journal.* 20 (April 16, 1988): 1024.

Reidinger, Paul. "Still Ticking After All These Years." *ABA Journal.* (September 1, 1987): 42.

Reuven, Frank. "Election Night." *New Leader.* 75 (October 5, 1992): 20.

Roberts, Charley. "Electoral College Placed Under Rare Scrutiny." *Los Angeles Daily Journal.* (May 27, 1992): 10.

Roberts, Charley. "The Perot Factor at Work." *Los Angeles Daily Journal.* (May 27, 1992): 1.

Rose, Jonathon. "The Rapid Rise of Special Interest Groups." *Scholastic Update.* 117 (October 19, 1984): 31.

Rosenthal, Albert. "The Constitution, Congress, and Presidential Elections." *Michigan Law Review.* 67 (November 1968):1.

Rosenthal, Albert J. "Some Doubts Concerning the Proposal to Elect the President by Direct Popular Vote." *Villanova Law Review.* 14 (Fall 1968): 87.

Schneider, William. "Electoral College's 'Archaic Ritual.' " *National Journal.* 20 (December 10, 1988): 3164.

Schneider, William. "An Insider's View of the Election." *Atlantic.* 262 (July 1988): 29.

Seligman, Daniel. "The Old College Tie, the Economics of Light Bulbs, Streetwalker Distribution, and Other Matters." *Fortune.* 110 (September 3, 1984): 105.

Sickels, Robert J. "The Power Index and the Electoral College: A Challenge to Banzhaf's Analysis." *Villanova Law Review.* 14 (Fall 1968): 92.

Sindler, Allan P. "Presidential Election Methods and Urban-Ethnic Interests." *Law & Contemporary Problems.* 27 (Spring 1962): 213.

Smith, Hedrick. "The Power Game: How Washington Works (Book Review), by Barry Gewen." *New Leader.* 71 (May 2, 1988): 17.

Spering, Howard S. "How to Make the Electoral College Constitutionally Representative." *American Bar Association Journal.* 53 (August 1968): 763.

Sterling, Carleton W. "The Electoral College Biases Revealed: The Conventional Wisdom and Game Theory Models Notwithstanding." *Western Political Quarterly.* 31 (June 1978): 159.

Sterling, Carleton W. "Electoral College Misrepresentation: A Geometric Analysis." *Polity.* 13: 1981.

"Swings and Roundabouts." *Economist.* 324 (September 19, 1992): 30.

"Unpicking the Republican Lock: The Campaign." *Economist*. 324 (August 15, 1992): 20.

U.S. Bureau of the Census, *Statistical Abstract of the United States*, 112th ed. Washington, D.C.: U.S. Government Printing Office, 1992.

"The Votes That Really Count." *Time*. 132 (October 17, 1988): 20.

Walsh, Kenneth T. "California Picks the President: The Golden State Is the Pivotal Electoral Battleground." *U.S. News & World Report*. 111 (December 30, 1991): 44.

Walsh, Kenneth T. "The Key States: The Longhorns of Texas and Laidbacks of California Will Be Kingmakers." *U.S. News & World Report*. 105 (August 29, 1988): 42.

Wechsler, Herbert. "Presidential Elections and the Constitution: A Comment on Proposed Amendment." *American Bar Association Journal*. 35 (March 1949): 181.

Weinhagen, Robert F. "Should the Electoral College Be Abandoned?" *American Bar Association Journal*. 67 (July 1981): 852.

Weisberger, Bernard A. "The Stolen Election." *American Heritage*. 51 (July/August 1990): 18.

Wildenthal, John. "The Role of the Electoral College." *Southwest Review*. 43 (1968): 113.

Wilkinson, Donald M. "The Electoral Process and the Power of the States." *American Bar Association Journal*. 47 (March 1961): 251.

Wilmerding, Lucius. "The Electoral College." *Columbia Law Review*. 59 (1959): 838.

Wroth, Kinvin. "Election Contests and the Electoral Vote." *Dickinson Law Review*. 65 (October 1960–June 1961): 321.

INDEX

About the Author

ROBERT M. HARDAWAY is Professor of Law at the University of Denver. He is the author of *Airport Regulation, Law and Public Policy* (Quorum, 1991) and *Population, Law, and the Environment* (Praeger, 1994).

ISBN 0-275-94569-3

90000>

EAN

9 780275 945695

HARDCOVER BAR CODE